INSIDE
the
CRIMINAL
MIND

INSIDE
the
CRIMINAL
MIND

REVISED AND UPDATED EDITION

Dr. Stanton E. Samenow

B\D\W\Y
NEW YORK

Copyright © 1984, 2004, 2014 by Stanton E. Samenow

Published in the United States by Broadway Books, an imprint of the Crown
Publishing Group, a division of Random House LLC, New York, a Penguin
Random House Company.

www.crownpublishing.com

Broadway Books and its logo, B\D\W\Y, are trademarks of Random House
LLC.

Originally published in hardcover in slightly different form in the United States
by Crown, an imprint of the Crown Publishing Group, a division of Random
House LLC, New York, in 1984.

Library of Congress Cataloging-in-Publication Data
Samenow, Stanton E., 1941–
    Inside the criminal mind / Stanton E. Samenow, Ph.D. — Revised and
updated edition, First paperback edition.
        pages   cm
    Includes bibliographical references and index.
    1. Criminal psychology. 2. Juvenile delinquents—Psychology. 3. Juvenile
delinquents—Rehabilitation—United States. 4. Criminals—Rehabilitation—
United States. I. Title.
    HV6080.S22 2014
    364.301'9—dc23   2014022399

ISBN 978-0-8041-3990-8
eBook ISBN 978-0-8041-3991-5

Printed in the United States of America

Cover design: FORT

20 19 18 17 16

In memory of Dr. Samuel Yochelson,
who taught and inspired me so many years ago
and
In memory of my parents,
Charles and Sylvia Samenow

CONTENTS

I am grateful to the following for reading the manuscript and making many thoughtful suggestions: Bryan T. Hodges, Senior Judge, State of Oregon; Terry Leap, Lawson Professor of Business, University of Tennessee, Knoxville; Joseph C. Lynch, retired attorney; and Joram Piatigorsky, PhD.

I also thank my wife, Dorothy K. Samenow, who, during forty-three years of marriage, has unequivocally supported me in everything that I undertake, while remaining in an ever-cheerful mood.

I also am deeply appreciative of Domenica Alioto, my editor, who has been keenly interested in this book, made marvelous suggestions in a positive fashion, and, overall, was a dream to work with throughout the entire publication process.

I was twenty-eight years old, two years out of graduate school, when, during January 1970, I joined Dr. Samuel Yochelson to work as a clinical research psychologist in his Program for the Investigation of Criminal Behavior at St. Elizabeths Hospital in Washington, D.C. Little did I realize that I had embarked on a career path I would follow well into my seventies. Dr. Yochelson launched in 1961 what remains the longest in-depth research treatment program of offenders conducted in North America. When he died on November 12, 1976, I became heir to his groundbreaking work and have continued evaluating and working with offenders, from petty thieves to spree killers.

For decades, the prevailing conventional wisdom about criminality has regarded the offender as a victim of forces over which he has little or no control. Virtually everything imaginable has been identified as a cause of criminal behavior, including poverty, bad parenting, peer pressure, violence in the media, and various types of mental illness. Dr. Yochelson and I subscribed to this premise when we began our work. From 1961 to 1978, we spent thousands of hours interviewing offenders and others who knew them well. Contrary to what we initially believed, we learned that these individuals were not haplessly molded by their environment. None of the widely accepted causes of crime withstood scrutiny. In addition, the offenders with whom we were working exploited our search for causes to offer even more excuses for their crimes. Referring to many months of psychiatric treatment, one man said to Dr. Yochelson in a moment of rare candor, "Doctor, if I didn't have enough excuses for crime before psychiatry, I now have more than enough after all these years." Once we extricated ourselves from the miasma of searching for "causes" of criminal behavior, we were able to develop a detailed understanding of how criminals think in all aspects of life, and to develop a process to help some of them change. Behavior is a product of thinking, and so it is incumbent upon anyone formulating policy or working with offenders to understand how criminals think.

After our work at St. Elizabeths Hospital was featured during a segment of CBS News's *60 Minutes* on February 17, 1977, I began receiving invitations to speak to professional groups in corrections, mental health, social work, substance abuse counseling, law enforcement, and the judiciary. Responses from my audiences included personal attacks (I was even denounced as dangerous) because I challenged the almost sacred theories about what causes criminal behavior and, further, asserted that a "criminal personality" does, in fact, exist. There seemed to be a difference of opinion between armchair theorists with little or no face-to-face contact with criminals and those who interacted daily with offenders. The latter group—correctional officers, counselors, law enforcement officials, and psychologists— embraced our work because it was in line with what they encountered every day on the job, and because it provided insights that helped them do their work more effectively.

The first edition of *Inside the Criminal Mind* was published in 1984, and a second edition in 2004. Now, a decade later, it is time to bring this work up to date. In this edition, you will come to understand in detail the thought processes and tactics common to offenders, regardless of their background or the crimes for which they are arrested.

Human nature does not change, and thus the criminal mind that I described in earlier editions of this book has not changed. However, a constantly changing society provides new avenues for the criminal mind to express itself. For example, bullying is not new, but cyberbullying is, and offers criminally inclined adolescents and adults a vast new arena in which to inflict great suffering.

The Internet provides a speedy and efficient means to conduct research, shop, plan travel, and communicate with others. Technology has opened this same world to criminals so they can conduct their "research" and implement their schemes. Using the Internet, criminals gain immediate access to do what they have always done—deceive, defraud, steal, and intimidate. Cyber-crime has become an increasing menace to individuals, businesses, and governments. Thousands of miles from their victims and out of the reach of law enforcement authorities, criminals can hack into government computer systems, steal personal information, commit identity theft, and destroy a company's valuable software or business records.

The 2004 edition of *Inside the Criminal Mind* included a chapter on the criminal's immersion in the drug world. This edition expands that discussion to include the alarming abuse of prescription drugs, and the manufacture and use of new synthetic drugs that add to an already enormous social problem. Drug manufacturing, distribution, and use provide the criminal intrigue, excitement, and financial gain.

In line with offering more detailed information about the criminal's patterns of thought and action (and less about alleged causes of criminal behavior), I devote a chapter to two cases in which two young men from very different backgrounds commit homicides. You will see that the thinking processes were extremely similar in the young man who came from a wealthy family and the youth who grew up in a chaotic inner-city home. Throughout this book, you will see a similarity in thinking patterns between white-collar criminals who commit multimillion-dollar crimes and street thugs who threaten an elderly person at knife point in order to steal twenty dollars.

I have added a chapter on sex in the life of the criminal. The pursuit of sex and the commission of sex offenses have little to do with sexual fulfillment. Rather, through sexual activity the criminal exercises power, nurtures his ego, and confirms his perception that he is irresistible. This concept is important to understanding the mentality of clergymen, coaches, counselors, and educators who manipulate others to gain their trust and then exploit their positions to sexually prey upon children.

The criminal simmers with anger because people do not satisfy his expectations. They fail to confirm his perception of himself as powerful, unique, and superior. What most of us find to be routine annoyances, the criminal personalizes as threats to his entire self-image. A chapter is devoted to discussing anger that, in a criminal, is like a cancer, metastasizing so that anyone or anything in his path can become a target.

No matter how much physical, financial, or emotional damage he causes, the criminal believes he is a good person. Maudlin sentiment and savage brutality reside side-by-side within the same individual. "I can change from tears to ice and back again," commented one violent predator. It is important to understand how a criminal fortifies his good opinion of himself so that he can do a kind deed for someone and then, shortly thereafter, wreak havoc. The criminal's view of himself as a decent person constitutes a major barrier to change.

Mental health professionals piece together information to understand perpetrators of mass shootings and other horrifying crimes. In some instances, these individuals have had *prior* contact with mental health professionals who tried in vain to evaluate, understand, and treat them. But such offenders are skilled at deception and do not want others to know who they are. They generally do not reveal their intentions. Although they may explain puzzling and extreme behavior in terms of mental illness, trained psychiatrists and psychologists often fail to recognize that they are dealing with the type of personality described in this book. You will come to understand why this happens.

When experts cannot identify a motive for a crime, they may conclude that the perpetrator was legally insane, that he did not know right from wrong, or that he acted on an irresistible impulse. Since writing the 2004 edition of this book, I have served as an expert witness in cases where an insanity defense was raised. This occurred during the trial of Lee Boyd Malvo, the younger of the two notorious Washington, D.C., snipers. Contrary to what many people think, acquittals due to a successful insanity defense are rare, and there is good reason for this. I will discuss a case in which I did find a defendant to be legally insane, a situation very different from other insanity cases in which I have participated.

There is also a widely held perception that seemingly responsible, levelheaded people are pushed by stressful circumstances to a point where they "snap" and commit a crime that is completely out of character. I have never found this explanation to be accurate, and you'll see why.

The acts of terror at Newtown, Connecticut; Aurora, Colorado; the Washington, D.C., Navy Yard; and the 2013 Boston Marathon are emblazoned in memory. Whether the carnage occurs abroad or at home, some acts of terrorism should be viewed in the context of people who embrace causes and utilize them as vehicles for the expression of an already existing criminal personality. We read accounts of men, women, and children becoming politically "radicalized." To understand fully what really happened in their lives, it is essential to consider the pre-existing personalities of those who place themselves in a position to be drawn into this process, then commit acts of terror.

A discussion of the thinking and behavior of offenders as they serve time in detention and correctional facilities will provide a vivid picture of what employees of such facilities contend with every day when they arrive at work. This edition takes a closer look at that world, including how gangs operate within prison walls, with their leaders having widespread influence not only on prison life but also outside the correctional facility.

The conventional wisdom about causes still guides the efforts of many who craft policies to combat crime. Policy makers waste billions of dollars as they naively seek to combat criminal behavior by eradicating its so-called environmental "root causes." Programs that employ traditional psychological approaches remain unsuccessful. For example, "anger management" programs are widely used in efforts to help offenders change. Such efforts are doomed, in that they actually legitimize anger. I shall propose an alternative approach.

Not surprisingly, the controversy continues unabated in the United States over the worthwhileness of efforts to help offenders change. Numerous facilities have adopted aspects of the approach that Dr. Yochelson and I developed decades ago at St. Elizabeths Hospital. This process entails helping offenders identify "errors" in their thinking, come to terms with the destructive consequences of that thinking, then learn and implement corrective concepts. With increasing budgetary constraints, resources directed toward programs for change in America's correctional facilities have become extremely limited. Nonetheless, it still is true that almost every man, woman, and child locked up today—with the relatively few exceptions of those serving life sentences without parole or on death row—will at some point be released onto the streets of America. While a small number may change on their own after having experienced the loss of their freedom, most will remain unchanged, with many returning to prison. As we learn more about the criminal mind, we shall be in a better position to help some offenders change so as to live productive and responsible lives.

Removing a Barrier to Understanding the Criminal Mind

The major purpose of this book is for you to understand the criminal mind. The chapter "Parents Don't Turn Children into Criminals" introduces the thinking patterns and tactics of individuals who, before reaching adolescence, grow increasingly irresponsible and commit crimes. Later chapters reveal thinking patterns in adults that become habitual and result in massive injury to other human beings. There's always the danger of developing a case of "medical students' disease" in which you start thinking, "My husband does some of these things. My son does them as well. And I think some of this applies to me." You may begin seeing criminality everywhere.

Bear in mind, there is a continuum with respect to most aspects of personality. Take anxiety as an example. It's normal for a person to experience some anxiety while anticipating the results of a diagnostic medical test. At the other extreme, a person might be paralyzed by anxiety to the point where he is housebound, phobic about going outside. Just contemplating a trip to the grocery store could trigger a full-blown panic attack.

The concept of a continuum is also essential to understanding the mental makeup of individuals with a criminal personality. Lying is a case in point. Nearly all of us tell small lies. A two-year-old knocks over a glass of milk and points to the cat as the culprit. Your friend asks if you like her new hairstyle and, to avoid hurting her feelings, you claim to admire it even though you think it doesn't do her justice. Exhausted and wanting a day off, you phone work to take sick leave although you are not truly ill. You assure your child the medicine won't taste bad in order to persuade him to swallow it, even though you know it is bitter. But there is a significant difference between a person who tells a relatively innocuous lie to avoid embarrassment or hurting someone, and the individual who lies as a way of life. The criminal lies to cover his tracks (he has a great deal to conceal) and to get out of a jam that he has created for himself. He lies to preserve a view of himself as special and powerful, a self-image that he fortifies every time he succeeds at deceiving others. More will be said about the chronic lying of the criminal in subsequent chapters.

Consider the failure to take into account someone else's feelings. We occasionally cause distress to others by single-mindedly pursuing what we want. We may cut someone off in the middle of a conversation or, with a dismissive remark, inadvertently belittle the importance of someone's recent achievement. But once we realize what we have done, we suffer regret over the harm we have caused. In contrast, criminals are uncompromising. In pursuing an objective, they are heedless as to the collateral effects of their behavior. They view other people as pawns to manipulate. Any means to achieve a desired end is acceptable. An offender commented in all seriousness to his probation officer, "This empathy thing; what's in it for me?"

The continuum concept also applies to anger. Some people have a sunny disposition and seldom get angry. They maintain equanimity even in the face of major challenges and disappointments. At the other extreme is the criminal who simmers with anger throughout his life. When people fail to fulfill his unrealistic expectations, he reacts as though his entire self-image is at stake. Throughout his life, he is infuriated because people do not conform to what he wants, and he is unable to control them.

Psychology and sociology have long advanced the view that the criminal is basically like everyone else, but becomes destructive because he has been traumatized or stymied in fulfilling his aspirations. A teenager "falls" in with the wrong crowd and joins a gang because he has never had a decent family life. Or a drug trafficker plies his trade because his skills qualify him only for jobs that pay minimum wage. Thus both are perceived as people who are shaped by circumstances outside their control, ignoring the fact that most youths from dysfunctional families do *not* join gangs, and that the drug dealer's lack of education and job skills is a *personal* failure, not a societal one. In many circles, the criminal is seen as a victim, not a victimizer.

Those who hold this view go a step further, asserting that we are all, in a sense, "criminals" because we lie, lust, and yield to temptation. But it is absurd to equate the rare small lie of the responsible person with the gigantic network of lies of the criminal. Equally absurd is to equate a child's pilferage of a small toy with a delinquent's stealing practically everything that isn't bolted down. It is misleading to claim that the criminal wants what the responsible person wants, that he values the same things a responsible person values. Both may desire wealth, but only one will work steadily and honestly to acquire it. The criminal believes that he is entitled to it and grabs it any way he can, not caring whom he injures, and then wants more. Both may desire a family life, but the responsible person shows the give-and-take, the thoughtfulness and caring, that it requires. The criminal often pays lip service to hard work, integrity, and responsibility, but his actions demonstrate that these concepts are antithetical to the way he lives his life.

In discussing the thinking patterns and tactics of criminals, it is essential to avoid simplistically dividing all of humanity into good or evil. During a well-publicized interview that appeared in the November 1976 issue of *Playboy* magazine, former President Jimmy Carter stated, "I try not to commit a deliberate sin. . . . I've committed adultery in my heart many times." Like President Carter, we often have thoughts that, if acted upon, would result in harm to other people or ourselves. Sinful (to use President Carter's terminology) thoughts flash through our minds, and we easily and quickly push them aside. They disappear and do not recur. We may struggle with other thoughts because they occur over and over. In all likelihood, however, we do not harbor thoughts of committing major crimes such as robbery, arson, rape, or murder.

Criminals often react to daily frustrations and disappointments in ways that differ dramatically from the reactions of ordinary people. A motorist cuts us off on the highway. Most people shrug it off and continue on their way. The person with a criminal mind, however, may pursue the offending driver, escalating the conflict into violent road rage. When treated rudely by a clerk in a store, most people simply ignore the bad behavior. The person with a criminal mind, however, may launch into a profanity-laced tirade and, possibly, a physical attack. In response to whatever transpires in our lives, we have thoughts and make critical choices about what to do with those thoughts. The person who is basically responsible thinks about consequences and has a conscience. He therefore does what President Carter described—he tries "not to commit a deliberate sin."

If one believes the statistics, nearly half of American marriages run aground, leading to separation and divorce. There are different ways to respond to marital conflict. If a person commits adultery, other people beside his spouse and children may be ensnared, including extended family, neighbors, coworkers, and friends. The lying and living a double life that are endemic to infidelity are similar *in degree* to the behavior of the criminal. However, in other aspects of life, the person who commits adultery may be honest, empathic, and responsible.

You might argue that criminality is relative. What constitutes a crime today may not be a crime tomorrow if the laws change. This was the case when Prohibition was repealed. Some behavior may be extremely hurtful, but not illegal. There are individuals who are "criminals," as I am using the term, no matter what the laws are. Consider the rapist who declared, "If rape were legalized today, I wouldn't rape. But I would do something else." For this man and others like him, doing whatever is forbidden is key to their self-image. There are also "non-arrestable criminals," and you probably know some. These are extremely self-centered people who incessantly lie, betray trust, build themselves up by tearing others down, struggle to control others, ignore personal and financial obligations, and blame other people for their wrongdoing. They may not commit arrestable acts (or perhaps are slick enough not to get caught), but they are very destructive to their families, coworkers, and anyone else with whom they have significant contact.

As you enter into the mind of the criminal, it is essential to remember that the thinking patterns and tactics described exist as a matter of degree. Having interviewed criminals for forty-four years, I had hundreds of cases from which to choose while writing this book. I deliberately selected as examples men and women who are at the extreme end of the continuum of criminality. When you understand the extreme manifestation of a pattern, it is easier to recognize it in a less extreme form.

If a man, woman, or child is extreme in all the characteristics I am describing—self-centered, controlling, dishonest, irresponsible, and callous—the whole is greater than the sum of the parts. The result is a human being who holds a radically different view of himself* and the world than does a person who lives a basically responsible life. That individual has a criminal personality.

---

* Throughout this book, the male pronoun "he" will be used, even though male and female criminals have the same thinking patterns and deploy similar tactics.

1

The Failure to Identify Causes of Crime

When I began working as a clinical research psychologist, I believed that people turned to crime largely because of factors outside of themselves. I regarded criminals mainly as victims. Working with my mentor, Dr. Yochelson, we eventually found this view to be completely in error. We became increasingly skeptical of self-serving stories in which criminals justified what they did by casting blame on others. As we challenged their accounts and interviewed those who knew them well, they became more forthcoming. We modified some ideas, discarded others completely, and discovered new topics for investigation. The evidence that we accumulated by spending thousands of hours interviewing criminals from a variety of backgrounds compelled us to take our sacred theoretical cows to pasture and slaughter them. We called ourselves the "reluctant converts" because we were so hesitant to abandon our theories, beliefs, and what we had learned in our professional training about why people turn to crime. Once we ceased perceiving the criminal as a victim, a new vista opened. Unfettered by "why" questions, we turned to developing an understanding of *how* criminals think.

We took a scratch-on-the-table approach. You do not have to know why a table is scratched. Rather than be concerned about how it was damaged, you need to examine the table to determine what it is made of and assess its condition in order to determine whether it is restorable. How does a criminal make decisions? What are his expectations of himself and of other people? How is it that he can pray in church at ten o'clock but, two hours later, terrorize a homeowner during a break-and-entry? Behavior is a product of thinking. By focusing on thinking patterns rather than causes, we eventually laid the foundation for a method to help offenders change their thinking and behavior

The search for the causes of crime is unending and is somewhat comparable to scientists' efforts to understand the causes of cancer. We think that if we discover the cause of what baffles and terrifies us, whatever the scourge is, it can be eliminated. Unlike with cancer, there should be no expectation that even if we succeed in identifying the "root causes" of criminality, we will discover a cure. Rather than generate successful strategies to confront and combat crime, the preoccupation with a search for causes has served as a distraction from understanding who the criminal is.

A view that has persisted for more than a century is that criminals are victims of sociological, psychological, or biological factors over which they have little or perhaps no control. Some sociologists maintain that crime is an understandable, adaptive, and even normal response to conditions of grueling poverty that deprive people of opportunity and hope. They also cite the stressful, competitive life in the suburbs as contributory. Some attribute criminality to misplaced values in society that alienate citizens from communities, the workplace, and the government. Psychologists emphasize the role of early experience in the family and point to parental deficiencies as causative of criminal conduct. In the nineteenth century, the theory was advanced that criminals were born "constitutionally inferior." Now, in the twenty-first century, scientists are returning to that idea as research findings point to a biological basis for criminal conduct.

In the 1957 musical *West Side Story,* Stephen Sondheim parodied what was then current thinking about causes of juvenile delinquency in the song "Gee, Officer Krupke." In that song, delinquents were misunderstood rather than no good. They suffered from a "social disease" and society had "played [them] a terrible trick." These lyrics were expressive of a view that their criminality was symptomatic of deep-seated psychopathology or of socioeconomic deprivation. In a 1964 article, the noted psychologist O. Hobart Mowrer questioned whether psychoanalysis actually encourages "sociopathy" (now officially called "antisocial personality disorder") by providing more justifications for crimes.[1] He addressed this issue in a psychiatric folksong:

> At three I had a feeling of ambivalence toward my brothers
> And so it follows naturally I poisoned all my lovers
> And now I'm happy, I have learned the lesson this has taught:
> That everything I do that's wrong is someone else's fault.

The thinking about causes of crime satirized in the 1950s and 1960s remains alive and well today. Every day new headlines appear in journals or pop up in the media pointing to yet another alleged cause of criminality:

> Disaffected Youth Identify with the Infamous[2]
> Slave Syndrome Argued in Boy's Death[3]
> Violent Games Cause Violence[4]
> Angry Outbursts Linked to Inflammation in the Body[5]
> Sleep Disorders May Underlie Aggressive Episodes[6]

Soda Linked to Behavioral Problems in Young Children[7]
Japan's Graying Criminals . . . Loneliness Is to Blame[8]
Candy Causes Adult Violence[9]
Violent Crime and Cholesterol[10]

The quest to identify causes of crime in the environment persists. The *St. Louis Post–Dispatch* of June 10, 2008, reported, "Crime may have declined in the 1990s because lead was removed from gasoline 20 years earlier."[11] In *USA Today,* an item appeared on July 17, 2009, with the headline "Top 10 'bad boy' baby names."[12] And an article in *Science News* dated August 2, 2013, cited shifts in climate change as strongly linked to violent conflicts across the globe.[13]

Although innumerable aspects of the environment have been identified as causing people to behave in a criminal manner, one that continues to command public attention is the alleged connection between exposure to violence in entertainment and violent conduct. This linkage is not new. Forty-two years ago, in his book *Seduction of the Innocent,* Frederic Wertham characterized comic books as "primers for crime."[14] Violent films, violent television programs, and violent video games all have been associated with violent behavior. Media critics have suggested editing newspaper content to avoid providing an impetus to the commission of "copycat murders."

Millions of people watch violence in films and on television programs. For more than fifty years, moviegoers have flocked to James Bond films that are saturated with violence. Millions of children and adults play violent video games. Responsible people are not transformed into killers because of what they watch or play for entertainment.

Statistics indicate that youthful violent crime has decreased as video game sales have skyrocketed. *The Harvard Mental Health Letter* of October 2010 cites research indicating that "use of violent video games may be part of normal development, especially in boys—and a legitimate source of fun too."[15] And when the Supreme Court ruled in June 2011 that video games should have the protection of free speech, it also noted that the psychological research on violent video games had methodological shortcomings.[16]

Copycat crimes do occur. On January 25, 2014, a man killed two people and injured another at a mall in Columbia, Maryland. The *Baltimore Sun* reported that the "killing spree" had been "inspired by the 1999 Columbine High School shootings" in Colorado.[17] The shooter waited to open fire until the exact time that the Columbine massacre had occurred. Imitating one of the Columbine killers, the shooter placed a gun to his mouth and pulled the trigger. Millions of people are aware of the infamous shooting in Colorado that remains in public consciousness. The same is true of subsequent mass shootings at the movie theater in Aurora, Colorado, at Sandy Hook Elementary School in Newtown, Connecticut, and at the Washington, D.C., Navy Yard. Millions of people who are aware of these horrific events through media coverage would never think of copying such crimes. What is critical is *not* what is on the movie or television screen, in newspaper reports, or in video games. Crucial is the psychological makeup of the individuals who watch the television programs, view the movies, or play the games.

In the scientific community, discussions of causes of crime have become more sophisticated, in that seldom is a specific factor singled out as "the cause" of crime. Instead, social scientists toss everything into the mix and speak of "risk factors," and of crime being a "biopsychosocial" phenomenon.

Why is there this persistent focus on causation? Kevin Dowling, a criminal investigator and member of the U.S. Secret Service, commented on the discredited notion that phases of the moon have a "quantifiable impact" on the incidence of domestic violence.[18] He explained that such beliefs arise from "a deep-rooted human need to find recognizable patterns in our experiences and to be in control within an otherwise chaotic world." In other words, if we think we know the cause of something that disturbs us, we will feel better, even if we cannot do much about it.

No single factor or set of conditions adequately explains the causes of criminal behavior. Writing in his book about juvenile delinquency, sociologist Robert MacIver stated, "To ask why any delinquency occurs is like asking why human nature is what it is."[19] This statement, made in 1966, applies every bit as much today. Even though the emerging field of "neurocriminology" may shed light on the origins of criminality, we are perhaps no closer to a full explanation of causation than we were decades ago.

The Environment Does Not Cause Crime

The earliest statement citing a causal link between poverty and crime has been attributed to Roman emperor and philosopher Marcus Aurelius (121–180 AD), who said, "Poverty is the mother of crime." Nearly half a century has passed since former U.S. Attorney General Ramsey Clark declared, "Poverty is the fountainhead of crime." In remarks made on September 18, 1968, to the National Commission on the Causes and Prevention of Violence, Mr. Clark expanded the list of causes of crime, citing "a clear connection between crime and poverty, disease, poor housing, lack of opportunity, segregation, injustice, [and] despair."[20] He asserted, "America must be stimulated to understand the nature and causes of crime . . . and to address them boldly." What followed was a plethora of government programs designed to improve opportunities for people who suffered from the deplorable conditions that Mr. Clark described. No doubt, many people benefited from those efforts and improved their lives significantly. However, crime remained an intractable problem in our society. Still, the bedrock belief persists that poverty causes crime.

Crime is not limited to a particular economic, ethnic, racial, or any other demographic group. Most poor people are not criminals, and many wealthy people are. Department of Justice statistics from 2010 revealed that thefts committed by students from households with an income of $75,000 or more were nearly triple the rate of thefts committed by students who came from households earning less than $15,000.[21] So-called white-collar offenses are not new. They began receiving widespread media attention at the end of the twentieth century and continue today. Although sensational cases receive the most publicity, our society has long had embezzlers and fraudsters preying upon vulnerable citizens, including their own families. They behave like this not because they are poor or lack opportunity, but because they believe they are unique and can ignore rules that apply to others.

But the conventional wisdom about poverty as a cause of crime, alive in the 1950s, '60s, '70s, and '80s, remains with us. In 2005, the United Nations General Assembly cited the "crime and poverty trap" to which certain regions of the world are vulnerable.[22] And in a 2006 publication, Joseph Donnermeyer and his colleagues pointed to "social disorganization" as facilitating crime in both rural and urban areas.[23]

Growing up affluent has also been cited as a cause of crime. On June 15, 2013, a Texas teenager killed four pedestrians as he was driving while intoxicated. His lawyer told the judge that the youth suffered from "affluenza."[24] The attorney explained that the boy's wealthy, indulgent parents were so preoccupied with their own problems that they failed to set limits for their son. Consequently, the teenager did not understand that there are consequences to misbehavior. "Affluenza," which of course is not a legitimate psychological diagnosis, was denounced in many quarters as "psychological mumbo jumbo." Nonetheless, the defense was effective in that the youth served no time in jail, but received ten years of probation.

During the past two decades there has been a slight shift from dwelling on "root causes" of crime to identifying so-called risk factors. Writing as a social science program specialist for the U.S. Department of Justice, Michael Shader noted that, having spent "much time and energy attempting to understand the cause of delinquency," researchers finally concluded that "there is no single path to delinquency."[25] Instead, they are applying to crime what has served as a successful model for medicine, in which factors are identified that put people at risk for developing diseases such as cancer or heart disease.

In 2011, the Centers for Disease Control and Prevention published a list titled "Risk Factors for the Perpetration of Youth Violence."[26] Eleven "individual risk factors," eight "family risk factors," six "peer/social risk factors," and six "community risk factors" were cited. The CDC cautioned, "Risk factors are not direct causes of youth violence." In what appears to be a hodge-podge list of thirty-one risk factors, the CDC identified almost any social or familial adversity one could imagine. Some "factors" identify conditions of a person's life over which he has no control, such as "parental substance abuse" or "high concentration of poor residents." Some of the risk factors should not have been termed "risk factors" in that they actually are descriptive of outcomes. "Association with delinquent peers" is not a risk factor. It is a result of the choices a person makes and characteristic of juveniles who commit crimes. "Antisocial beliefs and attitudes" do not place a person at high risk. The word "risk" is superfluous, because a person's antisocial thought processes virtually guarantee that the person will behave in a manner that injures others. "Involvement with a gang" requires participation in criminal activity. This is what gangs *do*, hence not a risk factor.

After identifying risk factors, the CDC listed "protective factors" that "buffer young people from the risks of becoming violent." In essence, these are antidotes to risk factors. It is difficult to see what is illuminating from the CDC's protective factor list, which includes items like "high grade point average," "positive social orientation," and "commitment to school." It does not take a social scientist to figure out that most children who do well in school, associate with responsible peers, and share activities with their parents are unlikely to be involved in criminal activity.

A person might demonstrate many of the risk factors and still remain law-abiding. Conversely, an individual might manifest many, or even all, of the protective factors, yet still commit crimes. I have interviewed adults and juveniles who have shown the following "protective factors" yet still engaged in illicit conduct: "high IQ, high grade point average," "religiosity," and "involvement in social activities."

A risk factor for criminality can be an incentive for self-improvement and hard work. What continues to impress me over these many years is not the circumstances and risk factors that people encounter but how they choose to cope with whatever life hands them. I have interviewed many criminals reared in poverty and chaotic homes, living in neighborhoods where firearms and drugs were as easy to obtain as cigarettes. They and their families certainly faced obstacles that citizens from more privileged backgrounds do not have to contend with. In nearly every instance, these individuals had a sibling who encountered similar risk factors and challenges while living in the very same environment, but they did not choose to follow a criminal path. Watching a parent or sibling destroy his life by participating in criminal activity has inspired many a person to embrace opportunities to live responsibly.

The concepts of risk and protective factors are applicable to cardiac disease or cancer. But with respect to criminality, this is old wine in new bottles. What are deemed to be "risk factors" take us right back to thinking that has been around for many decades, a conventional wisdom that has proved bankrupt.

If poverty causes crime, then one might have expected a surge in crime during the severe economic recession that began during 2008 and lasted through 2011. Actually, homicide rates throughout the United States plummeted to the lowest level since 1964, confounding criminologists, economists, and politicians. (It is worth noting that after the 1929 stock market crash, the incidence of crime also dropped dramatically.) Robberies significantly declined as well. *Washington Post* columnist Richard Cohen concluded, "The latest crime statistics strongly suggest that bad times do not necessarily make bad people. Bad character does."[27]

In the professional literature, a new twist has recently appeared in the perceived relationship between poverty and crime, namely that crime causes poverty. For example, if a person's home is invaded, robbed of valuable possessions, and he is assaulted and badly maimed, the economic impact would likely be devastating. Aside from the loss of property, the home owner might miss weeks or months of work, have to pay for costly medical care, then allot scarce family funds to install security devices for future protection.

Making changes in a particular environment can reduce opportunities for criminals to strike. An article in the *Washington Post* from March 2013 pointed out that, during cold weather, people leave their cars unattended while they warm up the motor.[28] A police officer observed that leaving keys in the ignition affords "a prime opportunity for someone to pass by and hop in." Architects, planners, and builders can create safer environments with preventive measures such as putting in bright security lights, installing deadbolt locks, and locating communal spaces in full view of the public. When the Washington, D.C., subway system was built, the planners avoided constructing pillars and alcoves where offenders could hide.

The criminal cases out places for opportunities, no matter where he is, even in jail. If the conditions in a particular environment make it difficult for him to commit a crime and avoid apprehension, he will go elsewhere. Efforts to change the criminal by changing the environment remain doomed to fail.

Biological Factors May Contribute, but Biology Is Not Destiny

In the late nineteenth century, Cesare Lombroso, an Italian physician, stated that some individuals are born criminals, the products of unalterable genetic factors. He regarded criminals as biological anomalies, savages in a civilized world. The concept of criminals having a constitutional defect endured.

In 1924, Richard Loeb, age eighteen, and Nathan Leopold, age nineteen, murdered fourteen-year-old Bobby Franks in Chicago. This crime had all the characteristics of a senseless "thrill" killing. In arguing at their trial to spare these young men the death penalty, attorney Clarence Darrow described their crime as "the act of immature and diseased brains." Writing in 1961, psychiatrist George Thompson stated that histories of psychopaths "reveal brain disease in 75 percent of cases."[29] And, in 1972, Clarence Jeffrey, a sociology professor, predicted that future decades would see "a major revolution in criminology" as biological aspects of behavior became better understood.[30]

For decades, it was not politically correct even to investigate whether biological factors play a role in criminal conduct. This was due to apprehension that identifying criminal genes would lead to selective breeding and genetic engineering, a throwback to Nazi eugenics. Now Jeffrey's 1972 prediction has come to pass, as the new field of "neurocriminology" emerges.

Dr. Adrian Raine, perhaps the leading spokesperson in the area of neurocriminology, stated in his book *The Anatomy of Violence,* "Criminals do have broken brains, brains that are physically different from the rest of us."[31] While observing that damage to the prefrontal cortex "can directly lead to antisocial and aggressive behavior," Dr. Raine conceded, "prefrontal damage doesn't always produce antisocial behavior." Dr. Raine also identified low heart rate as "a biomarker for the diagnosis of a conduct disorder," after which he noted, "of course, not everyone with a low heart rate becomes a violent offender." Dr. Raine issued a clarion call to social scientists "to reverse-thrust on their long-held beliefs and embrace the anatomy of violence." He asserted that focusing on biological factors is critically important to the development of public policy and to treatment that "will work more quickly and effectively than repairing the complicated social factors that also contribute to criminal behavior."

Other scientists and practitioners think that neuroscience promises considerably more than it delivers. In *Brainwashed: The Seductive Appeal of Mindless Neuroscience,* psychiatrist Sally Satel posed what she termed "one of the most daunting puzzles in all of scientific inquiry" by asking, "Can we ever fully comprehend the psychological by referring to the neural?"[32] Dr. Satel observed, "Mental activities do not map neatly into discrete brain regions." While not dismissing "brain-behavior relationships," she cautioned, "there are so many levels of influence on human behavior beyond the brain."

The emphasis of the new neuroscience has been on learning how the brain shapes the mind. However, the reverse is also true: the mind shapes the brain. Alterations in the brain are reversible, according to David Deitch, professor at the University of California, San Diego.[33] If a drug addict stops using drugs, this will have a profound effect on his brain. Reflecting on research about the brain and the mind, Adam Gopnik, writing in *The New Yorker* in September 2013, commented, "The lesson of neuro is that thoughts change brains" as much as the other way around.[34]

Studies of adopted children have provided evidence of the heritability of criminality. Most often cited is the large study in Denmark reported in 1984 by Sarnoff Mednick from the University of Southern California.[35] Dr. Mednick found that adopted children of criminal biological parents were more likely to be criminals than adopted children of noncriminal biological parents. Later adoption studies have confirmed his findings.

Biology need not be destiny. A person with a biological predisposition to alcoholism does not invariably become an alcoholic. There are people who have a type of brain damage that has been implicated in causing criminal conduct, but by no means do they all become criminals. As Dr. Raine pointed out, "The same biology and temperament may result in different life outcomes." The research of neurocriminologists deserves serious attention. So does Dr. Satel's caution that we "extract the wisdom neuroscience has to offer without asking it to explain all of human nature."

AS YOU CAN see, the theories about potential causes of crime are wide-ranging and endless. What follows is a tour inside the criminal mind. If you try to understand criminality with an open mind, perhaps you too will no longer be mired in myriad theories about why people become criminals. Instead, focus on the criminal himself, how he thinks and behaves in daily life. This may help you avoid becoming embroiled with such people in business or intimate relationships. Understanding how the criminal mind works is essential to developing public policy and to helping criminals change and become responsible human beings.

2

Parents Don't Turn Children into Criminals

The Child Rejects the Parents

Psychologists and other professionals have long blamed parents for nearly all the problems of their offspring. It seems to be a given that if you have a delinquent child, there must be something wrong with you.

Studies dating back to the early nineteenth century report that parental inadequacies are causally tied to juvenile delinquency. That view predominates today both in the professional literature and among the public, not just in the United States but in other countries as well. Children tend to be regarded as similar to unformed lumps of clay; they enter the world to be molded by their environment, mainly by their parents—upon whom they depend not just to meet their physical and emotional needs, but also to serve as role models. Blame for repeated juvenile misconduct rests mainly at the parents' doorstep. Authoritarian parents receive criticism for causing their children to become hostile, resentful, and aggressive. Permissive parents are criticized for spoiling children and giving them a sense of omnipotence. And parents who are democratic in their child-rearing are criticized for fostering a sense of entitlement. Parents of juvenile offenders are presumed to have any or all of the following deficiencies:

- They communicate poorly

- They fail to provide nurturance and support

- They do not institute appropriate discipline

- They do not monitor their children sufficiently

- They are rejecting

- They are abusive

- They are grossly inconsistent in their treatment of their children

One problem in making an accurate assessment of the family is that juvenile offenders frequently lie, especially when they are trying to create a favorable impression and avoid punishment. Their parents become a convenient target. Compassionate mental health professionals who do not know how offenders think, and who are unfamiliar with their tactics, are quick to buy into what these kids tell them. I have interviewed juvenile and adult offenders who portray their parents as monsters. However, their siblings describe these very same parents as loving, caring, generous, and devoted. I have also encountered mothers and fathers who, from any perspective, do a poor job of parenting. In nearly every instance where this is the case, the offender whom I am evaluating has a sibling who grew up under the same circumstances but did not commit crimes.

You cannot predict how children will turn out simply by knowing their parents. In a book, aptly titled *Stranger in the Nest*, psychologist David Cohen notes that a "strong inborn potential can trump parental influence" with the result that "one's child may seem like a perfect stranger." He argues that "parents have much less influence on a child's psychological development than is commonly supposed."[1]

Developmental psychologist Richard Trembley has written about parallels between criminals and toddlers.[2] Both are self-centered and lack a conscience. Both are physically aggressive in order to get their way. However, it is a misconception to equate criminals with very young children. Just beginning their journey through life, most toddlers respond positively to parents and others who help them solve problems in a responsible manner and without resorting to violence. The criminal, on the other hand, has been repeatedly exposed to socializing influences and has rejected them.

Child-rearing is not a one-way street. The child brings up the parent as well as vice versa. As any reader of this book with more than one child knows, children differ in temperament from birth. They differ in level of activity, the manner in which they interact with the environment, fearfulness, and other aspects. In a book titled *Understanding Your Child's Temperament,* psychiatrist William Carey points out that parents "cannot change their child's basic temperament," but they can control the way they respond to it.[3]

Consider the following situation. I was the tenth mental health professional to whom Ms. Patterson had turned when she consulted me about a crisis that had just occurred between her and her teenage son Tom. It all started with an innocuous request: Ms. Patterson asked Tom to turn off a movie he had begun watching because she thought its content was unsuitable for her younger children. She did not forbid him from seeing the film but asked him to view it later in private. Tom refused and responded with a string of expletives. During this meltdown, he ripped wires out of the DVD player, dashed toward his mother, knocked her down, then dragged her along the floor by her hair. As the younger children screamed in terror, he shoved her out the front door and she toppled down three cement steps.

When Ms. Patterson tried to reenter the house, he pushed her away, then locked the door. Entering through a different door, Ms. Patterson immediately phoned the police and filed charges against Tom for assault and battery and destruction of property.

In telling me about Tom, she recalled that when he was born, he cried constantly. Ms. Patterson could not soothe him, despite breast-feeding and attending to him constantly during his first year. She recalled his pediatrician assuring her that Tom was "a typical child" and nothing was wrong. She commented wryly, "This typical child kept me occupied fifty-five minutes out of every hour, day, and night." The situation did not improve. Tom was in constant conflict with other kids at preschool. His first-grade teacher seated him next to her desk because he was so distracting to the other children. Again, the pediatrician assured Ms. Patterson that Tom was just being a "typical boy." Tom could be sneaky or brazenly defiant. The Pattersons wondered whether to become stricter or loosen up. Nothing they did made a difference. Tom's parents were dismayed that he was commanding their attention at the expense of their other children, who posed few behavioral problems. He made life so unpleasant that it was often easier to capitulate to his demands or ignore his acting-up than deal with his rage and destruction.

Approaching adolescence, Tom seldom sought permission for anything and refused to say where he was going when he left the house. Mr. and Ms. Patterson felt more like police officers than parents. At the time his mother first met with me, she reported, "He goes into my room whenever he pleases, steals money from my purse, and throws away things that are not his." She and her husband began locking their bedroom door, and she was careful to hide her purse. Tom regularly reduced his little brother and sister to tears by fighting with them and breaking their toys. He refused to participate in family activities and, if forced to go along, he would ruin the event. Having a hair-trigger temper, he took offense instantly at any reprimand.

On one occasion, he became so enraged that he struck his father while Mr. Patterson was driving to church.

By seventeen, Tom had been badgering his parents for a driver's license for more than a year. When they refused to sign for him to obtain one, Tom launched an ongoing war to wear them down so they would change their minds. The Pattersons were adamant; they would not put innocent people at risk or render themselves liable by allowing their irresponsible son to drive. Lacking a license did not deter Tom. He would sneak out at night, grab his parents' keys, and cruise around. When the Pattersons discovered their car had been moved overnight, they hid the keys.

After Tom was arrested for the assault on his mother, he served a period of probation and then was sent to live for a year with his grandparents in a farming area in the Midwest. Living in a small rural community where everyone knew one another, Tom was under close scrutiny and had few opportunities to get away with egregious misconduct or criminal activities. Tom's behavior improved superficially, although he remained difficult and defiant toward his grandparents. That is the last I heard about Tom.

Mr. and Ms. Patterson had consulted one mental health professional after another. At one point, Tom was on lithium, prescribed for a mood disorder. There was no noticeable change in his behavior. The Pattersons invested considerable money and time on psychiatric and psychological evaluations of Tom. He thwarted all attempts at therapy or counseling. He defiantly shut down and disclosed little, or he fed the therapists what he thought they wanted to hear. One counselor insisted that Tom would be treatable only as an inpatient at a psychiatric facility. Insurance would cover only a brief stay, however, and the parents could not afford to pay thousands of dollars out of their own pockets. In addition to the many mental health consultations,

Tom's mother had attended numerous lectures and courses that addressed the topic of how to deal with difficult teenagers. Disillusioned by what mental health professionals had to offer, she remarked, "We could probably have done better doing anything other than wait for the 'educated' answer."

When I interviewed Tom shortly after he was placed on probation, he declared that his mother was the one with "a serious attitude problem" and proclaimed, "I have no rights whatsoever." He said about the incident leading to his arrest, "I grabbed her and dragged her out the door. My rights were threatened." He readily acknowledged that he had skipped not only individual classes but also entire days of school. Stating he had "no motivation" for school, he complained that he was forced to repeat junior year of high school because of poor grades. Asked about his experiences with counselors, Tom asserted, "I'm not the problem" and said, "They didn't change me." Asked if there was anything he thought he should change about himself, Tom replied in a challenging manner, "Like what?" He snapped, "People don't understand me. I think differently from most people."

Tom made it clear: other people were the problem. He saw no need to account to anyone for what he did. "My mom just tells me what to do, and I don't do what she says," he asserted. With respect to the arrest for assaulting his mother, Tom seemed to shrug it off, commenting that the real problem was that "the police officer didn't like me." As for his poor academic performance, he asserted, "I knew more than the teacher. He didn't like me." Although Tom acknowledged "I don't have a lot of friends," he did not attribute this to any deficiency within himself.

Like the Pattersons, many mothers and fathers of delinquent kids are superb role models, responsible, honest, diligent, nurturing, and firmly committed to their children no matter how difficult they turn out to be. Baffled as to how to cope with their offspring, they seek help, to no avail. Despite all the heartache, they do not reject their child. Rather, their child rejects them.

There is a lack of communication in homes like that of the Pattersons, and invariably the parents are faulted. One teenager told me defiantly, "I communicate to the point that it makes *me* happy. *They* need to communicate with me. I don't really want to hear anything they have to say. I don't have anything to say to them. We're just different kinds of people." Delinquent children do their utmost to keep their parents in the dark. They respond angrily to inquiries by mothers and fathers who they claim are nosy and have no right to pry into their "business."

Parents want to trust their children, and most children earn that trust. The criminal as a child makes up lies on the spot to get out of a jam. The day-in-and-day-out lies of omission, often about relatively mundane matters, provide unwelcome surprises. The child will claim that he is receiving good grades, that he has no homework, that he is doing well on tests, only to have his parents receive a report that he is failing several subjects and is missing assignments. This sort of youth is perfectly capable of being truthful. He will look a parent in the eye and tell the truth if he thinks it will achieve his immediate objective. Even then, he likely will relate only part of the truth—enough to lull a parent into believing him totally. During a counseling session, one teenager acknowledged, "If I tell the truth, it gives me room to get away with a lot more on the side."

Lies that seem to have no purpose roll off the tongues of such individuals. Mental health professionals consider this apparently "senseless" lying to be compulsive and pathological. However, once you understand the mind of the liar, you know that neither is the case. The "purposeless" lie has a purpose. Some of the lies the delinquent child tells are for the sheer excitement of it. Believing he can pull the wool over the eyes of others leads him to feel special and powerful. Speaking of how she had behaved since she was in middle school, one young woman explained, "I lie to make my life more exciting. The lies always start with a kernel of truth. That makes them more plausible." The only remorse these young people have about lying is getting caught. One boy told me that he lied because it was so easy to get away with it. He realized that, generally, people trust one another, and he took full advantage of this fact at every opportunity. His sole concern was that he had told so many lies to different people that, if they compared his stories, he might be found out and ostracized. From his standpoint, the only thing wrong with lying was getting caught. Parents of such children contend constantly with this mentality. If you have ever lived with an incessant liar, you know how unsettling it can be. You want to believe the person. Then you are at a loss as to what to believe. Eventually, you doubt everything he says.

Parents who are constantly lied to are sometimes faulted for not knowing or caring about what their children are doing. The professional literature identifies a lack of "parental monitoring" as a contributor to juvenile delinquency. You may remember, from some years ago, brief television spots that flashed on the screen asking, "Parents, do you know where your child is?" Parents like Mr. and Ms. Patterson think they do know. But the Pattersons would have had to hire a full-time private investigator to keep abreast of the whereabouts of their son, who lied to them regularly.

Of course, some parents do not adequately supervise their children. This may be because they are neglectful and don't care. More frequently, it is because they are stretched so thin by commuting, work, and other commitments that they cannot be physically present. Consider the "latchkey" child who arrives after school at an empty house. Without supervision, he has plenty of opportunity to get into trouble. Most such children are not juvenile delinquents. Upon arriving home, they dig into their homework or entertain themselves. I interviewed a single mother who worked at two jobs to support her two sons. She arranged for the boys to stay at a neighbor's home after school where an adult was present. Each afternoon, she called to check in. If either son wanted to do something out of the ordinary, such as visit a friend, he had to call with the details and obtain permission. One boy complied, while his brother exploited the situation. After his mother touched base with him, he would wander through the neighborhood and hang out with older kids, and he became involved in vandalizing property and shoplifting. Eventually he was caught concealing merchandise he had not paid for. In this situation, two boys responded completely differently to an identical set of circumstances. You could speculate that had the mother been home, the delinquent boy would have been reined in and not gotten into trouble. This might be true, but her staying home would not produce a change in her son's personality. The compliant youngster was trustworthy whether or not he was being watched, whereas the other was headstrong, sneaky, and dishonest.

As the personality of the criminally inclined child unfolds, his parents are gripped by apprehension that something terrible is going to happen. As their concerns mount, they try new ways of coping with his misbehavior. They more closely restrict his movement and privileges, but end up suffering more than the child, who sneakily circumvents the restrictions or blatantly defies them. In fact, it is a relief to the parents if they can bring themselves to lift the restrictions. Then there are fewer battles. Few parents want to function as a police officer!

In some of these families, corporal punishment is an unpalatable response because the parents prefer to talk to their kids and reason with them. They believe that resorting to violence is no solution. Those who do hit their offspring find that it has no long-range positive impact. The child absorbs the physical punishment and shows he can take it. He still does whatever he pleases.

Child abuse and criminality have long been linked. The theory is that the abused child identifies with the abuser (i.e., a bad role model) and becomes like him. Either because of that identification or because of displaced anger resulting from being abused, the child lashes out at others. There are serious consequences to this widely held but flawed theory. Criminals often are untruthful. They claim they were abused when it never occurred.

Professor of criminal justice Elaine Gunnison writes, "Physical abuse experienced by females has been linked to the onset of involvement in criminal activity."[4] Bear in mind that most children who are abused do not become criminals. The abuse has an impact, but victims of abuse deal with what happened to them in different ways. They may become withdrawn, anxious, depressed, or even think they deserved the abuse. Some are angry. And then there are those who resolve that they will never be like the person who abused them. These resilient individuals get along well with others, enjoy successful relationships, and become good parents. We don't hear about them because their stories do not make news.

And then there are the false allegations of abuse leveled by juveniles who want to get others into trouble and remove the focus from their own misconduct. Arnold, a twenty-five-year-old man, was temporarily living at his parents' residence while he prepared to take the bar exam so he could practice law. Living there had its challenges because he had to contend with Frank, his teenage brother, who had a violent temper. Arnold's father regularly had difficulties with Frank, who had kicked him, punched holes in walls, and been expelled from school. During an outburst, Frank had spat in their dad's face, then attacked and injured him, resulting in his receiving medical treatment. The police had been summoned to the house on several occasions. Major altercations often grew out of trivial disputes. Arnold and Frank were once arguing over who was to use a particular bath towel. Frank became furious and lunged at his brother. Trying to ward him off, Arnold raised his arms defensively and knocked into Frank, who tripped and fell, then rushed to the phone and dialed the police. An officer arrived, interviewed Frank and questioned him about the bruise, which Frank claimed his brother had inflicted upon him (it was caused by his fall), then arrested Arnold.

Arnold had to appear in court and hire an attorney; then he came to me for a psychological evaluation (recommended by his attorney). Arnold knew that his entire career could be jeopardized if he were convicted of assault and battery. After several interviews with this young man, I found him to be a quiet, shy fellow. He had no previous arrest record, never used illegal drugs, and drank only an occasional beer. Arnold felt badly about what had happened and wished he had handled the situation better. I found no evidence of a pattern of violence. Before this particular incident, Arnold had often endured abuse from Frank. I wrote the court that Arnold's striking Frank was accidental, "a situational response under unrelenting provocation." A judge dismissed the assault charge.

If you had a child who turned every request into a battleground, a child who disrupted family functions, a child you could not trust and who was defiant and destructive, don't you think it likely that, one day, you might run out of patience and slap him? I recall a father whose daughter, Janet, started taunting him and cursing when he asked her to help load the dishwasher. This was not the first time that he and other family members had endured Janet's defiance, temper tantrums, and threats. That evening, it was the one time too many. Frustrated, her dad slapped her with his open hand on the arm. Janet reported to her school counselor that her father had beaten her. Shortly thereafter, this man had a representative of a state agency investigating him. Worried about a possible criminal charge, he feared that he might lose his highly classified job. I stepped into this situation and told the social worker about the emotional volatility and physical aggressiveness of this girl, and related how her parents and younger brother constantly walked on eggshells for fear of upsetting her. I was not defending the father having slapped his daughter. Having counseled Janet for months, I provided the investigating officials with a context in which to evaluate what had happened. No finding of abuse was made. Again, as with Arnold, the abused person was not the delinquent child, but a member of the family. The complainant was in fact the abuser!

As I've indicated, one must dissect allegations of "abuse" to see what they really entail. Suffice to say, "I'm going to report you for child abuse" is a powerful weapon in the hands of young people like Janet and Frank. It removes the focus from their conduct and can result literally in putting their parents on trial. I have seen jobs and marriages imperiled by delinquent children making false claims of abuse. Psychologist Neil Bernstein termed these kids "self-proclaimed victims"—who enlist others' sympathy by "twisting words or actions around into personal affronts."[5]

Neglect and abuse are the most frequently cited examples of bad parenting that contributes to criminal conduct. However, the claim is also often made that children become delinquent because their parents overindulge them to the point that they constantly expect the world to cater to them. But like neglect, "spoiling" leads to different outcomes. Whereas some overindulged children remain self-centered and dependent on others, they do not function criminally. Pampered youngsters are jolted into reality once they leave home, and life's challenges force them to become self-sufficient. When a counselor attributes delinquent behavior to the overindulgent attitude of the parents, it is often based on appearances. The counselor sees that the child is behaving outrageously and seems to be suffering no consequences. But the counselor likely does not realize that for years the child has thwarted nearly all parental attempts to discipline him. Rarely is he behaving irresponsibly simply because his parents gave him free rein. The reality is more likely to be that consequences imposed so far have had no impact.

Mr. Cowell felt like a soldier engaged in constant battle with an enemy—except the "enemy" was Don, his fourteen-year-old son, who meant more to him than anyone else in the world. To outsiders, it appeared that Don could get away with anything, that he was totally undisciplined. The reality was that his dad was not a permissive parent. Mr. and Ms. Cowell had been struggling for years to socialize their son, and had clearly articulated expectations and established rules of conduct that Don regularly flouted. Mr. Cowell described his son as sneaky, defiant, and violent. Don urinated in a trash can, scribbled on walls, lied for no apparent reason, and refused to take responsibility for any misconduct. When confronted about his misbehavior, he smirked and appeared amused at his parents' dismay and anger. Even in the face of "evidence," he denied wrongdoing, blamed a sibling, or offered an excuse. Mr. Cowell remarked that Don appeared to delight in outwitting people, getting the better of them, and was never sorry for what he did. Told to go to his room, Don would refuse. His father would physically escort him to his room but, as soon as his back was turned, Don would sneak out. Don responded to parental discipline by screaming, cursing, slamming doors, and destroying property, including his own belongings.

The delinquent bullies siblings, helps himself to their belongings, and pins the rap on them when discipline is about to be meted out. This behavior is far more extreme than the usual rivalry that exists among brothers and sisters. Not only does the criminal child appropriate toys, DVDs, and clothes without permission, but he also destroys or loses them. He shakes down his siblings for money. They are cowed into submission, warned to keep their mouths shut, and threatened that if they squeal they will regret it. Some boys and girls suffer in silence because they retain a sense of loyalty to their sibling. One boy told me that he feared that if he complained too much, his parents would send his brother away to a school for bad kids. No matter how terribly his brother mistreated him, he did not want to shoulder the guilt for causing that to happen.

As long as the delinquent lives at home, his brothers and sisters know few peaceful moments and have little privacy. Worn out and on edge, their parents have less of themselves to share. Their attention has been stolen, leaving little time for the well-behaved children, whose problems are treated as less urgent, and so they feel shortchanged. The family is not really a family. The moments they do have together are often conflict-ridden. Once the delinquent leaves home, it is amazing to see that some extremely troubled families are instantly at peace.

After I lectured to an introductory college psychology class, a young woman approached me and said that she grew up with a brother who had the very personality I had just described. She said that she never skipped a class or day of school, was an honor student, and never caused her parents grief. As a child, she was resentful and baffled as to why she received so little attention and recognition from her parents. Only recently had she come to realize how challenged and exhausted her parents were from trying to cope with her extremely difficult brother. She urged me to advise parents not to ignore the children in their family who are doing what is expected.

When families remain under siege, parents find themselves experiencing emotions that they never thought possible; the most alarming is dislike for their own child. The prevailing thinking among professionals and in society has long been that children turn to crime because they are rejected by their parents, who are hostile toward them. Time after time, I have seen the opposite.

The parents never completely give up on their offspring, no matter how destructive he is.

I recently counseled seventeen-year-old Sam, who resided with his mother and stepfather, Linda and Max Spence. This teenager lived in affluent circumstances, attended an excellent private school, enjoyed membership to a gym where he regularly worked out, and wanted for nothing except a car, because Ms. Spence wisely refused to sign for him to get a driver's license. Despite the material advantages, neither Sam nor his siblings were overindulged. But Sam behaved as though he were a privileged character to whom rules did not apply. In contrast to his siblings, Sam was self-centered and constantly made demands of others while refusing to do a favor for anyone unless it suited him at the moment—which was rarely the case. Sam's grades dropped. He started sneaking out of the house at night to party with his buddies, returning home under the influence of alcohol or marijuana.

Sam endeavored to transform our counseling sessions into a court in which he was putting his mother and stepfather on trial, then trying to enlist me as his ally. He wanted to live with his biological father, who was single and had a laissez-faire approach to child-raising that was in stark contrast to Mr. and Ms. Spence's approach. Sam proclaimed that in several months, when he turned eighteen, he would walk out forever and live with his father. Mr. and Ms. Spence consulted me about what to do in the meantime. Ms. Spence, who did not work outside the home, was raising three younger children. She saw Sam setting a terrible example for his siblings, continually provoking arguments and behaving in a shockingly disrespectful manner to her. In desperation, she tried to improve their relationship by taking Sam on a trip to visit colleges, which he had requested. She was pleasantly surprised that they got along amazingly well. Of course, the reason for their good rapport was that Ms. Spence had engaged in an activity of her son's choosing. As soon as they returned home, he reverted to being the same nasty, defiant person he had been before their sojourn. Ms. Spence felt horribly guilty for disliking her own son. Although she never stopped loving Sam and worrying about him, living with him had become intolerable and was detrimental to the younger children.

Ms. Spence began thinking that, with the school year ending, perhaps it was time to allow Sam to live with her ex-husband even though she knew the loose bachelor-pad environment was unsuitable. Tearfully, Linda Spence told me that she felt like she was throwing her son out of the house and jeopardizing his future—that this is not what a good mother does. I reminded her that her three younger children have just one childhood and it was being ruined by Sam. She had done everything she could to help Sam, including taking him to counseling. I reminded her of the extremes to which Sam had gone in placing the entire family in danger, legally and financially. Assisted by his biological father, Sam had filed a complaint with the authorities that he'd been physically abused by his stepdad. The Spences had been compelled to hire a lawyer and appear at a hearing. Once the judge had obtained the full picture of what was happening in the Spences' home, he dismissed the charges and admonished Sam for claiming abuse when it had not occurred. In light of all that had happened, and with the prospect of Sam hanging around disrupting the household all summer, Ms. Spence was prepared to let him leave. I agreed, for there was nothing more that she or her husband could do to help their son.

A situation in which a son or daughter is of legal age to live independently but refuses to leave his parents' home is no easier. The parents may be afraid that if they force their offspring out, he will do something drastic. One mother said, "We've been through a flaky suicide attempt. He slashed his arms close to the wrist. Believe me, I hope I never have to go through anything like that again. My intense feelings of dislike after he was in the hospital scared me. Sometimes I think I need an analyst. These kids don't realize what they do to their parents."

Delinquent children deploy a formidable barrage of tactics to gain the upper hand as they are locked in battle with their parents. They do regularly what many well-behaved kids do on rare occasion. There is far more combat than conversation. Their tactics are designed to divert the focus from their irresponsible conduct to what their parents have allegedly done, thereby placing the parents on the defensive. Delinquent children tune their parents out, then claim they never heard them. They say they were confused because their parents failed to be clear. They accuse their parents of failing to listen or insist that they misunderstood. Constantly, they level accusations of unfair treatment and demand a rationale for whatever a parent says or does. They minimize the seriousness of what they did by citing their good intentions. Delinquent children accuse their parents of expecting perfection and placing too much pressure on them. They may appear despondent and make statements indicating they cannot do anything right and are total failures. Claims that their mom and dad don't care about them, don't love them, and are ruining their lives are often effective in inducing guilt. Feeling guilty and exhausted, the irate parent hastens to reassure his offspring, then softens disciplinary measures; and the misconduct, which is the main issue, is not addressed.

Some marriages crumble under the onslaught of kids who are chronically oppositional and defiant. It is not unusual for parents to have different perceptions and approaches to the same child. One may be firm and attempt to hold the youngster accountable for his behavior. The other supplies sympathetic explanations, unintentionally enabling further misconduct. When parents do not have a united front, the child divides and conquers. He plays one against the other, aligning himself with the more lenient parent while vilifying the stricter one. He then seeks sympathy from others, telling them how his parents fight all the time and how dreadful his home life is, failing to disclose that his misbehavior is the genesis of the discord. I have seen parents blame themselves and each other with disastrous consequences to the marriage.

The emotional and financial toll that this takes on the parents is staggering. The guilt is tremendous as parents psychologically beat themselves up, wondering what they should have done differently. "Did we put too much pressure on him and create a monster?" one mother asked me. Another speculated that she and her husband had erred because "we didn't give our son the playtime he needed when he was younger." These parents experience physical symptoms, depression, and anxiety. Rather than serving as a refuge from pressures of the outside world, their homes are filled with tension. Every time the phone rings, the parents' hearts sink. What is it this time—a distraught neighbor, the school reporting a fight, the police, or, worst of all, a hospital informing them that their child is injured or dead?

Few parents remain indifferent or give up. They continue to seek solutions—spend more time with the child, enroll him in a different school, support his joining organized sports and clubs, send him to a counselor, seek counseling themselves. Grasping at solutions, their soul-searching continues. Mothers and fathers blame themselves, each other, and people and events outside the family.

Often out of uncertainty, fear, and a sense of obligation, mothers and fathers will bail their offspring out of trouble. I have met a number of parents who went into debt posting bond, hiring a defense attorney, and securing other services for a child who was facing serious criminal charges. Even after experiencing disgrace in the community, parents continue to offer support. One father told me, "He's still my son. I need to stand behind him." This parent had refinanced his home in order to hire a top-flight attorney to defend the fifteen-year-old boy. He received no gratitude in return. His son expected the help. "He has no idea of the hardship he's caused the family. He thinks we're responsible for fixing his problem," the father remarked.

A divorce is tailor-made for these youngsters to maneuver and exploit parental differences. Emily's parents, Mr. and Ms. Douglas, shared joint legal custody, with Emily living primarily with her mother. Ms. Douglas, who had two younger children, was by far the firmer parent in setting household rules, requiring accountability, overseeing homework, and monitoring Emily's whereabouts. She maintained that her ex-husband was a permissive parent who "gets mad and walks away." Mr. Douglas acknowledged to me, "I've probably been too easy setting limits." But, from time to time, he too would reach the end of what he could endure, then resort to measures such as taking Emily's phone away and removing the door from her room.

Emily had been a real handful but, after the parents' separation, she became incorrigible. Both parents had to contend with Emily's constant lies, running away, sexual promiscuity, panhandling, vandalizing property, smoking, and physically attacking her siblings. The Douglases watched their daughter—whose intelligence was in the superior range—skip classes, refuse to do homework, and not open a book to study for tests. Her mother described Emily as abusive and having "an unbelievably foul mouth." The Douglases were constantly at odds over how to help and discipline her. Whereas Mr. Douglas was prepared to send Emily to the local public school and considered it a waste to pay for private school, Ms. Douglas paid for their daughter to attend a private Catholic school where classes were small and she would be closely monitored. Emily swore she would never set foot in the door of the parochial school and demanded to live with her father. Claiming that all her mother did was "cut me down," Emily declared she no longer wanted to have contact with her. Emily characterized her siblings as "little devils who kiss up to my mom." She denounced her dad, asserting, "He always favors my brother and sister. He yells and screams at me." As to her father's alleged favoritism toward the other children, Mr. Douglas acknowledged, "My other kids are fun to be with." Being a parent to them was far less stressful.

Emily's mother had dragged her to a therapist who concluded that the teenager's main problem was being "in the middle of a parental situation." She said that Emily had no "serious disorder" and attributed the girl's difficulties almost entirely to the "poor functioning" of her parents. There was a "parental situation" all right—created mainly by Emily behaving in a calculating and deceptive manner, and becoming extremely adept at playing one parent against the other. She favored whichever environment seemed less restrictive at the time. Her prescription for resolving all problems was that others should capitulate to her demands. The entire family, especially the younger children, were psychological prisoners of Emily.

The therapist was dead wrong in attributing Emily's behavior to parental dissension. The fractious relationship between Mr. and Ms. Douglas provided opportunities for Emily to drive an ever greater wedge between them, create distractions, then do whatever she wanted while they fought. The family remained in chaos as this teenager almost instinctively cased out family members for vulnerability and preyed upon them. Emily's problems were characterological far more than "familial." I advised the parents to seek co-parenting counseling so they could be more functional as a team. Family systems therapy, which her therapist had recommended, would have been a colossal waste of time. If the parents didn't have enough problems before family therapy, they'd have had more than enough after. I have encountered refugees from family therapy where all that the parents had to show for the experience was large bills and more stress. I recommended that Emily see her own therapist, who would address thinking patterns that were continuing to result in behavior that was destructive to others and, ultimately, to herself.

A mental health professional can always fish for some underlying problem and spot conflict in any family. Family systems therapy assumes that one member's problems are symptomatic of a disturbance in the entire family. One underlying theory is that a child may become delinquent because he has become the scapegoat whom the family unconsciously selects to act out the other members' forbidden fantasies and impulses.

It may well be that a disturbed family system can give rise to isolated cases of antisocial behavior, but there is as yet no convincing evidence from treating entire families that the disturbed system is the *cause* of a child's expanding and intensifying patterns of delinquent activity. In fact, what often happens in treatment is that the delinquent child scapegoats the family. While insisting that he is all right and does not require treatment, he capitalizes upon the therapist's view that the family is to blame because it is "sick."

I receive countless letters and e-mails from frustrated parents and stepparents throughout the United States who are locked into unceasing struggles with children like Don, Sam, Tom, and Emily. They report that when they took their children for counseling, the counselor immediately assumed the parents or stepparents were to blame. They became the focus of the counselor, an experience similar to being put on trial. Meanwhile, little was done to help their children. Clearly, some parents need help. Unfortunately, even if they make changes, this by no means ensures that their offspring will become a responsible human being.

Sometimes stepparents can have the psychological distance to be more objective than biological parents. They discover that despite unceasing devotion to their stepchildren, their best efforts are spurned. Tamara had struggled to be good to Tony, whose own mother had died when he was eight years old. She became more and more dismayed at the path Tony was taking—the friends he chose, his disinterest in school, his sneaking around and lying, and his disrespect for anyone who told him what to do. She found herself walking a tightrope. While trying to nurture and show affection to the young teenager, Tamara found that Tony balked at nearly every request or requirement that came from her lips. When I spoke with Tony about his relationship with his stepmother, he was quite caustic. He complained, "She makes a big deal out of nothing" and asserted that he prefers not to talk to her at all. "She doesn't have a lot of trust in me, and I don't have a lot of trust in her," he said. Tamara commented, "I can't live with a child who does not want me in his life. I've tried. I saw him as a child who needs to be loved." Their relationship had soured to such a point that she acknowledged with great sadness, "I don't like this kid." Tamara decided to reach out to Tony in writing. Her letter expressed sentiments similar to those I have encountered time and again as stepparents try valiantly to relate to this type of child, but receive repeated rejection. Tamara described finding not only that she had failed in her relationship with her stepson, but also that her marriage had been shaken to its core.

It is becoming pretty apparent that you and I are not going to be able to live together in a peaceful positive relationship. I am more sorry for this sad state than I'm sure you'll ever believe.

You have the tools to make changes in your life but you don't appear willing to use them. . . . It's frustrating to me to see you waste your great potential. It is wrong of me, but I'm afraid I take your actions very personally, feeling that they are directed at me, the intruder in your life. This feeling may or may not be justified.

I honestly do not feel that I have expected more of you than the other kids. . . . Two and a half years I loved you. Two and a half years ago I wanted to hug you, let you laugh your joy or cry your fears on my shoulder. I have wanted so much to be a good part of your life. . . . Now two and a half years later my desire is to smack you a good one to see if that would get a response, any response at all from you. I much prefer love to hate, hugs to smacks. I much prefer the love I had 2½ years ago to the anger and tension that is in me now.

We seem no closer to a solution now than at any other time. I have an overwhelming need for peace and warmth in my life and home. So much anger, tension, and frustration is killing your dad's and my relationship and destroying me.

You need to know these things and I need for you to know these things. I claim my share of responsibility. Your dad loves you very much and sees the good in you. I wanted to love you but love only grows if it is fed. I see good in you but also a need for firm guidance. Perhaps some day you'll decide to let the Lord guide you and then life will be much easier for you. Love . . .

Tamara had reached a critical point both in her relationship with her stepson and with her husband. Moreover, she had started to dislike herself because she realized she was behaving precisely opposite to what she had envisioned when she became Tony's stepmother. Striving to be nurturing, loving, and supportive, she had been rejected. And she felt despondent that her husband was thinking he had to choose between her and his son. Refusing to give up on her marriage or on Tony, she agreed to participate in couples counseling.

It is not unusual for parents who divorce and remarry to encounter difficulties when it comes to stepchildren accepting them. Blending families requires a lot of work, and sometimes professional assistance. However, the type of child being discussed here seizes upon any aspect of a stepparent's personality, or just the fact that the individual is not his "real" parent, in order to justify misconduct. One boy told me that his stepmother, who was younger than his biological mother, would ground him or tell him to go to his room. He said tersely, "Sometimes I did; sometimes I didn't. There was nothing she could do. She wasn't my mother. No one who's not old enough to be my mother can tell me what to do." He mocked his stepmother's voice and imitated her facial expressions and mannerisms.

Occasionally, a delinquent child sets out to convince his parents that he is trustworthy. He unexpectedly shoulders responsibility at home, is cordial toward his parents, and shows a better overall attitude. It is as though the sun has broken through the dark clouds. This turns out to be a con job, a front calculated to lull his family into thinking he is changing his ways. The motivation is generally to obtain something he wants and has been denied, or to have a disciplinary measure retracted. It is reverse "behavior modification." The child seeks to convert the parent to his point of view, then "reward" the parent by good behavior. He expects a temporary positive turn to blot out all prior transgressions. The improvement in behavior does not last.

After years of assault upon their own values, some parents gradually adopt views that previously were unacceptable. In one case, a mother steadfastly opposed to illegal drugs began to soften, then became an advocate for legalizing marijuana. This was after recognizing that she was helpless to prevent her child from using the substance, and after being convinced by him that everyone else was using it. Such shifts in attitude grow out of a parent's desperation to draw closer to a child who appears increasingly estranged.

Nancy Lanza was the mother of Adam, the Newtown, Connecticut, school shooter. From information that has emerged since the 2012 shooting, it appears that Ms. Lanza sought to help her son but also enabled him. *Washington Post* columnist Ruth Marcus described how Adam's mother catered to him. "Certain types of dishware could not be used for particular foods. Birthdays, Christmas, and holidays were not to be celebrated. The mother got rid of a cat because the shooter did not want it in the house."[6] Ms. Lanza did all the grocery shopping and cooked to her son's specifications. And she endured Adam's refusal to communicate with her except through e-mail, even though they resided in the same house. This mother indulged her son to the point that she "encouraged his interest in guns" and had a check made out to him to buy a pistol for Christmas. Ms. Lanza was a parent who took extraordinary measures to connect with her son, "seizing on a mutual passion"—guns.

In a calculating manner, a child can callously exploit a parent's desire to strengthen their bond. He believes that rather than risk a setback in the relationship, the parent will cave in on any number of issues. If one parent abdicates authority but the other does not, a major disruption to the marital relationship ensues.

The reader may conclude that I am letting parents off the hook, no matter what their inadequacies might be. This is not the case. Parents who are abusive, neglectful, inconsistent, and psychologically disturbed are likely to have an adverse impact on their offspring. This is not to say, however, that they will invariably produce criminals. Fortunately for society, most children who suffer neglect or abuse do not become criminals. Furthermore, it is striking to observe that some criminals are the sons and daughters of parents who are devoted, stable, and responsible. Unfortunately, the best efforts of parents to help and correct this kind of child can and usually do fail. As it turns out, the parents are usually the victims, the child the victimizer, not the other way around.

Some jurisdictions impose penalties on parents for their children's misconduct. If a youngster remains on the streets past a legally imposed curfew, is chronically truant, or engages in other violations, parents can be fined or jailed. I have interviewed beleaguered parents who have done everything in their power to guide, restrict, and discipline their incorrigible offspring only to have him continue to evade and brazenly defy their conscientious efforts. Punishing mothers and fathers for the delinquency of their children may be helpful when applied to parents who are irresponsible and neglectful. But such measures will only further undermine and demoralize conscientious parents who need help, not censure, from law enforcement and the courts.

Any parent who has read this chapter may be alarmed if he or she has a child who is showing any of the behavior just described. But before concluding that they have a budding criminal in the family, they should ask themselves whether their child is showing isolated instances of the behavior in question or engaging in *patterns* that are expanding and intensifying. Not every child who swipes a few coins lying on a table at home or steals candy from a store becomes a criminal. This chapter documents patterns in a minority of children who eventually inflict enormous damage upon society, no matter what their parents or others do to deter and help them.

Even when parents feel under siege and are frustrated and angry, they grieve. Many report that they can't stop thinking about their child and all his problems. One mother articulated the plight of many parents of delinquent kids when she said, "I feel so sorry for my fifteen-year-old child who harbors so much hatred for the world and those around him. I would give anything to have him come home and enjoy being one of the family. If I could wave a magic wand and make everything all right, I would sell everything I own to get that power. I can't stand having to watch this child ruin his life. I would love to hear the news that, just maybe, there is hope for him to become a relatively normal, happy teenager, one who is able to enjoy these precious years of childhood." Another mother, commenting about her massively irresponsible, rude, and self-centered daughter, remarked, "Over and over, I start having hope for her, but then she always does something awful. But without hope, what kind of mother would I be?"

Some exhausted mothers and fathers reluctantly conclude

that they have reached a point where they can do nothing to improve the situation. Still, it is extremely painful to do the only thing they can—sever the tie with their child.

"I'm learning to let go," said one father. "I don't want to tie my life to this problem. It's like a very ill relative. You prepare yourself for the death of that person." Still, the daily pain remains intense while commonplace events become sources of humiliation. What does a mother or father tell Grandma when she asks about her grandson? It is mortifying for parents to acknowledge to a school counselor that they cannot control their child at home, much less what he does in school. Each incident serves as a powerful reminder that they are failing at what they consider perhaps the most important experience in life—raising a child. Through it all, the child is without a shred of comprehension or concern about his parents' agony. When asked how he felt about his parents' distress, one boy replied coldly, "It's like an operation. They have to live with the pain. It's their problem."

3

Peer Pressure

No Excuse for Crime

"My buddies got me into shoplifting. My friends turned me on to drugs. Everyone I know does it. I'm just like any other teenager." These are typical statements I hear during interviews of young offenders. They contend that they were pressured, bullied, misled, or even compelled to commit crimes. This is what they tell others only *after* they are apprehended, when they are trying to avoid punishment. Many of their parents share the same view, explaining that their child is basically a good kid who was misled and corrupted by "falling in with the wrong crowd." The facts are very different.

Numerous professional observers contend that associating with delinquent peers is a "strong risk factor" for turning to crime. But this is like saying that diving into water gets you wet. It reveals nothing about causation, but a great deal about choice. "Us kinds find each other," observed a youthful offender. Criminals seek out one another for their own purposes. In radar-like fashion, they hone in on others who have similar interests. They are not enticed into crime against their will. If a basically responsible youngster makes an unwise choice and misjudges another youth who he discovers is up to no good, he will eventually extricate himself from that situation and most likely from the entire relationship.

There is no denying that peer pressure exists practically from womb to tomb. From preschool play groups into adult life, we experience pressure from people around us, especially our contemporaries. Every high school has its cliques and social groups—nerds, freaks, jocks, preppies, and so forth. The critical question is who a child *chooses* for peers.

In urban and suburban areas, kids flock to organized activities. As they meet new people and discover new interests, they become involved in sports, religious groups, scouting, community service, and school clubs. A process of socialization occurs as these children learn about cooperation, competition, sharing, and self-control. Whereas responsible children discover opportunities for fun and personal growth, the delinquent child experiences a gnawing restlessness and mounting boredom. Some delinquents refuse to participate in any organized activities. Others join but drop out. They resent having to fulfill requirements that others impose. One boy said that he quit Boy Scouts because "I don't like listening to adults and their telling me what to do." He denounced his fellow troop members as "nosy and annoying." He asserted, "I didn't feel like part of the troop. I just quit because I didn't like it." Such youths drop out of organized activities because they do not receive the commendation that they think they deserve. Invariably, they pick a fight with a coach, scoutmaster, or other leader. A responsible child may drop out of an activity because he grows discouraged and doesn't think he can measure up to what is required, or perhaps because he discovers a different activity that he prefers. The delinquent leaves faulting the organization, the leader, or the other participants. He seeks immediate recognition but does not want to do what is necessary to merit it.

Very young children do not divide the world into good kids and bad kids. But quite early they develop a sense of the boys and girls who do what they are told to do and those who cause trouble. The child who becomes delinquent is drawn like a magnet to others who are daring and disobedient. He gravitates to kids who are risk takers, doing things that they are not supposed to do. To gain acceptance, he must prove himself by demonstrating that he can fit in, that he is tough and can be trusted. He dresses as they do, mimics their language, follows them wherever they go, and does what they ask. In time, he is no longer considered a tag-along, but as one of the crowd. The criminally-inclined child has the utmost contempt for responsible boys and girls. I recall a fifteen-year-old scornfully asserting, "Preppies, they think they're so neat with their little alligator shirts. I'm not going to be a damned preppy." There was nothing wrong with this statement on the face of it. But with whom did he decide to associate? The kids who were skipping school, using drugs, and stealing from stores. Another teenager, speaking contemptuously of his brother, remarked, "To go to school, to come home and do homework and be with my parents; that's like being a dog on a leash." He rejected his more conforming classmates and gravitated toward older boys whose chief activity was "hanging out."

"Hanging out" is a common expression that does not necessarily have negative connotations. But when delinquent youths say they are hanging out and offer few specifics about what they are really doing, it is likely that they are up to no good. "Hanging out" translates into going places and being with friends whom their parents may not know, much less approve of.

Alan and his parents were referred to me by an attorney. The teenager had been spending most of his leisure time hanging out with several buddies. While his parents were at work, these boys would sneak teenage girls into the house, have sex with them, and film their encounters. When a boyfriend of one of the girls learned about this, he sought revenge and informed a school counselor. As a result, the youths ended up facing criminal charges. Alan saw nothing wrong with what he'd done and explained that he was "just being a teenager." There was plenty more that Alan did when he hung out. Skipping classes and entire days of school resulted in plummeting grades. Because he convinced his mother he was sick, some absences were marked as excused. Most of his truancy she did not know about. Left to his own devices, Alan did very little that was constructive, spending hours drinking with his buddies and playing video games.

Responsible youngsters "hang out" as well. But if one were to view a film of the conversation and activities of the two groups, striking differences would be observable. The issue is not simply where teenagers congregate but what they do when they get there. At a shopping mall, the more conventional kids might be spending their allowance or job earnings, engaging in window shopping, or standing around conversing about who is dating whom or what transpired at school. The delinquents would be wandering through stores, casing out merchandise, contemplating how to abscond with whatever seems appealing. Or they might draw attention by picking fights, making unsolicited and provocative comments to girls, singling out and taunting other kids, and being generally disruptive.

When both parents work, it is sometimes difficult for them to know their children's friends. Nonetheless, most parents endeavor to talk with their kids about what they are doing, where they are going, and whom they are with. They ask to meet these friends and develop some sense of who they are. The delinquent youngster keeps his friends away precisely because he knows his parents will not approve of them. Many parents have told me that they implored their sons or daughters to bring friends to the house. "I've tried so hard to make our home a pleasant place for my son to bring his friends," said one mother. "But he always goes out. They never come here."

The teenage delinquent's crimes become more frequent, daring, and serious. He is neither corrupted by others nor dependent on them for ideas. A torrent of schemes cascades through his mind, and he enacts those that are most exciting and feasible. He has plenty of his own ideas and is receptive to whatever others propose. The more he gets away with, the more emboldened he is. His offenses begin when he is very young and likely appear insignificant. As Sandy's grandmother was driving home, she saw in the rearview mirror that he was playing with a toy car that she knew he did not have before they had gone shopping. She turned the car around, drove back to the store, and marched him to the manager to return the pilfered toy. It certainly is not unheard of for young children to walk off with an item that was not purchased. However, once the transgression is discovered and they are punished, they rarely repeat the offense. Sandy was undeterred. The lesson he learned was that he needed to be more careful not to get caught. Stealing the inexpensive toy was only the beginning of a pattern that expanded to stealing money from his parents, then, as a teenager, joining other kids who were shoplifting, specializing in the theft of DVDs that they then sold. They embarked on a binge of slashing car tires and breaking into hundreds of vehicles. They enjoyed placing anonymous calls, delighting in "freaking out" people who were elderly. I learned about these offenses from Sandy while I was evaluating him at the request of staff from a juvenile correctional facility. Who knows how many other wrongdoings he did not disclose?

Parents, teachers, and others who think they know these boys and girls well are in the dark about their secret lives. If they had a film of their day-to-day existence, they would be astounded at the number and variety of crimes and their seriousness.

Preoccupied with fire, at the age of ten, Jonas burned ants in the driveway. He dipped arrows into paint remover, lit them, and shot them into trash cans of water. He learned to construct aerosol bombs, which he exploded. He acknowledged owning a dozen lighters, one of which he used to burn a bees' nest just to see what would happen. Jonas stole money from his parents, made prank phone calls, and frequently skipped school. He and a friend discovered a checkbook lying on the ground. Although he had no idea how to write a check, Jonas was quick to learn once his buddy started rattling off "all these neat things we could get." And so he forged a check in order to purchase a hundred dollars' worth of illegal fireworks.

Like many delinquent kids, Jonas's friends were older. He acknowledged, "Some have done lots of bad things. Some look mean and thuggy, but they're not." Jonas had not only engaged with peers in property damage, theft, forgery, and assault, but he had also, on his own, committed sexual offenses. Jonas exposed himself to a lady on a bike trail and repeatedly stood naked in a window of his house. He clandestinely entered a stall in the girls' bathroom at school so he could peek under partitions. At a swimming pool, he inappropriately groped a little girl. He was arrested for inducing another little girl to undress, then fondling her. Jonas told me, "Everything awful happens to me. I have bad luck!" He blamed his friends for leading him down a wrong path.

The delinquent is intent on conveying to peers an image of himself as invincible. As each youth is attempting to prove himself, he is also struggling to overcome intense fears that he is desperate to keep concealed. Fears of the dark, heights, water, and lightning persist into adolescence, sometimes into adulthood. These kids are also fear-ridden about their bodies. They exaggerate the significance of each ache, often to avoid fulfilling an obligation. However, their physical distress does not motivate them to go to a doctor, because they fear that even greater pain will be inflicted. Consequently, a minor ailment that is neglected may develop into an infection or a real illness. These youths fret over their height, weight, strength, and physical attractiveness. Some are so self-conscious about the size of their penis that they refuse to attend physical education classes in order to avoid undressing. Some, obsessed with developing their physique and gaining strength, spend hours a day working out—a self-discipline they never develop with respect to school or work.

Reputation is all-important. These youths build and maintain a "rep" for themselves through the way they talk, their style of dress, and the types of activities in which they engage. The profanity and street slang lacing the language of the middle-class delinquent is indistinguishable from that of his inner-city counterpart. Even as a small child, the delinquent accepts dares from others to convince them that he is not "chicken." These juveniles prove their mettle by jumping from high places, careening down steep hills on skateboards, riding the scariest roller coaster, racing a bike through someone's flower bed, competing to see who can swipe the most candy from a store. They play rough and take unfair advantage both in organized sports and in their own sandlot games. They prove to one another that they are physically tough by deliberately sticking pins in their arms or burning themselves with cigarettes. No tears at any time; they show that they can take it, whatever the source of the pain.

Children who are intentionally destructive can transform many items into weapons. The automobile broadens opportunities for all juveniles of driving age, and there may be a new set of pressures from peers. Responsible adolescents regard "having wheels" as lessening dependence on their parents to take them places. They may drive in a reckless manner to impress friends. Some take advantage of their new freedom and misuse the automobile by going places that their parents would highly disapprove of. A preoccupation with cars is typical of many adolescents, but what delinquents do with a car far exceeds the norm and has nothing to do with pressure from peers. Impatient to drive, many a delinquent is behind the wheel before he is licensed. His buddies allow him to drive, or he "borrows" the family car. The automobile is unleashed as a weapon, and the youth drives as though he owns the road. In a car, more territory is accessible for criminal activity. The city kid can hit the more affluent areas, and the suburban kid can make contacts in the inner city.

Hanging out with other delinquent kids and committing crimes is always risky in terms of the possibility of getting caught, convicted, and confined. There can be even more unintended and serious consequences. Tragically, for Mark it was the death of his best friend. He claimed that it was an accident but, since only he survived, there was just his version of what actually transpired. Mark despised school and refused to do homework. His father frequently grounded him so he would concentrate on schoolwork. Because his dad was rarely home to enforce restrictions, Mark would leave the house or invite friends to visit, which he was strictly forbidden to do. As to his father's comments about what a "bad influence" his friends were, Mark told me during an evaluation I was conducting, "He can't stop me from going out with them." He remarked, "The kids I hang around with, he'd be surprised. He wouldn't think I'd hang around kids who get into a lot of trouble at school." Mark said almost boastfully, "A couple of them have had experience with the police for a lot of fighting." He said that as though he regarded an encounter with the police as a badge of honor.

Mark wanted to be one of the "cool people." Rather than being pressured to join them, he sought them out. About his choice of friends, Mark remarked, "They were different. I don't consider myself a prep and never will. The troublemakers were the cooler people. They were like me. They'd disobey their parents and go out late at night." Mark did a lot of "hanging out" with buddies who would play "practical jokes," as he termed them. They would pick on other kids, make harassing phone calls, and toss fireworks into people's yards. They rang doorbells and vanished. He recalled hurling water balloons at kids he disliked. Vowing to even the score with a youngster who had offended him, he found a tree house that the boy had spent many hours constructing and tore it down. Mark acknowledged that he had been in fights but qualified this by saying they were all in self-defense.

I should note that, characteristically, kids like Mark tell adults that they do not start fights but are pressured by peers into fighting others with "a bad attitude." Or they inject themselves into a fight, later claiming virtuously that they were defending a friend. The emphasis is always on what someone else did to provoke a fight. One boy told me, "I don't see myself as a fighter." However, when he was nine years old, he was suspended from school because he knocked another student against a wall so hard that the boy's back was cut open. After this admission, he then boasted that he fights "to have a good time." After declaring, "I don't start fights with people," one youth qualified his statement to acknowledge that he had been in a dozen fights. He explained, "I don't stand there and let people do things to me. I stand up for my rights and defend myself. I'm not going to be a sissy; all my friends would call me a chicken."

Having insisted that he is not a fighter unless he gets forced into it, Mark eventually confessed that he enjoys fighting and stated that, while mastering martial arts skills, he discovered a way to "block out pain." Mark's fascination with guns prompted him to read about them in books and magazines. He collected toy soldiers and weaponry and regularly visited surplus stores where he acquired a uniform, badges, a gas mask, a helmet, and other battle gear. At nine he owned a BB gun, and at twelve he had a .22 caliber rifle, which he was allowed to use for target practice when he visited his uncle. Mark's father kept the .22 and a pistol in a closet and forbade his son from touching any weapon unless he was present. Mark ignored his father's warnings and restrictions. One incentive for his buddies to come over was that, in return for a pledge of secrecy about that visit, they could hold the weapons, which Mark would remove from the case. On one occasion, Mark aimed a pistol at boys who came over to hang out. Describing to me how they were messing up the house and kicking his dog, he explained, "I was having trouble keeping them under control. I was putting limits down, and they wouldn't respond. I thought they were my friends. They had been in before and nothing bad happened." He claimed that he had grabbed the pistol because "it was the only way I could control them."

On the day of the tragedy, his best friend, who had seen the guns many times, came over. Mark claimed that the boy "manipulated me" because he persisted in pestering him to take out the pistol so he could hold it. Certain the gun was not loaded, he handed it to the boy, who then wanted to play "keep away." Mark said, "I grabbed the gun and accidentally pulled the trigger just trying to get it away." After describing what transpired, he told me with chilling detachment, "His death was partly his responsibility."

Parents and counselors of kids like Mark attribute the child's choice of friends to low self-esteem, which results from their failure to fit in socially with others who are more in the mainstream. And it is true that many youngsters feel that they don't "fit in" because they are socially awkward or perform poorly in school. Comparing themselves to their more successful peers, some perceive themselves as outcasts. They would love nothing more than to be part of the mainstream. Many find ways to compensate for social or academic difficulties, including developing solitary interests or participating in activities where they can hold their own. But Mark's perception that he didn't fit in anywhere wasn't because he felt inferior. Quite the contrary. He held most of his peers in contempt. He mocked the "puny-eyed bookworms" and preppy conformists. When I interviewed Mark after his arrest, he acknowledged that he had no close friends.

Let's examine a relationship in which it appeared that a kid was led astray because he was weak and a follower. When Ronald met Larry at school, he was immediately drawn to him, although he had difficulty explaining exactly why. "I don't know what makes one person like another. We just think the same way," he said when I interviewed him. He explained that not only could he confide in Larry but that Larry "made it seem like he was making me a better person." Larry was instructing him how to "act cool" and how to "wear better clothes." Ronald was reluctant to go into detail, saying, "It's not a comfortable thing for me to talk about; I don't want to betray confidences." Ronald gradually let down his guard and opened up about his relationship with Larry. Larry flattered Ronald and sometimes paid him to do things for him. For example, Larry paid Ronald to write a term paper. When I pointed out that Larry had paid him to cheat, Ronald ignored the point and countered by bragging, "No one else can write like me." Ronald did whatever Larry asked. In return for driving him places, Larry demanded that Ronald pay. Requests for money continued, with Ronald paying for car parts, food, gas, a DVD. On one occasion, when Ronald refused to give him gas money, Larry threatened to maroon him without a ride. Ronald would spend the night at Larry's house but tell his parents he was having a sleepover at another boy's home. Unsupervised, into the early morning hours, the two would listen to music, drink wine coolers or beer, and smoke marijuana paid for by Ronald from his allowance and earnings from a part-time job. Before long, he had given Larry a key to his house, which was often empty on weekdays because both of his parents worked. Larry helped himself to liquor, experimented with expensive photographic equipment, and had sex with a girlfriend in a bedroom.

Ronald's mother disapproved of her son's friendship with

this boy, whom she saw as a manipulator and corrupting influence. She sensed that her son had become subservient to Larry and that their relationship had not one redeeming feature. Asked about his mother's view, Ronald snapped, "She assumes too much," pointing out that she had never laid eyes on Larry. This was true, of course, because Ronald would not allow Larry anywhere near his parents.

During counseling sessions, Ronald acknowledged that he was allowing himself to be controlled by his friend but remained unperturbed, remarking that he was having fun anyway. "He's cool," Ronald said, as if this explained everything.

Was Ronald simply an insecure, weak-willed kid who was suggestible and easily led astray? From among hundreds of fellow students at school and numerous neighborhood kids, Ronald was drawn to this one boy. Larry did not force him to be his friend. Larry opened up a world that Ronald was prepared to embrace, a life far more exciting than the comparatively mundane, conventional existence of most of his contemporaries. Ronald found his friend increasingly fascinating as he discovered more about Larry's criminality—his selling beer to minors, his network for drug distribution, and his widespread stealing.

Criminals perceive themselves as very much in charge, not in the least suggestible. To admit that he could be easily influenced by others is completely antithetical to a criminal's image of himself. He is suggestible to activities that are exciting and that will inflate his self-importance. Primed for action, he may require only someone else's urging to provide the impetus for a particular crime he already has in mind. A person's suggestibility depends on what is important to him. This applies to responsible people as well as criminals. A responsible merchant is not open to engaging in fraudulent practices, no matter how profitable they might appear. A dishonest businessman is quite amenable to committing fraud if someone makes a proposition that he thinks will enrich him. In short, a criminal is open to suggestion if what is offered is something that he wants.

All sorts of temptations exist for any youngster—an expensive leather jacket, a cell phone, an iPad, keys dangling in the ignition of an unlocked sports car, alcoholic beverages in his parents' liquor cabinet. Pressure from peers does not compel a youth to commit a crime. Responsible boys and girls will leave untouched what does not belong to them. Pressured to do something contrary to their idea of right and wrong, they choose not to participate. If, by chance, an otherwise responsible youth errs in judgment and succumbs to temptation, he is overcome by remorse when apprehended—sometimes even if his offense is not discovered—and is unlikely to repeat the behavior. In contrast, the developing criminal has no remorse about his crime. His only regret is that he got caught, and he resolves to avoid being apprehended in the future.

While I was interviewing Ronald, it dawned on him that Larry had not been a friend at all. Ronald commented, "I've had so much trouble keeping friends. I don't know which people really like me." He summed it all up when he stated, "I don't know how to deal with relationships. I ruin them. I'm a loner."

The characteristic of being a "loner" has been ascribed to a number of perpetrators of mass shootings. These young people allegedly sought revenge after being ostracized by their peers for being different. But it often turns out that they were shunned because they were menacing and scary to be around. During March 2005, Jeff Weise, sixteen years old, went on a shooting spree at a school in a small town in Minnesota, killing five students, a security guard, a teacher, and then himself. An article in the *New York Times* quoted Mr. Weise as saying, "I have friends, but I'm basically a loner inside a group of loners. I'm excluded from anything and everything they do."[1] The manner in which Mr. Weise behaved was unlikely to win friends. He "wandered around by himself" clothed "in Goth style," wearing eye makeup and dressed in a full-length black trench coat. He showed fellow students "elaborate, disturbing drawings he made in his notebook, some of them depicting people with bullet holes in their head [and] of half-living people with blank stares." He also posted a story on the Internet in which a school security guard had his throat "ripped out, replaced by a bloody mass of torn tissue." My point is that some perpetrators of horrific crimes are loners not because they are victims of others but because they drove others away by their behavior. Eric Harris and Dylan Klebold, perpetrators of the infamous 1999 Columbine High School massacre in Colorado, did not behave as though they wanted to be part of the mainstream. Like Jeff Weise, they were known to have dressed strangely and behave oddly. They displayed an intense dislike for entire groups of students. A national magazine characterized them as having compiled "an inventory of their ecumenical hatred: all 'niggers, spics, Jews, gays f—— whites.' "[2] Such individuals pride themselves on being different from their fellow students, for whom they have nothing but contempt.

In 2012, James Holmes killed twelve people and wounded fifty-nine others by shooting into a movie theater in Aurora, Colorado. Press reports characterized the twenty-four-year-old as being, like other mass killers, a person who put people off because he would not interact with them. The *New York Times* described Holmes as having "walked a solitary path . . . not engaged with people around him . . . [and] so uncommunicative that at times he seemed almost mute."[3]

After being expelled for repeated misbehavior and for threatening to stab a student, fifteen-year-old Toby was enrolled in a full-time therapeutic program designed to teach him social skills so he could have better relationships. His counselor stated that, upon entering the program, Toby was "completely mystified and baffled as to how to relate to his peers." She said that, despite the complete support that other kids offered him, he "hurled insults and vented inappropriate anger" toward them. She observed that the boy "seemed invested in having his peers reject him." Toby also isolated himself from the instructors. When they asked him to fulfill program requirements or to perform chores, Toby's response was to explode, hurling insults and death threats toward them. Eventually, staff members believed Tony had "made positive strides" in peer relationships. Less than a year after graduating from the program, Toby's parents consulted me about their son because he was displaying alarming behavior and they did not know how to cope with him. They thought he had made no improvement whatsoever in getting along with them or anyone else. Toby remained a loner. He said contemptuously about his fellow high school students, "There's not a normal person in my school. Everyone has emotional problems." He discussed his fascination with mass murderers, criticizing the Washington, D.C., snipers only because "they didn't give people a chance to protect themselves or run." He confided he "used to like Nazis because they'd kill big amounts of people." Immersed in books providing details of assassinations and massacres, he remarked to me, "It's interesting to see how a person can kill another." Toby's parents signed a release for me to bring this information to the attention of their son's new therapist, which I did.

In contrast to individuals who alienate people and scare them, some criminals are gregarious and charming. Because of their appealing personalities, they are able to draw others into their web and exploit or, in some instances, annihilate them. In a *Vanity Fair* article titled "The Roots of Evil," serial killer Ted Bundy was said to have maintained the image of "the pleasant adolescent" who became vice president of the Methodist Youth Fellowship and later "the rising star in Republican state politics."[4] Concealing the dark aspects of his personality, he was able to "disarm" those around him and succeeded in "luring the smartest, most beautiful coeds to their deaths."

Whether juvenile and adult offenders are scary like Mr. Weise or have magnetic personalities like Mr. Bundy, they are still loners. They do not permit others to get too close because they have much to hide. Focused on themselves, they have no concept of the reciprocity and empathy that is necessary to foster relationships. Love, trust, loyalty, and friendship are absent from their lives.

Grant returned home from prison. To his wife's dismay, instead of looking for a job, he headed to the streets, explaining he needed to get back to his buddies whom he hadn't seen for a long time. His wife asked where these so-called friends had been when he was in prison. Did they visit him? Did they offer to help her or their children in his absence? They were really not friends at all.

Bullying has been seen as a prominent factor underlying criminal conduct. The thinking behind this is that some youths are so psychologically devastated from being repeatedly targeted by bullies that they can endure no more and want to even the score. In other words, the victim becomes a victimizer.

Bullying is hardly a new phenomenon. Perhaps most readers of this book can recall episodes during childhood and adolescence of being cruelly taunted and pushed around by other kids. Bullies may inflict their particular form of venom by focusing on physical features, social awkwardness, race, ethnicity, sexual orientation, or any other characteristic that sets someone apart. A youth whom I interviewed teased unmercifully a boy who had a severe tremor when he tried to raise an ice-cream cone to his mouth. Another told me he hates people who are gay. He said, "I'd come down on them, make them feel like shit. If they touched me and I thought they were a faggot, I'd shove them against a locker or push them away." Bullying is a forerunner of future criminality. Bullies case out others to identify any vulnerability and pounce upon it. They achieve a sense of enormous power by intimidating others and watching them suffer. With the Internet and other forms of technology, bullies can inflict misery with the click of a button on a vastly expanded scale, without having a face-to-face encounter. Elizabeth Englander, a psychologist, cautions that bullying and cyberbullying start occurring when children are very young.[5] She states, "In Massachusetts, over 90 percent of third graders are already interacting online." Psychologist Michael Nuccitelli, an expert in the area of online predators, points out, "Bullying used to be confined to schools, neighborhoods, or some small geographic location that the bullied child could leave and seek respite. With cyberbullying, the target child has no escape from the taunting and harassment."[6]

Bullying causes intense emotional pain, as anyone who has been a victim recalls. Just as children react in different ways to parental abuse, the same is true with how they cope with the abuse meted out by bullies. Some children feel helpless and withdraw socially to the point that they avoid going anyplace where they might encounter their tormenter, even refusing to attend school. Some internalize the mean comments directed at them and lose self-confidence. Some become depressed. Some address the situation either by standing up to the bully physically or seeking adult help. The American Psychological Association reported the results of a Duke University twenty-year study of 1,300 children.[7] The researchers learned that, in contrast to children who were never bullied, those who were bullied "were at higher risk for psychiatric disorders, including depression, anxiety, panic disorder and agoraphobia." My point is that most victims of bullying, even though they may fantasize their tormenter's demise, do not grab a gun and massacre innocent people.

What about pressures experienced by youngsters to join gangs? It has long been thought by many who analyze gang membership that belonging to a gang offers young people the family experience that they have been deprived of. Ostensibly, a gang provides support, acceptance, and a structure, as well as a hierarchy of leadership and a path to approval and success. In a highly structured gang, a member can gain a sense of belonging, status, and power. Some social scientists contend that gang membership offers an understandable, even normal, means of adapting to circumstances that seem otherwise hopeless. If this were true, everyone who lives in an impoverished, decaying, or otherwise brutal environment would join a gang.

Contrary to what gang members say when held accountable, most were not coerced into joining. In neighborhoods where no gangs operate, delinquent youths in search of action will travel significant distances to locate a gang. Becoming part of the organization is not like joining most clubs. The prospective member has to prove his mettle through an initiation process such as getting "jumped" and engaging in combat with other gang members. Or he may be required to prove he is worthy of membership by assaulting someone.

I interviewed two young men, José and Pedro, brothers who grew up in a poor, gang-infested neighborhood in East Los Angeles. José joined gangs and spent most of his young adulthood in prison. He told me about the pressure to join, the turmoil in his home with a heroin-addicted father, and his belief that he would never amount to anything. No matter how many times he was arrested, he kept going back to "gang banging" and drugs. Asked why, José quipped, "Maybe they didn't punish me enough in prison." The fact was that nothing compared to the exciting life he lived as a gang member. José rejected overtures of counselors who were eager to help him while he was incarcerated and on probation.

Pedro was determined to become the opposite of his brother and father, and do everything he could to help his mother so she could afford to move out of the neighborhood and live a better life. Pedro reported being accosted repeatedly and badgered about joining a gang. He told me, "It was kind of expected you'll be a warrior. They'd catch me on my way home. I'd say, 'It's not for me; I'm not the gang type.' They'd call me names, jump me. They'd see I wasn't giving in. I was called a punk, and they'd spit at me." As he saw it, gangs offered a future of destruction, prison, and death. Pedro said, "Gang banging is a little thing in this big world. I wanted to be like Bill Gates, not the guy getting shot at. Teachers and coaches showed me there's another way out. They'd speak about colleges." Pedro maintained a vision of a world that offered boundless opportunity if he stayed out of trouble. Despite the turmoil at home and pressure from peers, he adhered to that vision and faithfully attended school, worked hard, played sports, and rejected the temptations around him— which, to him, were not temptations at all. As for his brother, Pedro commented, "My brother lived it, and I watched; I saw his mistakes."

In addition to excitement, gangs offer opportunities to feed one's sense of importance and fortify one's self-image as a tough guy. The purpose of a gang is not to provide a stable, nurturing, caring family environment. It is, as Pedro observed, a group of warriors who ruthlessly pursue their objectives, and who readily dispense with anyone who betrays them. In the family of the gang, anyone is expendable. Loyalty is demonstrated through a street code of "don't snitch." The primitive rites of initiation, the violence, and the drugs are hardly to be equated with the nurturing and support a real family offers. Many men and women who did not have a stable home life during childhood struggle to educate themselves, acquire skills, and work hard, hoping one day to have the family that they missed.

In Nicholas Pileggi's book *Wiseguy: Life in a Mafia Family,* former mobster Henry Hill attests to the critical role of choice in determining his path in life.[8] "At the age of twelve my ambition was to be a gangster. To be a wiseguy. To me being a wiseguy was better than being president of the United States. . . . To be a wiseguy was to own the world. I dreamed about being a wiseguy the way other kids dreamed about being doctors or movie stars or firemen or ballplayers."

If becoming a member of the mob seems to be extreme, consider a middle-class teenager I spoke with who clearly articulated the life she wanted. She boasted about her self-imposed separation from responsible peers, for whom she expressed complete disdain. She remarked, "What straight people do for fun, I'll never know. What do they do? If they started partying, they'd freak out." She remarked that she had nothing to talk about with "straight people," and affirmed that the kids she wanted to be with were similar to her. She made it clear: peer pressure had nothing to do with living in what she characterized and glorified as "life's fast lane."

4

"To Hell with School"

This is not a forum to discuss the shortcomings of schools or of our educational system. It is a place to describe how criminals function as children in whatever schools they attend. School alienation has been cited by the American Psychological Association as "a key factor in the development of both juvenile delinquency and school violence."[1] The fact is that the criminal rejects school long before it rejects him. He is bored and "alienated" from school because his objectives have little relationship to academic learning. Instead he exploits the school, using it as an arena for crime or as a cover for it. Like his parents, educators are unsuccessful in socializing and educating the criminal. Special education programs and counseling usually fail to assess the criminal student, much less change him.

There are three different patterns that criminals demonstrate in their approach to education. The first can be seen in the individual who drops out before completing high school. School is an arena for his criminal activity as long as he attends. These early dropouts pit themselves against teachers and the school administration. They do little or no work, disrupt the learning process for those children who want to learn, and leave as soon as they can.

A second group I call the "drop-offs." In the elementary years, they do not pose serious disciplinary problems. They are intelligent enough to get by, many excelling academically. The work is not that difficult and they get along reasonably well with others. They have one primary teacher, and they learn how to please her without making too many waves and getting into trouble. Upon entering middle school, they encounter teachers who impose a variety of requirements, including a significant increase in homework, more tests, and the imposition of deadlines for papers and projects. Because the minimal effort that they exerted in earlier years proves insufficient in meeting the new challenges, their academic performance drops off. Most drift through high school, and some enter college but do not graduate.

A third group excels academically. Highly intelligent, these students receive good grades and may achieve honor-roll status. Academic success enhances their overall reputation, thus giving them leeway to get away with whatever they want on the side. Some of these talented students graduate from college and go on to earn advanced degrees. We shall now examine these three criminal types: the dropout, the drop-off, and the high achiever.

The Disruptive Student Who Drops Out

Some delinquents are difficult to manage from the time they enter school. Many teachers tend to be sympathetic toward them and regard their misconduct as cries for attention. Understanding that children sometimes take time to adjust to school, they patiently try to guide them through whatever difficulties they are having. The problem is that the adjustment never occurs, and the teacher's kindness is exploited as weakness. Sympathy starts to wane as this child grows older and his behavior becomes increasingly disruptive and destructive. Some youngsters go on a rampage of theft and destruction. If they want something another pupil has, they help themselves. Belongings vanish from desks, coatrooms, and lockers, and items disappear from supply closets. Depending on the extent of security, the parking lot can become a treasure trove of unlocked cars for plundering. Youths with stolen goods find customers prepared to take hot merchandise off their hands. Drug transactions with an eager clientele flourish. Damage to property occurs during school hours and after-hour break-ins. Vandalism takes an enormous toll as delinquent students carve on desks, deface walks with graffiti, mark up books, shatter windows, and break furniture. Teachers find that it is more difficult to deal with one or two of these miscreants than to teach an entire class of pupils who want to learn.

It is extremely hard for a child to concentrate on the morning's math lesson after he has just been shaken down for lunch money and warned that he'd better return with more cash the next day. Studying is nearly impossible when a pupil has been threatened that unless he hands over money for "protection," he will be beaten to a pulp. Some children do anything to avoid using school bathrooms for fear of being victimized in unsupervised places. Fear stalks the corridors of schools where extortion and fistfights occur frequently. If enough delinquents are concentrated in one facility, the school is affected as though it were under siege. The entire educational process becomes hostage to youths who create a climate of fear and interfere with learning.

A school must choose which among a staggering array of problems merits concentration of precious resources. Behavior that is not terribly disruptive or longstanding may be temporarily overlooked. Nonattendance is one area in which some schools are lax in imposing penalties, at least until it becomes a frequent pattern. When the school does take action, the child may deny having been absent, compose his own excused-absence notes, and forge a parent's signature. Parents do not know that their offspring has skipped school, nor do they have any idea as to how he spent the time when he was truant.

School personnel walk a tightrope in managing disruptive students. If they must restrain or isolate a violent child, they risk getting into trouble with administrators or parents, dragged into court, or assaulted by friends of the delinquent. But school officials can also get into trouble if they take no action and a child is harmed. Suspension provides temporary relief, but rarely can the permanent expulsion of a disruptive student be justified, hence it is rarely a solution. An attempt to transfer such a child to a special program or facility meets with accusations that he is being stigmatized, deprived of opportunities, and dumped.

Schools often fail to report crimes to the police department. They prefer to handle them internally and avoid publicity. One reason is that administrators do not consider the behavior at issue to be a crime. A second reason is that reporting crimes brings in outsiders who want to conduct their own investigations, which can be disruptive. A third is that it makes the school look bad, and, by implication, the administration as well.

Many schools have law enforcement officers on the premises. For example, Washington, D.C., public and charter schools, during the 2012–2013 school year, had 102 armed school "resource officers" and 253 unarmed guards.[2] The presence of law enforcement officers constitutes a deterrent to some crimes. They are able to diffuse conflicts as well as to make arrests. (During 2011, D.C. school police officers made nearly five hundred arrests.) Some schools have security monitors, much like airports, that students must pass through when they enter the building.

Many schools, especially in inner cities, resemble war zones more than learning centers as delinquents stake out their territory and show who is in charge. In 2013, the American Psychological Association (APA) reported its findings from a survey of 2,998 kindergarten to twelfth-grade teachers.[3] Ninety-four percent reported students victimizing them in some manner:

44 percent were physically attacked, 72 percent were harassed, while 50 percent experienced theft or property damage at school. Violence against teachers has been termed a "national crisis."

The *Baltimore Sun* reported on February 16, 2014, that, during the past school year, there were 873 suspensions of students for physical attacks on staff. The report highlights the fact that employees of the public schools are injured more frequently than those working for any other Baltimore city agency with the exception of police department employees.[4]

A 2013 APA article recommended measures to prevent violence against teachers.[5] One intervention was to engage students in "positive activities" in the community in order to enhance their self-worth. Whereas this might be effective with many students, few delinquents have an interest in participating in community organizations. The article went on to report that "school based crisis-interventions" resulted in "positive changes from teacher and staff perspectives . . . but not from the students' perspective." In short, many delinquent students reject whatever is offered them because it is not in line with their interests.

Some school systems have adopted a "zero tolerance policy" in response to students who bring drugs or weapons onto school grounds. These policies have become increasingly controversial. Few people disagree with the need for strong measures to deal with students who are a threat to safety, but critics have denounced these policies as overreactive and ineffective. A task force commissioned by the APA declared, "Zero tolerance policies may create, enhance, or accelerate negative mental health outcomes for youth by creating increases in student alienation, anxiety, rejection, and breaking of healthy adult bonds."[6] Although this may be true in some instances, consider the type of child we are considering. Who alienates whom? The delinquent youngster is locked in combat with those who want to educate him. One teacher told me, "Brian has an 'I dare you to teach me' attitude." As a child, the criminal alienates the very people who want to teach and help him. He has no interest in forming "healthy adult bonds." Certainly it is true that any policy can be misapplied. Suspending a seven-year-old because he chewed a pastry into the shape of a gun and pointed it at a classmate is an overreaction. So is suspending a teenager who carries an aspirin in his pocket into the building. But surely, some form of "no tolerance" is necessary when it comes to dealing with students who are a menace to public safety.

Academically, most delinquent children function far below their potential. Because of strong social pressure and school attendance laws, they remain in school long enough to avoid hassles with parents, teachers, truant officers, and the courts. When they reach an age when the law no longer requires them to attend school, many leave.

A high degree of illiteracy among criminals is often attributed to their suffering from a learning disability. The theory is as follows. Because the child is learning disabled, he fails, becomes frustrated and resentful, and his self-esteem plummets. Receiving no attention that is positive, he compensates by seeking it in negative ways. Perhaps a small minority of delinquent children is truly learning disabled, but it has not been demonstrated that there is a causal connection between learning disabilities and juvenile delinquency. The reason most delinquent youngsters are illiterate is that they refuse to learn to read, not because they have a learning disability. Think about what reading requires—attention, concentration, repetition, sticking with a task that may seem tedious or difficult.

As a child, the criminal is certain that he is smarter than others. But he bristles at being told what to do and having to perform on others' terms. Typical is a statement by one boy who informed me, "I could get all A's if I want to, but school sucks." These youngsters do the minimum and care little about the end result. They determine the standard for what they deem acceptable. Some delinquents decide not even to go through the motions. One teenager said, "I didn't see the need for homework and told the teacher I wasn't going to do it."

School systems have a major problem when it comes to accommodating chronically disruptive students. One or two such pupils can rob an entire class of opportunities to learn. Almost every teacher has had experience with a defiant child or teenager who makes extraordinary demands on his time. This is not the chatterbox, "class clown," or child who requires constant prodding to complete projects or turn in homework. At their worst, these students commit crimes in the classroom—theft, assault, and vandalism. They usurp time, attention, and resources that should be expended on their classmates. They do not respond to ordinary disciplinary measures or to extraordinary efforts to engage them in academic subjects. Administrators do not always support the teachers who have to instruct these recalcitrant individuals. One teacher told me that administrators would tell the faculty, "If a student is misbehaving in your classroom, there's something you're doing wrong." She said that, with such an attitude, administrators would "just let the troubled kids stay at school and terrorize the others."

Suspending children with severe behavioral problems leaves them unsupervised at home or on the streets, since parents usually work. If they are placed in so-called alternative schools with others like themselves, they continue to be disruptive. All too often, such schools are dumping grounds for students.

But it is a travesty to allow these students to remain in regular classrooms and interfere with motivated students who want to learn. It is a terrible disservice to allow conscientious and well-behaved children to come to school each day terrified that they will be bullied, shaken down for lunch money, or threatened in other ways. For a minority of the trouble-causing students, referral for mental health services may be helpful. Most likely, these kids will reject whatever help counselors offer. From their point of view, the problem lies not within themselves but with others.

Early in 2014, U.S. Attorney General Eric Holder stated that zero tolerance policies which lead to student suspensions "disrupt the learning process" and contribute to a "school to prison pipeline."[7] Mr. Holder said that such measures have an adverse effect on young people, "increasing their likelihood of future contact with the juvenile and criminal justice systems." Might it not be that the cause and effect are reversed here? It isn't the policies that disrupt the learning process but rather the students who cause the disruption necessitating the policies. Nor is it the policies that result in young people ending up in detention. Perhaps errors have been made in applying severe sanctions to minor misconduct. However, when crimes are committed on school grounds, administrators need to take legal action.

If students who pose a danger to others are to be educated in the public schools, an investment must be made in developing closely monitored programs in a strict, highly structured environment, with a teacher and an aide in charge of a small number of these criminals-in-the making. If these students improve in their functioning, they can earn their way back into a mainstream classroom. Such measures are costly. But spending whatever funds are required will pay large dividends in educating boys and girls who want to be educated, and possibly in turning around others who seem hopeless.

The Drop-off

Some students perform very well academically during elementary school. They do not find the work difficult and exert little effort to achieve good grades. What little homework there is, they manage to finish in school or by dashing it off at home. They do well enough so that seldom is there a question about whether to promote them. They glide easily from grade to grade. Some of these children do so well academically that teachers cut them a great deal of slack when it comes to tolerating misbehavior. A fourth-grade teacher wrote on a boy's report card, "If he could adjust his behavior to the level of his academic capabilities, he'd be the most outstanding student in the school."

Nine-year-old Clark was one of these kids who seemed to have it all. He was good-looking, an excellent athlete, respectful to teachers, and he absorbed whatever was being taught like a sponge. Intelligence testing showed that he was at the upper end of the superior range. That Clark was highly competitive in every activity was a decided plus, but it also had a downside. A teacher pointed out that his "competitive nature" helped him excel in school subjects. However, she noted, "it sometimes works against him socially. He can be overly aggressive around his peers." Clark bullied other students and was aggressive playing team sports to a point of being reprimanded repeatedly for unnecessary roughness. Among an array of A's and "Outstanding" grades were three U's (for Unsatisfactory) in the categories of "shows respect for peers, property and authority," "gets along well with others," and "works collaboratively." The teacher seated Clark away from the rest of the class so he would not distract others or become distracted by them. In a note on his report card, she commented, "It is his social behavior that continues to be a concern and derails him from reaching his potential as a student and leader."

Clark was still very young, and of course the hope was that he would grow out of what was just a phase. Many children do go through times when their behavior is troubling. But they benefit from the correction and discipline of others, and learn from their peers. This is not what was transpiring with Clark, who seemed to get worse as the year progressed. There is little doubt that Clark will get by for quite some time because he is extremely smart, athletic, talented, and has a lot of charm. But all that will take him only so far. Whether he will be a drop-off in intermediate school or blaze an accomplished trail through college or beyond remains to be seen. What is very clear is that serious trouble lies ahead unless Clark corrects patterns that are already bringing him into conflict with teachers and other students (as well as his parents and siblings).

When boys and girls like Clark enter middle school, they often continue to do well academically at least for a while. The middle school experience is new, and they enjoy the freedom of moving from class to class and not being under the watchful eye of one teacher all day. They may excel particularly during the first grading period, because a lot of the work covers review material and is not that hard. But as the novelty of middle school wears off and the pace and difficulty of the work increases, they do not apply themselves, and there is an erosion in the quality of their academic performance. One student told me, after receiving outstanding grades for the first reporting period, that he subsequently became "disenchanted" and "disillusioned." His grades dropped from A's to C's. "I don't want to accept C grades. I'm not a C student," he declared, after which he acknowledged, "I lost my motivation and desire." The reality was that he found the work becoming progressively more difficult and he could not continue to earn the same high grades with minimal effort. The habits he developed in elementary school no longer produced the results he expected. And he just did not see any reason to work harder.

I was counseling James, a high school sophomore, who told me he had a history test the next day. I saw that he had come from school to my office carrying no books, and asked him about it. He replied that he knew he would ace the test and saw no reason even to glance at the textbook. When I met with James the next week, I inquired as to how he did on the test. By then, that subject was far from his mind, and he asked what I was talking about. James acknowledged that he had failed, but then faulted the teacher and the test. The failure taught him nothing. He continued to speak of his lofty goals. But they really were pretensions, not goals. He asserted that he could write "an unbelievable book" that would become a bestseller and result in an honorary degree.

This is how a criminal thinks. Just thinking something makes it so. When James stated he would receive an A without studying, this wasn't mere talk. He was positive it would happen. He didn't have to drag books home and spend hours reviewing to prepare for the test. When he received the test paper back from the teacher with a failing grade, he was livid. It shouldn't have happened. The teacher was an idiot. The test didn't reflect what he had learned, and so forth. When things do not work out in line with a criminal's expectations, it is always someone else's fault, no matter how unrealistic his expectations were to begin with. The blaming of others is habitual and without end: the school has a bad reputation, the teachers don't know how to teach, the teacher doesn't like him, and so forth.

If they do not fault others, these students claim they have an impairment, such as a learning disability. Perry told me that schoolwork was difficult because he had a "reading disorder." Not long before he said this, he mentioned that he was fascinated by a lengthy book about the arch-manipulator and murderer Charles Manson. When I asked if his "disorder" interfered with reading that particular book, he replied, "I read very well if it is a topic I like to read about. If it's boring, I don't know how to read it."

Kids like Perry might appear to take responsibility by making statements such as "I don't learn as quickly as others. I have trouble taking tests. I get easily frustrated." Rather than having a handicap, the truth is that such students do not learn quickly because they choose not to pay attention. They have difficulty taking tests, but it is because they don't bother to study for them. They also get easily frustrated because, when they don't grasp a subject immediately, they are unwilling to persevere until they do.

Drop-offs do just enough to get by. They "forget" to do

homework or neglect to hand it in. Projects and papers are ig-nored, or become slapdash enterprises engaged in at the last min-ute. One boy had nothing positive to say about the academic part of school but proclaimed that he really enjoyed it. When I asked why, he replied, "I party my brains out at school. School is the place I see my friends." To such a youth, academic subjects are of little interest. One teenager said quite seriously, "Why study history? It's all in the past." This is not a criticism of the school. If the curriculum included a course in arson, safecracking, and lock-picking, these kids might be challenged and interested. Some drop-offs have no problem digging into a subject in which they have an interest. This is in line with their attitude toward so much in life: "If I like it, I do it; if I don't like it, forget it." They perform especially poorly in subjects, such as foreign languages, that require drill, repetition, and memorization. They receive high grades in subjects they enjoy or find easy. Otherwise, they barely pass.

Parents are understandably upset when their drop-off son or daughter brings home a report card with low grades, espe-cially after they have been accustomed to seeing excellent grades earned in elementary school. How could their honor-roll student be failing tests and having teachers send home notes about his failure to apply himself?

Van presented a typical drop-off pattern. As a fifth grader of at least average intelligence, Van was receiving grades of D and F. His parents had him repeat fifth grade, which he said was "because I didn't use my potential to the fullest." He would ignore homework requirements, dash off an assignment at the last minute, and occasionally not turn in his work at all. In sixth grade, he was briefly suspended for fighting, which he justified as an act of self-defense. In middle school, he was repeatedly sent to the principal's office for talking back to teachers. He was kicked off the school bus for profanity and being generally dis-ruptive. And he received a brief suspension for smoking in the bathroom. In tenth grade, Van heard a rumor that his girlfriend was going to break up with him because she was interested in another boy. "The rumor made me mad," he recalled, and he responded at the time by threatening to kill his rival. Van stated that he never actually intended to carry out his threat but "was blowing off steam." Nevertheless, he was suspended for a week.

Van told me that it was "not cool" to do homework. He remarked, "There are some subjects I shine in." If he found an assignment interesting, he did the work. He read the classic novel *Fahrenheit 451* on his own initiative but refused to read the "boring, drug-out" short stories assigned in English. "It's doing things on others' terms," that galled him, he told me. And, he added, "I'm not a strong person when it comes to things I don't want to do." He thought it pointless to "do certain math you won't ever use." In contrast, he said, "Almost everything about science is interesting." Some history units he plunged into because he liked "learning about wars." However, he failed Spanish because he refused to put in the daily effort that learning a foreign language requires. Van's pretensions outstripped his performance. Shortly after receiving a report card showing he had a low C average, Van told me, "All I cared about anyway was passing. To get A's, I'd have to go home and work, and I don't want to do that." With considerably less than a stellar academic record, he still envisioned himself strolling the campus of an elite college. Desperate to find a remedy for their son's difficulties in concentrating, Van's parents consulted a psychiatrist. While in high school, Van started taking medication for an "attention deficit hyperactivity disorder" (ADHD). When it became evident that the medication was not leading to improvement in his grades or in any other aspect of his behavior, the physician discontinued the drug. This teenager barely managed to graduate from high school, then took a retail sales job. Van eventually ended up in jail, convicted on several felony counts of burglary.

The delinquent child appears to have a short attention span

for most classroom assignments. And if he is diagnosed with an attention deficit disorder, it is as though that explains and excuses anything, including criminality. Sixteen-year-old Andy was referred to me for a consultation after he had fractured a classmate's skull during a locker-room brawl. Andy's mother came prepared with a stack of papers, including reports from educational and psychological evaluations. The reports were replete with references to her son's recently diagnosed ADHD. Practically every difficulty this teenager had was attributed to ADHD, including low grades, emotional volatility, poor problem-solving skills, impulsivity, avoidance of challenges, and a negative self-image. I hadn't a clue how ADHD explained why Andy threatened to attack a boy, then delivered on that threat more than an hour later. ADHD also seemed irrelevant to the criminality that Andy revealed, including fights, dozens of shoplifting episodes, vandalism, thefts from his parents, truancy, anonymous phone calls, driving without a license, guzzling beer while underage, and smoking marijuana. Excusing the boy's behavior because of his diagnosis did nothing to help improve his conduct.

Educators and mental health professionals frequently latch onto a diagnosis, and it takes on a life of its own as it is invoked to explain almost any aspect of an individual's functioning. (According to *JAMA Pediatrics,* the rate of diagnosing ADHD has increased 24 percent since 2001.)[8] With Andy and others like him, the diagnosis may be in error to begin with. Andy could pay rapt attention when he was interested in what a teacher was presenting, something that many youngsters with ADHD cannot do without great difficulty. His mother observed him spending countless hours riveted to video games. And, she noted, on long trips to places that he enjoyed going, Andy sat in the car for hours without fidgeting. Another teenager's father related that his son, also diagnosed with ADHD, spent two full days assembling an intricate model airplane requiring him to meticulously follow complex, detailed instructions. However, in school, which he despised, he seemed unable to focus. Clearly, his difficulty stemmed not from a biologically based condition, but from an unwillingness to concentrate on anything not to his liking. Some teenagers like Andy find subjects of interest in vocational classes and learn to repair electrical problems, fix plumbing, or repair cars. Even in such classes, delinquent teenagers are difficult and challenging when they are bored, disinterested, and required to do something that is not of immediate interest.

At the age of sixteen, Warren underwent a comprehensive "psychoeducational evaluation." His parents were concerned about their son's difficulty paying attention, his disorganization, and his procrastination. Warren tested in the superior range of intelligence. The evaluation report included observations that he seemed not to care about school, made careless errors, and avoided tasks requiring sustained mental effort. The psychologist wrote that Warren had problems paying attention if he did not find the subject interesting, and that he got "distracted by the fact that he doesn't want to do the work." Moreover, he observed that Warren did not think he had any difficulties with school or any aspect of his functioning, apart from the fact that his relationship with his parents was strained. Ignoring all the motivational and attitudinal factors, the psychologist concluded that Warren's primary diagnosis was ADHD and recommended treatment and accommodations for ADHD. The psychologist even suggested that the boy be "provided with note-taking services to assist him when studying for exams," and that he be provided a copy of the teacher's lecture notes or a classmate's notes.

ADHD does not preclude achievement. Many boys and girls who have difficulty paying attention do want to succeed academically. These children show no signs of antisocial behavior. They do whatever is necessary to improve their school performance, including work for hours outside school time with a tutor. Or they try to compensate by excelling in areas other than academic endeavors, such as sports, the arts, or mechanical skills. Some benefit from medication. Thus far, there is no evidence that medication prescribed for an attention deficit disorder changes criminal thinking.

Readers may wonder whether having a diagnosis of ADHD places a person more at risk for engaging in criminal behavior. Some research studies suggest that this may be the case. However, there are two problems with these studies. First, there does not seem to be agreement as to how to assess ADHD. Second, to conduct a truly accurate evaluation, a professional would have to observe the subject engaged in a variety of tasks in different settings, which is rarely done.

Even when their students are unmotivated, inattentive, negative, or hostile, teachers tend to be sympathetic and want to help. They continue to believe that such pupils are emotionally disturbed. Their strategy is to develop whatever strengths their pupils have and to nurture a positive self-image. They encourage the delinquent at what he can do well and downplay his academic weaknesses and unruly behavior. Whatever good work he does is held up as an example to others. Encouraged, the teacher may relax disciplinary measures. Eventually, the student has the teacher where he wants her. He figures that the instructor won't keep the pressure on, because she'll want to keep the peace. If the teacher raises expectations, the close-knit relationship unravels and the student acts as though an ally has betrayed him. Faulting the teacher for whatever happens, he once again presents himself as a victim of injustice.

Teachers are especially challenged when gifted students fail. They provide extra attention and accommodations such as extending deadlines for homework and projects, providing one-on-one help, and referring these students to tutors and counselors. Educators remain dedicated to helping these boys and girls succeed. Some students benefit from these measures, but the delinquent youth exploits them.

Seventeen-year-old Brad was extremely capable, but unless

he found the subject matter easy or particularly fascinating, he refused to work. An educational evaluator observed, "He gets distracted by the fact that he doesn't want to do the work. He avoids tasks that require sustained mental effort." The evaluator recommended individual psychotherapy. Brad's parents dutifully took him to a therapist, but their son volunteered little information, then refused to attend any more sessions. He also refused to take medication. The evaluator suggested that Brad be allotted extra time to take tests, that he be tested in a small group or separate room to lessen distraction, and that he have "rest breaks" after every thirty minutes of testing. And he was to be allowed to redo work to correct careless errors. The school implemented these accommodations, none of which resulted in an improvement in Brad's motivation or academic performance. Brad took advantage of the special attention and continued counting on teachers remaining sympathetic and making additional concessions. As he mulled over which colleges to apply to, Brad was not doing the day-to-day work. Midway through senior year, he was failing science. His frustrated but still very devoted teacher wrote his parents, "[Brad] knows he can do the work but he does not actually want to put forth the effort. We discussed the fact that you can't just wish for what you want. You have to work for it." His mother reported that his teachers had "begun to praise him with the hope of turning his motivation up." There were two problems to this approach. First, Brad was doing precious little that merited praise. Second, Brad lacked internal motivation. The prospects were dim that, once he reached college (if he were admitted), he would spontaneously turn into a fireball of academic activity.

Chris was enrolled at a selective high school for students gifted in math and science. He was brilliant, the sort of student who potentially would be pursued by colleges when the time came for him to apply. Inexplicably, Chris's academic performance fell far short of his promise. By the middle of sophomore year, he was failing nearly all of his courses, virtually unheard of for a student at this particular high school. Teachers noted that Chris seemed distracted, that he wasn't completing homework, and that he was frequently absent. They seemed to concur that the source of his distraction was his nonstop attention to his laptop. Because the school had an abundance of computers, it was unnecessary to bring one's own computer to school. A recommendation was made that Chris leave his laptop at home, which he refused to do.

It turned out that Chris was focused on pornography to the exclusion of practically anything else. Since the age of eleven, when he first discovered pornography on a computer, he'd seemed obsessed with it. It was almost impossible to pry him away from his computer, as though an umbilical cord were attached to it. Chris had saved thousands of images and videos of the most violent, sadistic pornography imaginable, including anal rape and genital mutilation. He had also transmitted photos of himself in sexual poses, and traded pornography with other teenagers and with strangers all over the world. In addition, he had hacked into students' Facebook accounts. His parents struggled to limit his time on the computer. He would lie and tell them he needed access to it to complete homework. Chris began staying up until two or three in the morning immersing himself in pornography. Sometimes, he was so fatigued that he convinced his parents he was in no condition to go to school. He rejected all attempts to rein in his computer use, complaining about invasion of privacy. Once, when his mother managed to wrest his computer away and lock it up, he went on a rampage and destroyed property at the house.

School staff members did everything they could to help this boy. They conferred with his parents, who had him under treatment by a psychotherapist, a process he stubbornly resisted. Although his academic average dipped below what was acceptable in order to remain at the school, Chris was placed on probation and allowed to stay rather than be transferred to his neighborhood public school. Teachers did their utmost to encourage him, and continued to make accommodations and extend deadlines. Chris steadfastly insisted he did not have a problem and remained impervious to suggestions that were offered.

CLEARLY, THERE ARE students who drop out of school for reasons that have nothing to do with criminality. And many students who are not criminals are unmotivated academically. They avoid homework, care little about grades, and are not particularly interested in traditional school subjects. They may enroll in vocational programs and develop marketable skills. Superficially, they may appear similar to the criminal drop-offs I am describing, but their personality makeup is entirely different. They usually acknowledge mistakes and learn from them. They understand that it is necessary sometimes to do things they prefer not to do. They demonstrate they are trustworthy by being forthcoming about whom they are with and what they are doing.

A child's "job" is to attend school. At any job, one has to do things one does not want to do. The criminal as a child takes shortcuts, blames others for his difficulties, lies about what he has done or failed to do, and expects others to suit his requirements rather than suit the requirements of others. His expectations of other people are unrealistic, and he becomes angry when those expectations are not met. Dropping out becomes a way of life, not just with school but also with sports, religious school, organized clubs and activities, music lessons—anything that requires sustained effort and doing things on others' terms. The excitement he seeks is not to be found in the world of responsible living. The child rejects the school; it is not the school that rejects him.

The Good Student

College students experience a time of unparalleled freedom as they live away from their parents for the first time. It has been decades since college administrators fulfilled the role of *in loco parentis*. Students are mostly unsupervised, and their newly acquired independence offers a chance to experiment academically and socially. For young men and women with a criminal personality, college can be a playground. Well before entering the ivy-covered walls, they have already taken enormous liberties with whatever freedom they've had, and defied rules set down for them. Now nearly all restraints are off. To retain the privilege of remaining in college while someone else foots the bill, all they need do is pass and avoid getting caught for a serious rule-infraction or crime. In terms of academic performance, there are three basic patterns. Some of these students drop out or flunk out within the first year. Others limp through and graduate. And there are others who excel.

Parents may find it difficult to acquire information about their offspring's academic progress. Under the federal Family Educational Rights and Privacy Act (FERPA), when a student turns eighteen, many rights that parents had revert to the student.[9] Disclosure of a student's records to a third party requires the student's consent. Without that consent, his parents may remain completely in the dark as to how their son or daughter is faring academically. I have known of situations in which a student ceased attending classes for months, but based on what he told his parents, they had the impression that he was conscientiously applying himself to his studies.

Some criminals select a particular college because the institution has a reputation as a party school. One teenager told me he was only considering colleges where football was king, students were permitted to have a car freshman year, and fraternities welcomed first-year students. Specific course offerings were not a consideration. Delinquents who once behaved as though they were allergic to work continue to take the easiest courses and do the bare minimum needed to receive a diploma at the end of four years, although some drag it out longer. They size up what is required and try to figure out shortcuts to beat the system. They read summaries rather than the full assigned texts. They "borrow" work from classmates. Any means to an end is acceptable; cheating and plagiarizing being common. Because they know that faculty can use computer programs to detect plagiarism, some students simply hire others and pay them a fee to write papers for them. If a criminal cannot locate someone on campus to do this, he can find someone on the Internet who will.

Mark attended a small Midwestern college. Rather than attend classes and complete assignments, he established a cycle of staying up late at night playing video games, then sleeping through morning classes. He boasted that he made it to his 8 a.m. class only half the time, but still got an A. Intellectually curious, Mark spent hours every day browsing the Internet, reading about all sorts of subjects that interested him while putting off studying. Inclined to stick to himself, he grew bored spending much time secluded in his room. Eventually, he found others like himself and addressed his shyness by consuming alcohol as "a social lubricant." He was constantly figuring out how to get by academically because, if he flunked out, he knew his parents would insist he get a job that he feared would be "grunt work."

This young man was intellectually pretentious and considered most of the work beneath him. In speaking with me about his experience, he revealed that he had a low opinion of the other students, claiming he shared nothing in common with them and believed he was a lot smarter than they were. Writing poetry on his own, Mark despised his creative writing course. He regarded other students' poetry as "childish." Because of his admittedly "contemptuous attitude," he clashed with his instructor. When Mark came to class, he was usually unprepared and faked his way through it. He submitted papers late and performed poorly on tests because he refused to take time to review and study. Occasionally, Mark would skip a test altogether, which resulted in a failing grade. Jolted back to reality, Mark would make a fitful attempt at studying. As his grade point average slid, he told his parents and the dean that he was "overwhelmed" by the work. He told me, "I wouldn't tell them I didn't care." Complaining that he was at the wrong school, Mark declared, "I haven't learned anything I didn't learn in high school," which of course contradicted his lamentations to others that he was overwhelmed. Referring to college as "crawling through a rat maze," Mark continued to drink, use drugs, play video games, sleep late, and miss classes. With supreme confidence, Mark proclaimed, "I'm capable of sliding by." Uncertain as to how to "fix my motivation," he nonetheless planned to attend graduate school and become a teacher. Asked how prospective employers might evaluate his college transcript, he replied, "I wasn't thinking of the implication of college grades." This is yet another illustration of a thought pattern of the criminal mentioned earlier, namely that merely thinking something makes it so. He saw himself as a teacher standing in front of a high school class, and had no doubt that this would occur.

Unlike Mark, who barely graduated from college, other students with a criminal personality are motivated to do well and take challenging classes. A strong academic performance is their ticket to prestigious and powerful jobs. But although they may achieve academic honors, their conduct in other spheres of life is far from exemplary. They have trouble getting along with roommates, clash with students in campus organizations, and get embroiled in conflicts with faculty.

Ned was doing average work in academically challenging courses. He envisioned himself becoming a financial tycoon, a corporate executive with all the perks that CEOs often have. He attributed his mediocre grades and "incompletes" to procrastination. On weekends, he'd engage in heavy drinking. "I have a high tolerance," he remarked, and told me he regularly consumed four or five beers within two hours. On weekend nights, he would down as many as ten beers. One night, an incident occurred as Ned was engaging in his customary heavy drinking. A group of guys had gathered in his dorm room. Ned took offense at one of them lying on his couch with his shoes on. He reprimanded the boy, and the incident escalated quickly to the point that Ned flew into a rage. "I snapped and started yelling," he recalled. Not only did he scream obscenities, but he threatened the youth, who then called the university police. Ned was charged with disorderly conduct. He acknowledged to me that he'd had "temper problems" before this incident. Earlier, he had been charged with what he termed a "bogus weapons violation" that was ultimately dismissed. Ned grudgingly conceded, "My temper has festered, and I didn't admit it was a problem."

Some students with a criminal personality commit thefts, rapes, and assaults on campus. Most do not get caught. An article in the Penn State *Daily Pennsylvanian* discussed the underreporting of crimes on campus.[10] Among the reasons given was lack of evidence. A laptop computer may be stolen but there is no way to track how it happened. The victim may conclude that it is pointless to report it. Some crimes go unreported because a student fears the embarrassment that might occur if he was victimized while engaged in drug use or underage drinking. Date rape is the most underreported crime. Criminals often count on the fact that their victim will never utter a word about what transpired.

Doing well academically can camouflage criminality. A criminal is less likely to be a suspect if he has a reputation as a campus leader and an honor student. I have interviewed people who were stunned when someone who had an outstanding reputation was arrested for a serious crime. For some criminals, their high academic achievement paves the way for similar success in careers where they rise to positions of great responsibility and power. Their success provides a front of respectability that helps them get away with a great deal. In the next chapter, we'll look at the criminal who appears successful by any standard but for whom no legitimate success can ever be sufficient.

5

Work and the Criminal

Criminals approach work and education with similar thought processes. At heart, they are anti-work in that they attach little value to the tasks that they are asked to undertake. Some work rarely, if at all. Others hold jobs intermittently to appear respectable, meanwhile committing crimes under the nose of their employer. These individuals stick with a job until they become bored, or until they suspect that the authorities are hot on their trail. Others hold a job for a long time and perform well. Securing a good reputation makes it easier for them to indulge in illicit activities without being suspected.

For many criminals, to work is to become a slave. Yet, with few marketable skills, they refuse to assume the only positions for which they are qualified, often involving routine and menial work. Such labor is not in line with their inflated notion of the station that they believe they deserve. Rather than scrub floors, pick up trash, or tote luggage, they prefer to remain unemployed. One young offender who had no job skills and had dropped out of school was living at home and refused to consider working at a fast-food restaurant. He told me, "I'd rather die than have my friends see me serving up fries." Another offender complained that his employer was unfair and never gave him a chance. He then disclosed that he frequently showed up at work late and intoxicated. He ignored his manager's warnings and encouragement to seek substance abuse treatment. Finally, he was fired. Another, after being dismissed from his tenth job in one year, admitted, "If the job meant something, I would have been there."

I have asked many men behind bars what kind of work they want to do when they are released. Many responded that they desired to run their own business. One can hardly fault them for aspiring to achieve what, for many people, is the American dream. When asked what being an entrepreneur involves, most haven't a clue. Dwelling in the world of their own pretensions, they imagine themselves barking orders while others scurry to do their bidding. Rather than anticipating the endless problems that plague even the most conscientious people as they build and operate a business day to day, criminals focus on the enormous wealth that they are certain will be theirs. It is the "big score" notion—a huge bonanza obtained easily.

For some criminals, crime *is* their work. "You go to your job, I go to mine," said one man who worked what he termed "the daily grind." Each day, he went out shoplifting and selling drugs. He committed crimes numbering into the thousands as he did this day after day, month after month, and year after year. He was apprehended for none of these offenses, but was finally charged with carnal knowledge of a minor. This man regarded work as for suckers. He was able to live quite well on the proceeds of his crimes.

Aaron, age thirty-five, was convicted on multiple charges of possession and distribution of heroin and marijuana. As a teenager, he was committed to a residential treatment center because he was incorrigible, having shown total disregard for parental restrictions and rules. He had run away from home, engaged in shoplifting, refused to attend school, committed numerous traffic offenses, and repeatedly violated probation. He was a law unto himself. A report from the youth center stated, "He has consistently strived to be a free agent." When I interviewed Aaron, he was anything but free. He was in jail for drug trafficking.

"I haven't found anything that motivates me," Aaron said. Although highly intelligent, Aaron grew bored after three semesters of college and dropped out. His drug use began when he started smoking marijuana at age thirteen. Not long after, he was using cocaine and heroin. He prided himself on becoming a businessman, not an addict. When he was twenty years old, he "went into business" with another man selling large quantities of marijuana. He found a major buyer out of state and made more than $2,500 on his first venture. Two years later, he began selling heroin because it was more remunerative. Describing himself as "self-employed," Aaron was earning nearly $100,000 "tax free" per year. Nonetheless, he was thousands of dollars in credit card debt. No matter how much he earned, Aaron continued to spend more. Obsessed with appearing successful, he spent a small fortune amassing a huge wardrobe, including more than two dozen pairs of pants and three dozen sweaters. "When you look good, you feel good," he commented. Mainly, he spent money living high—furnishing his luxury town house, eating at pricey restaurants, gambling, and traveling. His rationale was that there is an enormous demand for drugs, so why shouldn't he meet that demand and profit? He emphasized that he was an honest dealer, not one of those slimy people who adulterate drugs and cheat customers. His probation officer indicated that he had imported nearly half a ton of marijuana into the Washington, D.C., area as well as smaller quantities of other drugs. Aaron did not think that his business harmed anyone. His sole regret was that he got caught.

Aaron had few friends and no intimate long-term

relationships. A psychological test profile stated, "Quite outgoing and sociable, he has a strong need to be around others. . . . although his personal relationships may be somewhat superficial. Individuals with this profile usually have a history of risk-taking behavior and relationship problems that are likely to continue. They are usually not very motivated to change their behavior." Aaron had scarcely begun serving his probation period when he was arrested and charged with speeding and driving without a license. He also tested positive for drugs on several urine screenings. He expressed contempt for drug programs, which he characterized as requiring that "you leave your ego at the door." Rejecting drug treatment, he asserted, "I'm not going to be as miserable as you all want me to be." Aaron then complained that probation was more wretched than time spent in jail. After urine test results indicated that he had violated probation, Aaron said, "I'm tired of others' opinions of how I should live." He said he was prepared for revocation of probation and to serve the remainder of his jail time. The consequences of failing to remain a "free agent" did not alter his view of himself or of what he considered important in life. Asked if he wanted to change anything about himself, Aaron tersely replied, "I like myself fine."

The criminal's fantasy has long been that, were he to deign to work at a legitimate job, he would stride through the door, snow the interviewer, and land a high-paying position. He assumes that he will be a resounding success at anything if others will only recognize his talents and surrender the reins of authority to him. He readily envisions himself as the manager of a department store, but would never consider sweeping the floor of that very store. With some education and experience, he may present himself so impressively that he persuades a company executive to offer him a position carrying considerable responsibility.

Daniel, an honor-roll student in high school, gained admission to a first-rate state university. He dropped out before his junior year. "I wasn't a good student; I wasn't studious," he admitted. While in college, Daniel had begun dabbling in real estate. Scornful of any job that required him to work regular hours, he fantasized being a real-estate mogul who, as a self-employed entrepreneur, would earn a fortune. Daniel invented a "dream world" in which he saw himself living in a mansion, wearing custom-made Ivy League–style clothing, and being consulted by others as a guru for advice on hot real-estate investment prospects.

Daniel was arrested for a series of burglaries that netted him more than $15,000 from selling the items he stole. Before these crimes, he had a history of living large but earning little income. Borrowing money from a wealthy young man he'd persuaded to trust him, Daniel established a land development company. He opened a fancy office and hired a secretary, but his company was never able to cover its overhead and was forced to close its doors. Impressing an executive during an interview, Daniel landed a job as a top agent for a real-estate company. He was dismissed when that firm suffered severe financial problems. Rather than hunt for a job, Daniel chose not to work at all.

Rosalind, Daniel's wife, said that for as long as she had known him, he never held a "real job." Rosalind commented, "He seemed to always have a deal in the works." However, none of the deals ever panned out. Nonetheless, Rosalind believed that Daniel had many redeeming features, and she had continued believing in his ability to fulfill his ambitions. By the time I spoke with her, however, she had become completely disillusioned. She had always left management of the family's finances to her husband, because finance was his area of expertise. She was shocked to find checks being returned because there was no money in their bank account to cover them. More than a hundred creditors were pursuing Daniel. His car had been repossessed. What Rosalind found the most difficult to cope with was that Daniel had invaded their children's accounts to pay bills. Rosalind decided she could no longer remain married. She commented, "We're better off swimming alone than drowning together." After she and Daniel separated, her husband seemed totally unconcerned about paying child support. "I wish he'd jump in a lake and leave us alone," she said, then added, "I feel sorry for him." Rosalind was angry, but also sad because this talented, promising man with whom she had fallen in love had squandered so many opportunities and destroyed his life and that of his family.

Daniel refused to get a job. For months he lived without earning any income but accepting a monthly stipend from his parents. (Daniel recalled having been scathingly critical of his father for being "too tight" while living on a budget.) Finally concluding "I shouldn't be in real estate," he admitted that an "ego problem" was preventing him from taking any job that wasn't up to his standard. He had difficulty imagining himself in any work setting where he was not attired in a suit and tie. Daniel's thinking bounced from working at a gas station to being an executive. "My thinking pattern isn't normal. Is this an illness?" he inquired. This rhetorical question was followed by his proclaiming, "I want to do work that I enjoy." He said that "low echelon" jobs were not exciting, and he could not imagine work that was not exciting.

Most people want to enjoy their jobs, at which they spend a major part of their waking hours. However, because of circumstances beyond their control, many men and women find their work tedious or downright disagreeable. Because obtaining the necessities of daily life compel them to work, they do what is required. Not Daniel, who longed to enjoy the fruits of his labor without actually having to labor to obtain them. Even before he had his first job, he envisioned himself as a fabulously successful entrepreneur and his own boss. It was not incumbent upon him to complete college and enroll in a graduate program that would provide knowledge and skills to help him fulfill his lofty ambitions. He never gave serious thought to the value of gaining experience by working for someone else. He remained unemployed, voicing the hope that "I'll fall into something I really like. I keep waiting for something to happen." When I told him that he could support himself temporarily by working as a waiter at a downtown upscale restaurant, Daniel looked at me in horror and remarked that he would constantly be comparing himself with the diners he was serving. Daniel indicated that he was embarrassed for resorting to burglary, which he scornfully referred to as "a blue collar crime." As long as I was counseling Daniel, he refused to work. His eventual solution was what many refer to as "the geographic cure": to move out of the area.

Criminals often establish their own businesses through which they purport to provide services or deliver products and then do neither. The home-repair business is one of many that are plagued by fly-by-night operations. A contractor drives around a neighborhood, offers homeowners a good price for driveway resurfacing, pockets a deposit, and is never seen again.

Some criminals are steady jobholders because they realize that employment is their badge of respectability. If a criminal works, others ask fewer questions about how he spends his time. (Often parents, spouses, and counselors think a criminal is mending his ways just because he holds a job.) When he chooses to put forth effort at a job, he learns quickly and is a fireball of energy. His employer values him, and he earns promotions. At least for a while, he basks in the recognition because it conveys publicly what inwardly he has been certain of all along—that he is a cut above the ordinary. But that is about all it means, for he still does not think of himself as a regular workingman like his coworkers, and more than likely he has contempt for the job and for the very people who promoted him. Nonetheless, he knows that just as good grades at school helped him or his buddies get away with things on the side, so can an impressive résumé.

Status and authority are far more important to the criminal than the quality of the work he does. To rise meteorically to the summit is his due, just because he is who he is. On the job, he maintains that his way is the only way. He provides unsolicited advice and imposes his opinions. A ruthless critic of others, he bristles at anyone who offers even a minor suggestion to him. Coworkers resent his dogmatism, inflexibility, and closed mind. He locks horns frequently over trivial issues with fellow employees, subordinates, and supervisors. He abuses authority that he holds legitimately rather than exercising it in ways beneficial to the company. As an executive, he reaches decisions in isolation rather than through consultation. He states opinions and conclusions as decrees. In the short term, the employee's self-confidence and certainty may be so highly valued by his supervisor that his shortcomings are overlooked. His executive style creates a convincing front until it becomes evident that he is not only antagonizing people, but also has no in-depth knowledge of the business.

Some criminals are smooth rather than contentious, ingratiating rather than surly, devious rather than intimidating. They pretend to be interested in what others say. Appearing to invite suggestions, they inwardly dismiss each idea without considering its merits. They seem to take criticism in stride, but actually ignore it and spitefully make a mental note of who the critic was. They misuse authority and betray trust, but are not blatant about doing so. With the criminal at the helm, employee morale deteriorates. His method of operation sooner or later discourages others from proposing innovative ideas and developing creative solutions.

For the sake of perspective, it is important to remember that people who are not criminals have similar personality flaws; it is a matter of degree. Some executives would be far more effective were they less dogmatic, more self-critical, and generally more sensitive to the needs of others. Still, they value their job, loyally give their best to the firm, and do not intentionally exploit their coworkers. A criminal values his job mainly as an arena for power-seeking. He attains power at the expense of others, sometimes quite ruthlessly, and exercises it to further his own objectives.

It is the routine of a job that gets to many criminals, who seem allergic to routine anywhere in life. In order to overcome the tedium, some use drugs while at work. When the criminal is high, his day is bearable, for drugs help his mind soar from the mundane to the exciting. In addition, there is the intrigue of finding out which fellow workers are users too, identifying new sources for buying drugs, or discovering markets in which to make sales. Because he performs satisfactorily at his job, the criminal's drug use is unlikely to be noticed by management. If he becomes lackadaisical or careless, his employer reprimands him and perhaps assumes that something is temporarily troubling him. If the poor performance persists, the criminal may be fired, but without his boss ever suspecting his involvement with drugs. In the unlikely event that the criminal is caught red-handed using drugs, his boss may advise him to seek treatment, perhaps at company expense. Some employers even shoulder part of the blame. Rather than penalize the user, they assume that unsatisfactory conditions at work drove him to use drugs. The worst that may happen is that the criminal loses his job, which to him may not be a particularly severe penalty.

Criminals often utilize jobs directly for crime. Businesses suffer more from insider theft than from pilferage by customers. Employees abscond with millions of dollars' worth of merchandise and embezzle substantial amounts of cash. It has been estimated that between 30 to 60 percent of small business failures are attributable to employee theft. In addition, companies contend with cyber-attacks in which computer systems are targeted by viruses. A 2013 study based on a representative sample of sixty organizations in various industry sectors indicated that the average cost of cyber crime was $11.6 million per year, the range being from $1.3 million to $58 million per company.[1] Businesses also have to contend with cyber-thefts, in which criminals use computers to commit fraud and embezzlement, and to steal personal or financial data. A Forbes publication reported that thefts of trade secrets have affected companies to the point that they have "suffered crippling financial losses, been forced to eliminate jobs, and scaled back or even terminated their operations."[2]

Criminals who appear to be solid, reliable employees seize upon opportunities to enrich themselves at the public's expense. Educated and skilled and without any prior criminal record, they have little difficulty qualifying for federal, state, or local government jobs. Wanda worked for a county agency handling registrations for hundreds of adult education courses. During a three-year period, she diverted nearly a quarter of a million dollars in funds from county coffers into an account bearing her name. At first, she was using the money to pay extraordinary medical bills of family members. Then, as she put it, she "got way over my head" and spent thousands of dollars on lavish vacations and jewelry. As to why she embezzled the money, Wanda told me, "I tried to keep everyone happy," referring to her parents, husband, and children, who were beneficiaries of some of her spending. Then she said, "I try to please people too much."

Wanda said she had quickly noticed that the other accountants who were her work colleagues "weren't the swiftest," and considered them inattentive to detail and careless. Moreover, monitoring of the registration fees was lax, and her overworked supervisor trusted her completely. Wanda always had to be in control. Seldom would she admit that she didn't know something or needed help. She said that, in school, she would have been mortified to ask a teacher to explain something she didn't understand. Because Wanda rarely extended herself to others or confided in them, she had few friends and no close girlfriends. She said, "I'm more of a controlling person. I don't talk to anybody about anything." That included Peter, her husband.

Peter could not believe that his wife and the mother of his

children was capable of stealing a candy bar, much less embezzling such a huge sum. Because she was an accountant, he left it to her to manage the family's finances. He had no idea there were any problems paying the bills. He assumed that whatever Wanda told him was true. Wanda took advantage of her spouse's accepting nature. She racked up bills on three charge cards, reaching the maximum allowed on each and paying in excess of 20 percent interest on unpaid balances. To purchase a brand new car, she took out a five-year loan. When she could no longer make payments, the dealership repossessed the vehicle. Wanda said about her husband, "I've never seen anyone as unargumentative as he." Wanda pushed him around and micromanaged his every move. "My husband won't even make the bed," she commented, "because he knows I'll redo it." Asked if her controlling perfectionism got on Peter's nerves, she replied, "I'm sure it does. He doesn't say anything." Wanda acknowledged that there was absolutely no need for her to embezzle the funds from her job. "We always had everything we really needed or wanted."

Peter was heartsick when Wanda was indicted for embezzlement but remained loyal, stating, "I told her we'll get through this. I wasn't going to leave her. She has a great heart. I love her to death." His wife had told him that they could afford to take two cruises because she'd found bargain rates. As for the jewelry, he commented that he didn't see a lot of it and really wasn't paying attention to what Wanda owned. "I didn't know one stone from another," he told me. Peter confirmed that his wife was a perfectionist. Referring to making the bed, he said that it "has to be perfect—military style." In general, Wanda "has to do things her own way."

Wanda struggled to remain firmly in control at home and did not tolerate criticism. She interpreted the most mild suggestion as an insult. While awaiting sentencing, Wanda had taken a clerical job where she apparently had a boss similar in personality to that of her husband. She said that her immediate supervisor was reluctant to make a suggestion or deliver a criticism if he thought anything was wrong with what she was doing. At this new job, if she had a question, she did not ask it, because she wanted to avoid appearing "ignorant." She'd take her chances that she could figure the problem out on her own. "I've never talked to anybody about my problems," she commented. A psychological test revealed the following: "She has strong underlying tendencies to rationalize hostility, to covertly blame others, and to externalize problems. She tests as overly sensitive, easily hurt, and irritable. She would be acutely sensitive to criticism. She could rigidly overcontrol her hostility for long periods of time with rare but dangerously explosive outbursts."

Wanda's mother described her daughter as the most independent of her four children. Asked what she meant, she responded, "Very controlling" and spoke of Wanda trying to boss around her siblings and fighting continuously with them. Without wanting to blame Wanda for her financial excesses and the crime she'd committed, this lady lamented, "This generation wants everything now" and contrasted her daughter and son-in-law's extravagance with the frugality of her husband, who had worked more than three decades to finally afford several luxury items they now enjoyed. "What could Wanda possibly have done with that money?" her mother asked. She wondered why her son-in-law didn't question Wanda about her purchases. "He just went along with it," she remarked.

Wanda's situation reflects a pattern common to criminals who steal from the job. Controlling others is a major source of their self-esteem. They are adept at masking their criminality behind a facade of intelligence, competence, and devotion to their jobs. They ferret out and exploit vulnerability in coworkers or weakness in the way the system operates. Because they appear to perform their duties so well and their demeanor is intimidating, nobody challenges them. They engage in deceptive conduct over a long period of time until, finally, they are discovered.

Criminality in corporations is not new. It began to receive attention in the media during a stock market decline between 2000 and 2003. During the great recession that started in 2009, titans of finance contributed to the collapse of banks and brokerage firms. Headlines appeared regularly about predatory lending and mortgage fraud. Most notorious was Bernard Madoff, who managed billions of dollars for investors. Mr. Madoff operated a Ponzi scheme disguised as a hedge fund and swindled thousands of investors. He pled guilty in March 2009 to eleven counts of fraud, money laundering, and perjury and was sentenced to 150 years in prison. Madoff's criminal enterprise was a classic affinity scam. Many Jewish organizations and individual Jewish investors had invested with Madoff, who was Jewish, assuming that one of their own would be absolutely trustworthy and work for their best interest. However, as *Newsweek* columnist Joseph Epstein pointed out, "Madoff bilked his own family, so to say."[3] Subsequent investigations suggested that as early as the 1970s, Mr. Madoff sent employees out to purchase drugs for company use, and that his workplace was "rife with cocaine [and] sex." There were allegations that Mr. Madoff used investor funds to pay for escorts and masseuses. An article in the *New York Times* stated that Bernard Madoff "might have stolen simply for the fun of it, exploiting every relationship in his life for decades while studiously manipulating financial regulators."[4]

The mentality of the executive who misuses corporate or investor funds is the same as that of the armed bank robber, for neither is in desperate need of money. The amount of money gained in the crime is an index of how skillful the person is. The bank robber extracts money by force. The corporate executive does the same through sophisticated and wily schemes and deceptive maneuvers. Both know right from wrong, but eliminate such considerations from their thinking. Both the bank robber and the corporate crook calculate how to avoid detection, and revel in their success at pulling off the job. And neither cares about the impact of his conduct on others.

In the case of the white-collar criminal, he is beyond suspicion because of his accomplishments and the esteemed position he holds. Victims are reluctant to come forward because they know it is their word against that of a highly regarded professional. The criminal counts on the victim remaining silent. If his wrongdoing is discovered, he mounts an attack on his accuser's credibility.

With respect to the contribution of environmental factors to corporate crime, the conventional wisdom is that if temptation is dangled in front of an ambitious individual, greed may override integrity and sound judgment. Analysts of financial crimes have maintained that illegal activities are more likely to be perpetrated when oversight is lacking. In February 1995, the 233-year-old Barings Bank—noted for financing the Napoleonic wars, the Louisiana Purchase, and the Erie Canal—collapsed, due primarily to the activities of one person. After engaging in unauthorized futures trading, Nick Leeson forged documents and concealed trading losses of $1.3 billion. Mr. Leeson served a prison sentence in Singapore, where he had been a general manager of Barings' operation. In an interview in *Research* magazine, Mr. Leeson was reported to have blamed the "failure of Barings' risk management that enabled his fraud to metastasize."[5] Mr. Leeson also ascribed his fraudulent activity to his inner drive to be "a success." Nick Leeson told a symposium gathered in Miami in 2005, "The word 'criminal' is an ugly word. I don't think of myself as a criminal. It was something I fell into."

Weak regulation does provide more opportunity for men and women of dishonest character to exploit such situations for their own benefit. Those who are honest will do the right thing whether or not someone is looking over their shoulder. Again, it is the individual who decides how to function, whatever the environmental conditions may be. Nick Leeson offers a prime example of a criminal ferreting out weakness in a system and capitalizing on it. Professor Terry Leap, of the College of Business Administration at the University of Tennessee, points out that rising executives who unexpectedly turn into monsters had "serious character flaws that were either hidden or ignored for years."[6] These superstars were commended and promoted for their dedication and hard work. Personal shortcomings were tolerated and overshadowed by their accomplishments. If a person excels at what he does, he is a valued member of the organization. His dishonesty, irresponsibility, and rough interpersonal edges become increasingly visible when he reaches an executive position and has far-reaching power. Even then, his talent and productivity appear to outweigh his negative characteristics until his corrupt practices come to light.

Lester, a highly regarded attorney, was arrested for embezzling millions of dollars from client trust funds. A high-salaried professional, he did not steal the funds out of financial need. "Most of it just got spent leading the good life," Lester told me while speaking of expenditures on fine wines, art, custom-tailored clothes, jewelry, and travel.

His wife, Joann, said that she had always regarded her husband as "perfect." However, she said he was extremely judgmental. Tearfully, she said, "I never did anything up to his standard of perfection." She did her utmost not to provoke his wrath because the consequences were hard to endure. "When Lester got angry, it was terrible—he looked like he hated me," she remarked. Joann said that once her husband made up his mind about something, there was no dissuading him. Consequently, she left most decisions to him, including the purchase of an "enormous" home with a three-car garage and pool. "I'd never have bought it, but I did all the things you'd do as a homemaker and made the best of it," she told me. Lester paid cash for a time-share, and she didn't question it. "I signed the papers. I figured Lester was in control. He handled it. I thought, 'He's an attorney,' and I never paid attention." Despite doing so well professionally, Lester insisted that Joann continue to work even when she became ill. Although Joann readily acknowledged that Lester was very controlling, she pointed out that he was also very giving. Never having spent more than $150 on a dress before marriage, Joann was allowed to spend more than $1,000 for an outfit. She was also the recipient of jewelry, which, in the past, she never cared much about. Joann never suspected that the life she and Lester were enjoying was a result of ill-gotten gains. "Our whole marriage has been a lie," she told me after her husband's arrest as she was sinking from an opulent lifestyle into one of austerity, with the bank about to foreclose on their home. Despite all that had transpired, she emphatically told me, "I still love Lester" and insisted, "His basic character is very moral."

Lester disagreed with his wife's characterization of him. "My view of Joann is that she's the typical spoiled only child." He acknowledged that, whereas he could be judgmental, part of the problem was his wife's tendency to "put those who she truly loves up on a pedestal." As to her fear of making him angry, Lester dismissed this when he asserted, "She never appeared to be walking on eggshells." As we spoke, Lester was able to articulate how it was that he was able to commit fraud over a long period despite the knowledge that it was wrong and could lead to the end of his professional career and to the loss of his freedom. As to the wrongness, he said, "I was able to block it off. I could open a little door and out would come the wrongness about it. I could shut it back in a soundproof room and no one would hear the screaming. On the whole, that worked." He observed, "If people don't have the ability to block things out, then you almost can't get through life." He explained, "I was sheltered through that time span. Nothing bad happened. No one walked in and said, 'I need the money out of my trust.'" And, he pointed out, "Regardless of how much you try to convince yourself that you will repay the money, it never, never happens. You only dig yourself a deeper and deeper hole."

Lester described an aspect of his motivation that recalls Nick Leeson when he commented that his numerous extravagant purchases "were symbols of what I was trying to be, not of what I was." He recalled that, since middle school, he "always needed to be bigger," by which he meant more important. Being a big shot was how he defined success.

Why would a person successful in his profession take such risks? It goes back to the criminal's basic view of work being for slaves and suckers. Reaching the highest rung on the corporate ladder is not enough. Holding a trusted, esteemed position as a doctor, teacher, lawyer, or financial advisor is not enough. Whatever legitimate rewards a criminal's job offers, they do not satisfy him. The criminal never has enough power, control, and excitement, which are the oxygen of his life. Over and over, he must demonstrate that he is more clever, more capable, more ingenious than others. And so he pursues his objectives by violating employer policies, breaking rules, and manipulating others into serving his own objectives.

For more than a decade, an official of the Environmental Protection Agency took extended periods away from work, telling his supervisors that he was on a secret assignment for the Central Intelligence Agency. He cheated taxpayers out of $900,000 as he received his federal salary, a bonus, and other benefits for work that he never did. The *Washington Post* reported that the defendant said in court that he was motivated by "a sense of excitement and the rush of getting away with something."[7] The ex-EPA official was sentenced to serve thirty-two months in prison and to make restitution for his ill-gotten gains.

Trusted public servants have exploited their positions and abused the trust vested in them. Massive cheating scandals have been reported in which it is not just students who cheat, but also their teachers and school administrators, who manipulate test scores for appearance's sake or to maintain accreditation. This occurred in what has been called the largest cheating scandal in recent history. In Atlanta, Georgia, during 2013, thirty-five educators were indicted, including a former school superintendent. According to one report, the indictment stated, "For at least four years, between 2005 and 2008, test answers were altered, fabricated, and falsely certified."[8] System-wide cheating has been reported in a number of other jurisdictions across the United States. In addition to the legal consequences, a nationwide controversy has been fueled about the pressure on teachers to orient their curriculum around testing. Pressure has been particularly intense when teacher evaluation is largely based on test scores as a measure of student achievement. This is not the place to discuss that particular controversy. The point is that, although there may be external pressure from peers or administrators to alter test scores, it is the individual teacher who decides whether or not to engage in such fraudulent activity. In news reports, we learn of educators who succumb to such pressure but not about the majority who do not.

When Dr. Yochelson and I conducted our original study of criminals (1961–1978) at St. Elizabeths Hospital in Washington, D.C., among the questions we asked was "When you were growing up, what sort of job did you hope to have?" A significant number responded that they had wanted to be a police officer. They were attracted by the symbols of power as well as the exercise of power. The attractions were the uniform, badge, fast police cruiser, the gun, and the ability to pursue and arrest bad guys. Their motives had nothing to do with serving the community and making it a safer place. By the very nature of their job, police officers have legitimate authority to enforce the laws. They are for the most part honest, dedicated to their work, and make personal sacrifices and endanger their lives to help others. However, a person with a criminal personality who becomes a police officer is likely to misuse the power he is entrusted with and become embroiled in conflict within the department as well as in the community. A police officer with a criminal personality may take bribes, use excessive force while making an arrest, and, in general, seek to gratify his own needs ahead of serving others.

Former police officer Drew Peterson's alleged murder of two wives was a high-profile case. I have not interviewed Mr. Peterson but, for years, he was a focus of media publicity and a notoriously fascinating figure to the public. In 1979, he was named "Police Officer of the Year" by the Bolingbrook Police Department in Illinois. In 1985, he was fired for disobedience, conducting a self-assigned investigation, failure to report a bribe immediately, and official misconduct. He was indicted on charges of official misconduct and failure to report a bribe. The charges were dropped for lack of evidence and, the following year, he won reinstatement. In May 2008, Mr. Peterson was charged with a felony: unlawful use of a weapon. When police searched his home, they found eleven guns. The charges again were dropped.

Mr. Peterson's third wife, Kathleen Savio, died in a mysterious bathtub mishap on March 1, 2004, just before the financial settlement for their divorce was reached. Between 2002 and 2004, police had been called to the Peterson home numerous times for domestic disturbances. An autopsy revealed that Ms. Savio's death was a murder, not an accident, as investigators had previously concluded. During October 2007, his fourth wife, Stacy Peterson, disappeared. Her relatives said that Stacy, a mother of two young children, would never have run off with another man, as her husband suspected. Early in 2009, Christina Raines, who was engaged to become the fifth wife of Mr. Peterson, moved into his home with her two young children. On May 7, 2009, Drew Peterson was indicted for two counts of murder and was taken into custody. In February 2013, he was sentenced to thirty-eight years in prison for murdering Kathleen

Savio. According to news reports, he showed no remorse and complained about false police reports and "rumors, gossip, outrageous lies and, most importantly, unreliable hearsay."[9] Moreover, Mr. Peterson alleged, "the state took an accident and staged a homicide."

For years, Mr. Peterson was able to evade the consequences of his actions. His criminal behavior, or at least allegations of such conduct, apparently had not begun with the homicide of Ms. Savio. He was able to evade charges of misconduct and retain his job as a police officer. Moreover, since he was intimately familiar with how the police work, he was able to literally get away with murder for years, thumbing his nose at the cops. He became a media sensation, maintaining his innocence on national television shows and appearing on the cover of *People* magazine. He mocked the investigators and predicted he'd be tried and acquitted. According to a *Chicago Tribune* report, "Drew Peterson carefully appraised each prospective juror [and] remained closely involved as the final jurors were selected."[10]

The cases described above are illustrative of how wide-ranging and widespread corruption is in the lives of criminals who are often admired for their success at their jobs. They mistreat others in the workplace and do the same to family members. They leave a trail of destruction affecting their colleagues, families, and the community. For most, their chief regret is getting caught. Even after being convicted, many deny their guilt and charge that others have treated them unfairly.

6

"Life Is a One-Way Street— My Way"

Thinking Errors and the Criminal Personality

The criminal craves power for its own sake, and he will do almost anything to acquire it. He values people only insofar as they bend to his will or can be coerced or manipulated into doing what he wants. The criminal has been this way since childhood, and by the time he is an adult, he believes that he is entitled to whatever he desires. To him the world is a chessboard, with other people serving as his pawns. He is constantly sizing up his prospects for exploiting people and situations.

The criminal expects to prevail in every situation. He considers himself the hub of the wheel, never one of the spokes. As one man reflected, "I made myself a little god at every turn." The criminal's attitude toward people is mercurial, dependent on whether they are of use to him at the moment. They are like property. He does not regard himself as obligated to anyone and rarely justifies his actions to himself. (The justifications come later, and only when he has to defend himself to others.) Just the fact that he has decided on a course of action legitimizes it. The criminal strives to gain the upper hand, but not through fair competition. Instead, he operates by stealth, loading things in his favor. His secrecy offers him great advantage and provides him with a sense of power. Others are unaware of the sinister intentions that lurk behind an often benign facade. Only he knows when and where he will strike. Assuming that everyone plots and conspires as he does, he enjoys playing games with people's minds and catching them off-guard.

The criminal's appetite for conquests can be temporarily appeased but never satisfied. No sooner has he achieved one triumph than he pursues the next. Rarely does the career criminal stick to one type of crime. Clearly, for our system of justice to work, there must be a presumption of innocence. However, people who conduct background investigations and evaluate offenders should be aware that an arrest may represent only a fraction of crimes committed, and an attempt should be made to determine how extensive the prior criminality has been. This would be relevant to sentencing decisions, for judges are permitted to consider prior convictions when imposing a sentence.

You may say that the title of this chapter, "Life Is a One-Way Street—My Way" applies not only to criminals. We have all known people who are extremely controlling with their attitude of "my way or the highway." It is extremely distressing to have to cope with a family member, work colleague, or friend who is uncompromising even with respect to seemingly trivial matters. Even if they do not commit illegal acts, these individuals have their victims.

Larry and Trevor made headlines for committing murder. Larry, a middle school dropout, was raised by a single mother in an impoverished minority neighborhood of a small southern city. Trevor, a college student, grew up in a suburb, raised by two parents amid affluence. Whereas the two young men share little in common in terms of family background, their thinking patterns and personalities are similar. After describing these young men, I'll explore several of what I term their "errors in thinking." Of course, we all make errors in our thinking *to a degree*. However, people who injure others day in and day out are so extreme in these thinking patterns that they have a radically different view of the world from those who live basically responsible lives. Criminals like Larry and Trevor do not seem to resonate to other human beings, in that they show no empathy and are indifferent to the suffering that they cause. They leave in their wake a trail of emotional, financial, and physical carnage.

Errors in thinking are pervasive in the lives of offenders from different backgrounds and who have been arrested for different types of crimes. Larry and Trevor provide examples of the following:

- The lack of a concept of injury to others

- Claiming to be a victim and blaming others when held accountable

- An ability to shut off conscience

- An extreme sense of entitlement

- A sense of uniqueness

- The lack of a concept of obligation

- An ability to shut off fear

Larry

Larry was in his early twenties when he and a friend spotted an elderly gentleman walking out of a store. "We just wanted to have something to do," he told me when I interviewed him in jail. And so, feeling "bored," he and a buddy accosted this man, a complete stranger, and repeatedly struck him with a baseball bat. The blows knocked him to the ground, at which point the attackers started kicking him, then grabbed his wallet and left him bleeding on the sidewalk. According to the autopsy report, the victim died of "multiple blunt impacts" to his head.

The basic facts are these. Larry was a "full-term baby" without any complications associated with his birth. His parents separated when he was in middle school. Larry and his five siblings went to live with Edna Green, their mother, in dilapidated public housing known as "the projects." According to a court-ordered probation department study, Ms. Green, who was unemployed and receiving public assistance, was unstable and had difficulty supervising her children. Larry's father told the investigating officer that his ex-wife and the children had "street fever," and that the kids behaved like "wild animals." Mr. Green held a regular job and sometimes brought food over and paid the bills of his ex-wife. Neither parent had ever been convicted of a felony. Larry maintained a C average until ninth grade, when he got fed up with school, stopped doing any work, and began skipping school, eventually dropping out at age fifteen. Other than doing occasional yard work, the longest that Larry held a job was for one day.

I spent nearly ten hours interviewing Larry, as well as others who knew him well. I also reviewed court and probation records. Larry responded readily to all questions I asked except those having to do with the homicide. He had nothing positive to say about his mother, declaring, "Me and my mother hate each other" and denouncing her as mean and uncaring. Criticizing her for often losing her temper and slapping him, he said he wished he had a different mother.

There is little question that Ms. Green had her own problems and limitations. The home environment was chaotic, and supervision of the children was erratic. However, none of the other children had a criminal record, with the exception of one who was charged with disorderly conduct as a teenager. When a criminal is interviewed after an arrest, he is likely to present himself as a victim of circumstances—family, poverty, peer pressure, and so forth. When I interviewed Ms. Green, she did not fit the picture of an uncaring and hostile parent. She lamented how difficult Larry had been to raise. He did not get along with teachers and resented them telling him what to do. "At school, he'd always fight and talk back," she said. Larry complained about his mom "always fussing." Ms. Green agreed that she did a lot of that because her son "just didn't want to mind me." Wherever he went, he was fighting. "He'd just go out there and pick a fight with his friends," she recalled. What she found intolerable was the cruel manner in which he brutalized his siblings, which went far beyond teasing them. When one of his brothers accidentally awakened a sleeping younger brother, Larry erupted. Ms. Green recalled, "He got mad and jumped on him. He hit him in the head, and kicked him on his side." Larry became so infuriated at another brother that "he almost choked him to death." Ms. Green said, "None of his brothers or sisters like him too good. They call him crazy." When she pushed him to get a job, he would retort, "I don't need no job. I can go out there and steal if I need something." Asked what her son did all day, Ms. Green replied, "Sat around the house, listened to the radio, looked at TV," and visited a grandmother in the neighborhood whose daughter had a little son. "He was crazy about that little boy," she said, and noted he had developed a crush on the boy's mother. Larry came and went as he pleased, turning a deaf ear to his mother's entreaties to do something productive.

Ms. Green said that Larry's temper constantly got him into trouble. "The way he talked to people and picked on people. If you just look at him in a store, he'll say, 'What you lookin' at me for?'" She said, "I brought my kids up to not hurt nobody. I don't hurt nobody myself. I wish he had listened to me a long time ago." Saddened that her son seemed to hate her, she wistfully said, "I wonder how you could talk bad to somebody who helped you through your life." Devastated by Larry's arrest for murder, she said, "It's just crazy, messin' with a man who wasn't bothering anybody. I wish that man would come out of heaven and talk to him so he can sit back and think about how he treated people." She indicated that if she'd had a premonition as to what was about to happen, she would "have pushed that man out of the way and let him beat on me." She continued, "I love my son but I didn't teach him to go out there and hurt nobody."

Larry's sister, Caroline, attributed his problems to his attitude. She said, "If anybody try to correct him, he like to be right all the time. I guess he wanted everything to go his way, to never be wrong." Others saw a softer side of Larry. The grandmother in his neighborhood who had the little grandson said, "Larry treat me like a mama. He go to the store for me and take no money. He'd come around and take my grandchild to the store." Larry's father perceived his son's choice of friends to be the cause of his downfall. "He wanted to be with the trouble bunch," he commented, adding, "They pick the friends they want to be with." Mr. Green contrasted his other children with Larry. Speaking of the next youngest son, he said, "He didn't hang around with Larry. He just didn't want to be with him. He wanted to stay out of trouble." Because Mr. Green wasn't around Larry very much after the boy went to live with his mother, he did not witness the raw anger and aggression. He was stunned when he heard on the radio that Larry was arrested for murder. He had fond memories of his son as a young boy drawing pictures and helping elderly people. Asked why Larry didn't remain with him, his father replied, "He wanted to get back with the wild bunch."

Larry insisted upon doing things on his own terms and tuned out anyone who disagreed with him. After leaving school, he spent his days wandering the streets, watching television at home, visiting women, and frequenting clubs. He started drinking, smoking marijuana, and trying other drugs. He said he dropped out of school because "my mind wasn't in it. It seemed like I was daydreaming. I would fall asleep. I didn't want to do my work. I quit. I wanted to do things my way instead of having people tell me what to do." After leaving school, he was home around his mother a lot more, and their conflicts escalated. He complained, "She was always telling me go out and get a job." Not for a minute would Larry entertain the idea of working at a fast-food restaurant. He exclaimed, "I don't want to work at no restaurant paying minimum wage" and asserted, "I'd like a high-paying job." Instead of earning money, he demanded it from his mother, then resented her when "she'd hesitate and get all pissed off." He went into a tirade proclaiming that his mother did more for her boyfriend than for him, and that she failed to treat him like a son. The altercations he had with his mother reached the point of Ms. Green threatening to summon the police because she was at a loss as to what else to do. Larry was venomous in his attitude toward police officers. He told me, "I'm tired of seeing cops. If a cop tells me to go home, I tell him I go where I want to go. Cops are dumb. They're not going to tell me what to do. They want to make arrests. It gives them something to do." Many times, he had given police officers a false address and a false name. He recalled officers stopping him at a festival when he was drunk and cursing at passersby. Instructed to go home, he appeared to leave, then slipped back into the park.

Rather than being defensive about his temper, Larry seemed proud of it. He volunteered, "If someone keeps arguing, my mind will snap." Even his girlfriend, the mother of the little boy to whom he was attached, experienced his wrath. "Sometimes when she talks about her husband I get mad and cuss her out," he said. Larry recalled a day when the young woman felt his head, thinking he might have a fever. Larry's response was to grab her wrist and bend it back. "She's seen me get mad a lot of times," he said. Asked whether he remained faithful to her or whether he had slept with other women, Larry responded, "If I didn't, something got to be wrong." Moreover, he said that when he has sex, "I don't use no protection because I got to have that feeling."

Larry and I had a surprisingly frank discussion about conscience. (Even though his formal education stopped in ninth grade, Larry was intelligent and articulate.) Speaking of situations when he becomes enraged, he said, "There's no telling what I might do. I just want to hurt the person so they know they shouldn't mess with me. If I see something in my sight, I might grab it and hit 'em with it. A lot of people tell me I've got a conscience. They don't know nothing about me. How do they know? They don't go through my brain. They think if I get in serious trouble, my conscience will bother me. I don't even think about it. They say I need help. They're the ones who need help. I don't have a conscience. If something happen, it happen. I've done a lot of things. I don't worry about it. Some people have a conscience. It's going to bother them. To me, it don't." Asked if he recalled ever being sorry for something he had done, Larry paused and thought, then replied, "Not really. If I have done something, I probably can't remember. I might tell someone I'm sorry. Mostly, I look at them and laugh." He said that if he had hurt a woman's feelings, "They brought it on themself. Not me." Larry stated, "I'm a good person. I don't like to bother nobody."

Larry's criminal record before the homicide was lengthy. It included arrests for assault, burglary, petit larceny, grand larceny, disorderly conduct, property damage, and shoplifting. Most were either crimes of opportunity or committed when he lost his temper. With respect to the former, he and some buddies were passing by a school at night and, on the spur of the moment, decided to break into it. There was nothing they wanted. "It just went through my mind to do it," he recalled. The youths smashed a window to enter, ransacked classrooms, turned over desks, then stole textbooks which they tossed into bushes. Larry was a one-man walking crime wave. He was arrested for only a fraction of the crimes that he committed. Completely cavalier about stealing, he said, "If I see something I want, I just take it. The price doesn't matter." He bragged, "I can steal without getting caught."

Larry reported being fascinated by fighting since he was nine years old and watched kung fu movies on television. He imagined himself "on TV doing it. Kung fu is like a dance movement." But he did more than admire the art form. He enjoyed fighting just to fight. "When I fight, I've got to kick." He observed, "One minute, I'm nice. Another minute I could get all mad and cuss and grab a chair and throw it." He acknowledged that his temper was more likely to explode if he was drinking. Asked if he had ever been attacked and beaten up, Larry responded without hesitation, "It makes me feel good, like I can stand the pressure. I've been hit in the head with broomsticks, bottles, and rocks. I can handle two people. It feels good to have somebody jump on me and know I can stand it." He mentioned a night when "two guys jumped me from behind. I had a knot on my head." He refused to go to the hospital because "I ain't too fond of them hospitals. Like I hate 'em. I'd rather suffer with my own pain." In discussing his involvement in illegal activities, Larry alluded to "peer pressure" but then indicated that he found it challenging to "to see how it is in the streets, to run in a gang and see how I can handle myself."

Larry served brief jail sentences, most having been reduced by a judge to provide him with opportunity to reform while on probation. Larry ignored probation requirements by refusing to get a job, moving without notifying the officer, and failing to turn in monthly reports. More than once, his probation was revoked, and Larry served additional time in confinement. When I asked about his frequent probation violations, Larry grew indignant and faulted the probation officer. "He doesn't know what he was talking about. His mind must have been gone. Maybe I just couldn't obey. I wanted to do things my way, not their way.

I'm not going to work in no restaurant or fast-food place. I might cut grass."

As I interviewed him in jail, Larry said, "I wish I could go to sleep and wake up, and it's all just a dream. I wish I could just wake up and see a whole new future in front of me." Just after saying this, he commented, "I don't consider myself being bad at all." With respect to a possible death sentence, Larry was quite clear: "I'd rather take my life than let them take it." He discussed thoughts about how he might commit suicide while in prison. He wanted total control until the very end. Issuing a warning to the judge, Larry said, "I don't care if the judge get mad. It doesn't scare me. My temper; they don't know how it is. They'll find out. All they can get me for is contempt of court." Although he gave inconsistent accounts about the homicide, he tried blaming it on a friend. Larry had emphasized how close he and this buddy were, having sworn a blood oath together. Now that he was in legal jeopardy, that oath meant little; it was every man for himself. "I'll try to save my neck. I've called police on plenty of my friends before. They never know what I'm going to do." Larry is serving a life sentence in the penitentiary.

Trevor

Trevor was raised in an affluent upper-middle-class suburban family. His two younger brothers excelled academically and professionally. Neither parent had a criminal record, nor did his brothers. Trevor was arrested for stabbing his father to death during an argument about whether he would agree to receive inpatient psychiatric treatment. I spent approximately twenty hours interviewing him for a psychological assessment ordered by the court.

Trevor admired his father, Mr. Winter, for having a brilliant "encyclopedic" mind and for his accomplishments as an engineer. "Acquiring knowledge is sort of an adrenaline rush for him," he commented, something he couldn't imagine being the case in his own life. Harshly critical of his dad's personality, Trevor said that Mr. Winter charmed others but behaved like a demon toward him. He maintained that all that really mattered in his dad's "wretched existence" was money, material possessions, and maintaining a stellar image in the community. Calling his father a "workaholic," Trevor didn't see the point of all that work. Asserting that "work hurts my head," he thought having fun was far more important. Asked whether he was a beneficiary of his father's success, Trevor grudgingly conceded that he had a comfortable existence. However, he said that, rather than live in the opulent manner of his family, he'd be content with a small apartment and a routine, undemanding job. While disparaging his parents' values, he focused on their money. Calling Mr. Winter "a worthless human being except for his money," Trevor said, "It would be heaven if he never spoke a word and paid my bills." Whatever money he wanted that his parents didn't give him, Trevor helped himself to. He knew that if either parent missed money from a wallet or purse, they would assume the other took it. The thefts mounted into hundreds of dollars.

As for his mother, Trevor considered her simply a "mouthpiece" for his dad, and resented her for this. On the other hand, he felt sorry for her because she was submissive and never stood up to her husband. During adolescence, he recalled, "I always had anger on my mind when I was around her and enough energy to be in an ugly, foul mood." He recalled once becoming so infuriated that he grabbed her and spun her around "to get her attention." Trevor told me that his mom was basically a nice person who endured his meanness "because she thought I needed an outlet."

Characterizing his father as "emotionally sadistic," Trevor had in fact long been the truly sadistic member of the family. From the time he was in elementary school, he tortured his siblings, delighting in bringing them to tears while he pummeled them with his fists. Trevor was contemptuous of his brothers for embracing his parents' values. "My brothers were nice to me," he admitted, but he continued to attack them. "Whenever I saw them, I wanted to hit them or punch them." The only reason he supplied for this brutality was, "It just felt good." He claimed that he could manipulate his parents by pretending to be remorseful about his unprovoked assaults. "I wasn't. It was very fun. I got a lot of practice acting remorseful." No punishment that his parents administered put a halt to the physical abuse Trevor dished out. His frustrated mom and dad resorted to spanking or slapping him, which he listed among his complaints about their "harsh, abusive treatment" of him. Trevor characterized nearly any attempt by his parents to discipline him as physical or emotional abuse.

"Killing isn't new to my brain," he told me during one of our interviews at the jail. As a little child, he remembered "causing havoc with bugs." This was more than just stepping on an ant or bug in the house. He would hunt them down, then "stomp on a whole bunch of them and go out of my way to kill them." He recalled his "real violent relationship with toys," where it was "all about fighting." He got suspended briefly in school for injuring a boy during a fight. He became so enraged at his parents for something they did (he couldn't remember what it was) that he picked up a valuable porcelain sculpture and smashed it. Trevor pronounced himself an addict when it came to playing video games that featured mass killing. His fascination with killing was not restricted to characters in video games. Since he was in elementary school, Trevor would become so infuriated at his father that he fantasized different ways to kill him. He told me that he wished he'd "punched him in the face and strangled him a long time ago." He had similar, though less frequent, thoughts about his mother.

Trevor did well in school until he entered an intensely competitive high school. Initially, he earned honor-roll grades, then grew "disillusioned" and "sick of work." He found school boring and much of what he was learning irrelevant. To his parents' dismay, his grade point average plummeted as he skipped classes and ignored homework. If Trevor had a lengthy assignment or project, he would not mention it at home. "I'd never tell them I had anything big. I'd fake doing work, then watch TV and relax myself." The next morning he would "go into a work frenzy" and succeed in getting by, at least for a while. He complained that his parents were unrelenting in their pressure on him to earn high grades so he could gain admission to top-ranked colleges. He decided to rebel against them and their "conservative values" by "making a promise to myself I was no longer committed to good grades. I had a plan. I knew what I had to do to screw up."

Trevor was pleased when several elite colleges rejected his application for admission. However, to his dismay, he was admitted to a college with high academic standards that he knew he'd be forced to attend. Once on campus, he ceased working and failed several classes. Drug use, which started in high school, became the focus of his life. Pilfering money from his parents to purchase drugs, Trevor quickly attracted a flock of friends eager to leech off his largesse. Trevor told me, "I was never good at talking to people." He noted that, because he had the funds to purchase large amounts of high-quality drugs, "it was easier to hang out with people; but it did revolve around my having money."

At college, a dean who took an interest in Trevor reported to his parents that the harder counselors tried to help their son, the worse he did. Trevor lasted four months into his freshman year, then withdrew, ostensibly to return home to seek therapy, which he complied with in token fashion. Back at home, he immersed himself in watching television and playing video games, abstaining from drugs because his parents required him to undergo random urine tests. After spending what he termed "the most boring months a human could spend wound up as tight as a rubber band," he decided it was better to return to college, but this time to a less demanding institution.

Trevor appeared to take pride in the fact that no one ever knew him well. He was not close to any family member. He had no best friend. In fact, he was not close to anyone. Even when he held a job or played a sport, his interactions with others were superficial. He said that he was "not good at having conversations with peers" although he could get along with "people with a high intellect." His overall evaluation of his socializing skills was summed up in the comment "I'm as retarded as any human being can be." Asked why he thought this was the case, he dismissively said, "Just a host of horribly bad luck." He also maintained that he was "emotionally disabled" because he was "brought up by weird parents. They didn't do a good job raising me. They fucked up in every possible way." He accused them of "forcing me to live a life where I had to concentrate on my work." Emphatically, he declared, "I can't think of one thing that wasn't my parents' fault."

Trevor was a loner because he never cared about other people. He acknowledged that he had no interest in others "unless I can get something out of them that benefits me. How can I be interested unless it gets me something?" Instead, he preferred to isolate himself and play video games, several of which he stole from stores. (The reason he gave for stealing was not related to a lack of funds but simply "I thought I could get away with it.") His parents desperately tried to limit his time watching television and playing video games, but to little avail. Conflicts over this issue erupted almost daily and were so emotionally intense that they poisoned the atmosphere for Trevor's brothers. Trevor's parents backed off. Their other sons deserved better than having to cope with turbulence that they had no part in creating. Mr. and Ms. Winter just couldn't ruin their entire family life by fighting with him constantly.

Trevor returned to college, but to a school that he expected would be easier. He continued to use drugs heavily "to relax." As to what he was relaxing from, he replied that it was from having to go to class, attend to assignments, and study for tests. Trevor regretted that by arguing with his parents about drugs, he gave them "a window into my mind," letting them witness how unrepentant he was. To appease his parents, with their "draconian attitude" about drugs, he attended substance abuse education classes—but slept through sessions or skipped them.

Trevor's parents became increasingly baffled as to how to help their son. Trevor rejected their concerns and attempted interventions. From the time he was a young teenager, he resented what he termed their "interrogations" about his activities, and referred to them as "nosy bastards." He was in constant conflict with his father because the less he told him, the more questions his dad had. "I never wanted to talk to him. If I didn't answer, he'd get pissed. I tried to ignore him. Then he'd start yelling at me."

Trevor's mother and father never gave up trying to save their son from himself. While he was at college, they paid for a tutor. Trevor said, "My dad considered this a gift. I didn't want a tutor." However, he said the tutor helped him raise his grades so that, for a while, having the tutor "kept my parents off my back." His mom and dad were in frequent contact with school administrators, which Trevor resented as meddlesome. He thought, "On purpose, my parents are destroying my life." Killing both of them would be a relief. "I always fantasized about my dad being dead. Killing him would be heavenly. I just want my dad dead. His money is good. It'd be good if he was gone and his money stayed." He fantasized torturing and killing his father by strangling, stabbing, or shooting him. Trevor despised his dad more than any other human being on the planet. And he was furious with his mother for going along with her husband and echoing his opinions on everything.

During high school and after he failed at the first college, Trevor's parents had demanded that he go to a therapist. Trevor complied but did little more than occupy a chair in various offices, disclosing little. He told me he had nothing against the mental health professionals and thought some of them were smart and nice people. He just didn't see any reason to be meeting with them. Trevor had no interest in changing anything about himself. He did his utmost to convince the therapists that it was his parents who needed to change. He said that his parents desired that he be "fixed," but he wanted them "fixed" instead. The therapy was a standoff with nothing accomplished. "I'm not saying they weren't good at their jobs. I didn't need them," he said.

One of the therapists strongly recommended that Trevor enter residential psychiatric treatment. Mr. Winter diligently started looking into this. On a day that was like so many others, Trevor and his father got into a screaming argument about what he was doing, what he wasn't doing, and what he should be doing. Trevor became so infuriated that he grabbed a knife and stabbed his dad repeatedly. When I asked during one of the interviews in jail whether he was thinking about having murdered his dad and the consequences to the rest of the family, Trevor coldly responded that he had put it all out of his mind.

Errors in Thinking

Rarely do criminals think about the impact of their behavior. Larry didn't know anything about the gentleman who was innocently walking out of a store. Not that it mattered to him. Aimless and looking for excitement, Larry was intrigued by the prospect of "messing with" this total stranger. To reduce him to a quivering, pleading speck of humanity before totally annihilating him was the ultimate excitement. Larry might as well have stepped on an ant, so little significance did this man have to him. Not once during my interviews did Larry voice regret about what he had done. He wished he could turn back the clock, not out of regret over the homicide but so he wouldn't be contemplating spending the rest of his life in prison. That was his sole concern.

By killing his father, Trevor was able to rid himself of the individual whom he regarded as his lifelong nemesis. Trevor's crime was not against a stranger. But it might as well have been. Trevor knew his father mainly as his oppressor. He really had no interest in him as a person. Many times in his imagination, Trevor had eliminated Mr. Winter from the face of the earth so he could be completely free to do whatever he wanted. In jail, Trevor was giving little thought to the unending impact of his crime upon his mother, brothers, extended family, his dad's work colleagues, family friends, or on people in the community where they lived. Like Larry, Trevor's focus was on himself, and how he would live in prison. He refused to see visitors because he wanted no one from the past to intrude, asking questions or seeking explanations.

When criminals are held accountable, some pay lip service to having harmed someone. "I know the guy missed his stuff," said one burglar, "but I'm the one who has to serve time." The criminal's idea of injury is limited to leaving someone lying in a pool of blood. Watching blood ooze from his victim's wounds, Larry knew he had hurt him, but that did not stop him from continuing his assault until the man was dead. Criminals often blame their victims for being careless or provocative. "If he had locked the door, I couldn't have gone into his house." "She left the key in the car. That was an invitation to take it." "She was out late at night looking like she wanted to party; she had it coming."

Criminals prey upon vulnerability. Larry saw the elderly man walking alone as a convenient target, a way to relieve his boredom. After a crime like this is reported, law enforcement and mental health professionals search for a motive. Was it greed, lust, revenge, or passion? Some crimes elude such analysis, appearing senseless and without motive. In Erik Larson's best-selling *The Devil in the White City,* Detective Geyer tries to understand why a man would slaughter not only innocent young women, but also young children.[1] "Every crime had a motive. But the force that propelled Holmes seemed to exist outside the world of Geyer's experience. [Geyer] kept coming back to the same conclusion: Holmes was enjoying himself." If you understand the criminal mind, you comprehend that the seemingly purposeless crime has a purpose—to achieve a sense of sheer power, control, and excitement. Larry's victim was a stranger. "Let's get him" was the so-called motive—to get a charge out of knocking him down, subduing him, beating the life out of him, then robbing him.

You might surmise that individuals like Larry and Trevor completely lack a conscience. The truth is they have a tattered, threadbare conscience. Another way to put it is that they have elements of conscience. Like Larry and Trevor, criminals shut off considerations of conscience in order to do whatever they want and experience no lasting remorse. We have all hurt other people, whether inadvertently or deliberately. Afterward, we are likely to suffer pangs of conscience and, when possible, try to make amends. We learn from our experience and are more sensitive the next time. More often than not, conscience restrains us in the first place. Anticipating the harm we might do, we bite our tongues, rein in our impulses. The criminal is capable of experiencing fleeting regrets, but these do not deter him from future offenses. Upon learning that the home he had ransacked belonged to a lady suffering from a terminal disease, one offender was so remorseful that he arranged to have all the stolen items returned. However, this act of contrition did not restrain him from committing other burglaries. Larry recognized that other people have a conscience, but seemed almost proud that this was something he didn't have to reckon with. It seems as though he was able to totally shut off awareness of whatever conscience he had, long enough to pursue the objective of the moment.

Despite their very different family backgrounds, Larry and Trevor were similar in personality. Each had committed property crimes, used illegal drugs, and committed acts of violence. They had done far more that was illegal than ever came to the attention of the authorities. Both had a sense of entitlement. This error in thinking is vividly captured in the statement of another fellow I interviewed who recalled his frame of mind during a break-and-entry: "When I walked into that room, everything in that room belonged to me." This was not an indication of a mental illness. He knew full well that the DVD player, computer, jewelry, and flat-screen television belonged to the person whose home he had invaded. In his mind, however, these items were already his. All he had to do was take physical possession of them, figure out the best way to sell them, then dispose of the proceeds. Larry indicated that he thought the very same way when he said, "If I see something I want, I just take it." Trevor had the same outlook when he helped himself to money from his parents. He did not have to justify to himself taking the money. In his mind, the cash was already his, and he was planning how to spend it.

Criminals do not justify their crimes *before* committing them. They formulate their objective, decide how to pursue it, consider the chances of being caught, then strike. There is excitement in every phase of a crime—contemplating the end result, planning the crime, executing it, making the getaway, reveling in the success, eluding the police, and relishing the publicity that may attend the crime. Even when the criminal is caught, the excitement may not end. He now has to beat the system. There may be many people to outwit, among them police officers, detectives, mental health professionals, court service workers, and his own attorney. Justifications for what he did come into play *after* he has been apprehended and is held accountable. One man told me, "I don't steal from people. I steal only from stores. They can afford it. They rip people off. They won't miss it." This was all after-the-fact thinking. When he entered the store with the idea of stealing already in his mind, he spotted the jewelry, figured out how to take it, and made his exit. He acknowledged that, while committing the crime, he had no thoughts about whether the store could afford to lose the item or whether people were being cheated. For years, he had stolen from numerous stores and individuals, including his own mother.

We all want what we want when we want it. The questions are: What do we want? How do we try to obtain it? And what happens when we are thwarted? Two men walk into a store that sells DVDs. One is a criminal, the other isn't. The former picks up a DVD set. Paying for it does not enter his mind. He observes that the cashier is occupied by a line of customers, spots a nearby exit, and detects no evidence of security personnel or devices. "I could steal this whole place blind," he thinks, and grabs what he wants, quickly inserting the DVDs into a satchel he has brought in anticipation of the heist. The noncriminal picks up a DVD set that he has his heart set on but discovers it costs more than he thought. Reluctantly, he returns the item to the shelf, thinking, "I'll save up and buy it next month," then leaves. Stealing does not cross his mind. The practiced thief may steal an item even if he has money in his pocket to purchase it. "Why buy it if you can steal it?" asked one man who was well-versed in shoplifting. Some thieves give away or throw away what they have stolen. The act of stealing is more important than the proceeds. What the offender truly craves is the excitement that he derives from outwitting the merchants.

The criminal's desire to constantly fortify a sense of uniqueness is a driving force of his personality. Every human being is unique physically, psychologically, and experientially. A criminal may pay lip service to what he shares in common with others, but inwardly he believes he is like a fingerprint, one of a kind. He refuses to subordinate himself, at least for very long, to anyone else or to heed their advice. From his point of view, if he submits to others in any fashion, it is as though he is losing his identity. If nine criminals are on a baseball team, each thinks he should be the captain or the guy in charge. He expects others to fulfill his requirements, not the other way around. If they do not, he will abuse them or attempt to undermine them. Not receiving the recognition that he believes he is due, he becomes disillusioned and angry. Dropping out becomes a way of life. The criminal ceases participating in activities and organizations, and quits jobs. Trevor and Larry failed to get along with other people in part because of a sense of uniqueness, their belief that they were better than others and that what applied to others did not to them.

Criminals have no concept of obligation. From their standpoint, to be obligated is to be powerless. Criminals focus almost exclusively on what they perceive as others' obligations to them. They may appear to fulfill obligations but generally they do so to get others off their backs, or as part of a scheme by which they will later exploit the person they seem to be helping. Trevor had no appreciation of his parents' love and mounting concern about his well-being. While taking advantage of the comforts and opportunities they provided, he felt no obligation to them and yearned to be rid of them. This was far more than adolescent rebellion. He wanted them out of his life. Like all parents, Mr. and Ms. Winter had their flaws. But the other children managed to live with those shortcomings. In killing his father, Trevor never considered that he had any obligations to his family whatsoever. In jail, he counted on his mother feeling an obligation to him to hire a first-class defense attorney to represent him at trial. Larry had a mother, a father, siblings, and many relatives who had long prayed for him to change his ways. When they first learned about his arrest for homicide, even knowing Larry's problems, they were shocked and sickened. Neither before nor after the crime did Larry indicate that he felt any obligation to those who cared most about him, not even the young boy whom he'd befriended or the child's mother who had become his girlfriend.

Like Larry and Trevor, criminals frequently say they have nothing to do and complain of boredom. Highly responsible individuals say the same things. We may find a lecture boring or certain rote tasks tedious. At times, we yearn to get away from our daily routine. When criminals say they are bored, they may as well be on a different planet in terms of what they mean. Trevor grew bored with school—or, as he put it, he became disillusioned. He appeared to be clinically depressed. (At one point, Trevor defined depression as "the absence of fun.") But his depression developed in response to his parents' persistent efforts to keep him motivated and on track for college. Trevor said that he saw no reason to work, that the point of life was to be entertained, which entailed a social life revolving around drugs and spending hours playing violent video games. (The video games did not turn him into a violent person. He was violent *before* he played his first game.) Trevor was bored in the same way Larry was. Both young men had no close friendships. They rejected their families. They had no career aspirations. Totally self-centered, they lacked intimate relationships and were loyal to no one. These two young men had no sense of purpose from day to day. No set of principles inspired their lives. "There's nothing going on" means there is no excitement at hand. The same with "nothing to do." This discomfiting state of mind can be relieved when a criminal thinks about or engages in a self-aggrandizing and exciting activity, including planning and committing a crime. Because Larry's environment was chaotic and he had no one keeping track of him for very long, he had a much larger arena in which to operate than did Trevor while he was living with his parents. Once Trevor was on a college campus, he could immerse himself in whatever he wanted, the only interference being from his worried parents who were in touch with college administrators. Larry killed a total stranger while seeking something to do. Trevor killed his father not for lack of something to do, but because he feared being confined in a situation where he'd have almost no control over what he could or could not do—a residential psychiatric treatment facility, which to him was tantamount to jail.

Criminals know the potential consequences of their crimes. The "occupational hazards" are being caught, convicted, and confined—even being executed for crimes carrying the death penalty. There is also potential for being injured or killed during a high-risk crime. Criminals have a chilling capacity to eliminate from their thinking all these risks once they are poised to act. Their ability to shut off fear is so precise, it is like turning off a switch. In contrast, most responsible people have no need to shut off such fears because they are not contemplating committing crimes. In fact, the reverse is true. We experience fear and allow it to be a guide so we do not take imprudent risks and jeopardize our health and safety. Fear can be an ally or our enemy. Sometimes, we are not cautious enough. Occasionally, we are overly cautious. For a criminal, "fear" is a dirty word. To acknowledge being afraid is incompatible with his self-image. Having set his mind on a course of action, the criminal will not be dissuaded. He wants what he wants and nothing will interfere. No one knows how, when, or where he will strike. As he commits his crime, he has switched off deterrent considerations that might interfere with achieving his objective. Enough fear returns so that the perpetrator remains sufficiently vigilant to look over his shoulder for the police. In his mind, however, he is certain he will succeed at his undertaking.

If asked, Larry and Trevor could have foretold the possible consequences to anyone who killed a stranger on the street or a family member. But these did not apply to either of them at the time each committed murder.

7

Sex for Conquest and a Buildup of the Self

Criminals are often portrayed as having unusually strong sex drives. However, it is the excitement of making a conquest, not a biological urge, that provides the primary impetus for sexual activity. The desire to have power over others starts early. As a child, the criminal comes to discover that sex is one way of gaining that power. A twenty-five-year-old inmate in a county jail explained, "Before I knew about sex, between the ages of four and ten, I had a fascination over seeing girls cry. It wasn't that I liked seeing them get hurt. It was the equivalent of seeing them naked and it turned me on in a way that I could never really understand." He went on to observe, "Sex has always been the main objective in every relationship, if not the only objective." Often the criminal does not even conceive of his partner as a person, and so he has sex with a pair of breasts, buttocks, and a vagina. He brandishes his penis as a weapon before which others will succumb. A rapist commented with pride, "I'm well-endowed. I've stuck it into women like a murderer sticks a knife." Anyone may be a target—a tramp in a bar, the wife of a friend, one of his own children or stepchildren, a child whom he is caring for in his role as clergyman, teacher, coach, or scoutmaster.

Criminals find little that is satisfying in a consenting sexual relationship. Sex is mainly an assertion of their own power; they usually give little thought to the feelings of their partner. No matter who the partner is, the process of winning that person over is far more exciting than the sexual act. The criminal believes that others find him irresistible. If a female fails to confirm that assumption, she poses a challenge. He pursues his conquest through a soft sell of flattery and conning, or resorts to force. Some male criminals exploit men sexually. Those who engage in homosexual acts may be bisexual or exclusively homosexual. The sexual orientation is of far less importance than what a criminal actually seeks in his sexual life. The central motivation is the charge he gets from seducing, conning, or intimidating another human being into doing exactly what he wants. No sooner has he achieved one conquest than he is in pursuit of the next.

From adolescence, when the criminal refers to "my girl," he really is asserting that she belongs to him, but he considers her as disposable as an old tattered shirt. Seldom does he speak of love, nor does he have a concept of what a love relationship entails. While demanding that a woman change to suit him, he requires that she accept him just as he is. He insists that *his* girl be totally faithful, while he has sex with whomever he pleases. Once a woman presses a criminal for a commitment, she risks being discarded. Snapped one criminal, "This is a man's world. I don't want a bitch telling me what to do. Because she has a pussy, that doesn't mean she can control me."

Your initial reaction to the often graphic content that follows may be to think that the perpetrators of the crimes must be sick. You might think that no normal person has sex with his own young son, goes out at night peeping into windows, attacks and rapes a stranger, and so forth. The crimes may be sickening, but they are not products of a "sick" mind. The perpetrators know that rape, voyeurism, indecent exposure, and sex with children are illegal. Individuals who commit these crimes are rational human beings who have been massively irresponsible throughout much of their lives. A large number of sex offenders have committed other types of crimes. A study of adolescent sex offenders at a state correctional facility revealed that approximately two-thirds reported having been in treatment for offenses not of a sexual nature.[1] (Given that offenders are often untruthful, this is likely an underestimate.)

Voyeurism

Richard was arrested after years of peeping through windows at night and filming what he saw. In sentencing him to jail followed by probation, the judge emphasized that Richard had "violated the privacy and basic security" of numerous women. Before all this happened, Richard had been fired from his job after a "personality clash" with his supervisor, and his marriage started to crumble. With his life falling apart, Richard began walking out of the house at night to get away from his wife, telling her he was going for a walk. On one of his strolls, Richard saw through glass doors a woman changing clothes in her bedroom. Subsequently, he made it a point to walk by that house every night. "It became sort of a schedule for me," he commented. "I'd spend time there waiting and watching." These walks grew increasingly lengthy as he gazed into windows at other residences too. Prowling around and peering through windows offered a lot more voltage than the "humdrum routine" of his marriage. "It was exciting, daring, there was an element of risk," Richard said, and acknowledged, "I was very conscious of the risk. That was one of the reasons I did it."

Not content with just looking, Richard purchased a camera and began filming what he saw. He was regularly looking into the homes of more than a dozen women. He would view these films late at night and masturbate. Sometimes, he would masturbate without watching the films, reliving in his mind the excitement of lurking in the woods and looking in windows. This all came to an end when he brazenly entered the backyard of a home and was so wrapped up in his voyeuristic act that he failed to see a male advancing. This man knocked Richard to the ground while his wife phoned the police.

Reflecting on what he had done, Richard commented during my evaluation of him that "I was off in my own little world." His voyeurism was exciting in two ways. One was taking the risk; the other was in the sexual arousal that followed when he watched the films. He supplemented his own films with nearly five dozen sex videos from which he would sample each night while he masturbated. With respect to his illegal behavior, Richard said, "I knew it was breaking the law. I never carried it to the next level," by which he meant physically hurting another person.

When Richard was a young boy, his grandfather had molested him and sworn him to secrecy. After he summoned the courage to tell his mother, the grandfather moved out of the home and entered a psychiatric facility. To his credit, Richard did not use the molestation as an excuse or explanation for his voyeurism. "I see no relationship between this and what I've done," he told me, and noted that his parents remain "my very closest friends."

Richard regarded himself as irresistible, a trophy to women. "I'm a neat guy. I deserve a really neat girl," Richard told me. He thought he was too good to have either an ordinary woman or ordinary employment. After he was fired from his job, he continued to live a country-club existence, spending days on the golf course. He wanted the perfect job, which was to "own my own company and produce a tangible item." After his wife left him soon after his arrest, Richard was on a mission to find the perfect woman. He rattled off the characteristics of his ideal woman the way a person might list the options he wanted to order on a new car. As he was speaking about his relationships with women, Richard realized that he had never been in love. He recognized that he had been extremely self-centered and difficult, readily finding shortcomings in others, rarely in himself. Richard acknowledged how ornery he was at work, snapping and "flippantly using curse words to make a point." He seldom exerted effort at anything, whether it was building a career, establishing friendships, or making his marriage work. Unfaithful to his wife, Richard had blamed her for being domineering and unreasonable. As for his reluctance to look for a job, he mused, "I don't know where my ambition and drive are." The fact was that he always had ambition, but very little drive.

Although unemployed, Richard refused to read newspaper want ads or to search online for job postings. He admired a friend who was struggling financially for "doing what he has to" in taking a job at a fast-food restaurant. Richard was not inspired to do anything similar. There was nothing new about his pretensions and laziness. In college he was on academic probation before he dropped out. He always imagined himself living in a mansion, working at an executive position with "big-league players," driving an expensive car, and having a wife and family. Meanwhile, to raise cash he was forced to sell stocks that he had purchased years earlier when he was having modest success at his work. Playing at "upper crust" golf courses and participating in tournaments was costing him money that he did not have. Richard commented, "This is so easy, sitting around and pulling out money from savings. I'm flat-out lazy." Perhaps to assure himself (rather than assure me), Richard vowed, "I'll make money. I'm ready. It's going to happen." But then he remarked that his situation was similar to a man having a ladder but being unwilling to climb the rungs to reach his objective. This man was adept at articulating his inertia and at finding excuses to do nothing. He said, "I don't want to get rejected. I take rejection personally.

Any rejection hurts." This statement said worlds about him. He felt rejected whenever someone failed to recognize him as the irresistible, highly competent, superb human being he thought himself to be. He required others to confirm his lofty view of himself. In his voyeuristic acts, Richard experienced a sense of extreme power over women who did not even know him. Unsuspecting, they were providing him with excitement he lacked in his marriage or at a job.

After serving time in jail, Richard wondered, "Have I turned off my sexual mechanism? I'm completely uncomfortable with jumping in the hay at this point." Without engaging in illicit sexual activities, and while doing his utmost to deter even a single thought of voyeurism, Richard's sex drive was minimal. Upon his first attempt at sexual intercourse with a woman he had been dating, he was dismayed to find that he could not get an erection.

Richard was an uncompromising individual who had been destructive everywhere he went. Up until his arrest, the frequency of his voyeuristic activities had increased so that he was thinking about them day and night. There is no way to determine whether his sexual offenses would have evolved into more serious crimes if he had not been apprehended and prosecuted. John Douglas, a pioneer FBI criminal profiler, observed, "If you study the most violent of sexual predators . . . you will find in virtually all cases an escalation from relatively innocent beginnings."[2]

Indecent Exposure

Numerous theories purport to explain why men (it is almost always men) commit acts of indecent exposure. Psychoanalytic theory explains this act as being motivated by a desire to receive reassurance that one is physically intact—a defense against "castration anxiety." In a lengthy manuscript on exhibitionism,

Brett Kahr, senior clinical research fellow at London's Centre for Child Mental Health, wrote that this behavior also "serves as a communication of internal distress, usually linked to childhood trauma," as "an expression of hatred toward women," and as "a means of restoring damaged self-esteem."[3] Such explanations are difficult to prove scientifically. Whatever its origin may be, the perpetrator of indecent exposure finds it to be tremendously exciting.

For over twenty years, James had developed a routine for exhibiting his penis. As the weekend approached, his mind raced with anticipation at the thought. Telling his family he was running errands, he would embark on a hunt to identify places where he could position himself in order to surprise unsuspecting passersby. He frequented parks, bike paths, tracks, and wooded areas where he could hide and target people who were out for recreation. He became so focused on this activity that he began devoting time to it during his daily lunch hour at work. On business trips, he would select a hotel based not on cost or convenience to the work site, but on its proximity to a place that would offer opportunity for indecent exposure. His objective was to entice women who would discover him and stare at his genitals admiringly. Since most women reacted with shock and disgust, he was disappointed, but it was the attention that mattered. James became so obsessed with exhibitionism that it was on his mind from the moment he woke up. He became careless, losing track of how many times he had visited the same location. Finally, at a park that he had frequented numerous times, James was apprehended by police who had staked out the area.

Nothing that James told me supported the explanations frequently offered by mental health professionals for this behavior. James was not sexually deprived, as he had a wife with whom he had a sexual relationship. Nor was he exposing himself to gain relief from depression, anxiety, or any particular adversity. In fact, his life was going extremely well. James explained that, by displaying his penis, he was enjoying himself and finding excitement in every phase—thinking about where to go, stationing himself so he could be visible without being obvious, taking out his erect penis, anticipating the reactions of people who would pass by, then watching their reactions. James acknowledged that fantasies of rape raced through his mind. There is no way to know whether he would have started physically attacking women had he not been arrested.

Indecent exposure had become like a second career for James. He started missing work, lying to his family and colleagues, and betraying their trust. James was a tyrant at home, resulting in his wife and child walking on eggshells to accommodate his demands. His wife filed for divorce, and the agency that employed him in a high-level position let him go because he was no longer able to maintain a high-security clearance.

Louis's pattern was different. After his wife died, he lived a routine and lonely existence. Walking around nude inside his home, he frequently stood in a window, especially around the time two teenage girls were getting off the school bus. He watched their comings and goings—they were often in the company of boyfriends—and fantasized about their sexual activities. Louis was aroused by the thought that the girls looked forward to seeing him naked in the window. "I had a feeling they were looking for me, and I was pleasing them," he said. "When you see them, you think that's what they're looking for, and you just want to go ahead and let them see you." After he watched them, he would masturbate. Louis acknowledged that, while on the deck of his house, he began gazing into the bedroom window of the girls' house that was adjacent to his own, and was rewarded by seeing them in various states of undress. He thought they did this deliberately to tantalize him. He was encouraged by the fact that both girls spoke to him when they saw him outside. Louis proclaimed that what he did was completely harmless and assured me, "I'd never do anything to the girls."

Louis confessed that his wife used to admonish him about his carelessness in walking around the house unclothed. She worried that someone might see him. He acknowledged that, if she were still living, she "wouldn't put up with what I was doing." Louis then revealed that his wife "accused me of doing something" with a babysitter. He said he didn't recall exactly what it was but simply admitted, "I might have had a crush on her."

Because of my limited contact with Louis, there is a lot that I did not learn. I include his case in order to make several points. One is that the repeated incidents of exposing himself occurred after a major deterrent to such behavior was removed. With the death of his wife, he did not have someone constantly warning him about possible consequences of his conduct. Secondly, like James and others who engage in indecent exposure, he viewed himself as irresistible and harming no one. A third point is that his pattern included both exhibitionism and voyeurism. Finally, there is the intimation that his misconduct may have gone further, as suggested by the conflict he had with his wife over some manner of inappropriate behavior with a babysitter.

The frequent perpetrator of indecent exposure does not have to go out and search for places to station himself. With the use of a cell phone, he can engage in this behavior without leaving home. With the click of a button, a male or female can photograph his or her genitals and transmit the image. Some people who engage in "sexting" do so naively. This activity is extremely risky. Images can be appropriated and relayed to parties other than the intended recipient. They can be used for retaliation and blackmail. A minor can send a photograph of himself to another minor, resulting in charges of production and distribution of child pornography. Cell phones have also provided an outlet for voyeuristic activity when, without the knowledge of the participants, sexual activity is filmed and watched by others. Undoubtedly, there is a continuum ranging from a youth who mischievously engages in sexting, to the person for whom the activity represents another dot in the landscape of his criminal activity.

Rape

Innumerable professional articles and commentaries have described rape as a crime that has little to do with sex but far more with power and conquest. It is important to understand the act of rape within the context of the perpetrator's entire personality. Rapists do not necessarily hate women, nor are they sexually deprived. At stake in a rape is the criminal's affirmation of his image of himself as powerful and desirable. The assailant believes that his target already wants him, or will want him once she gives him a chance. Her attempts to ward him off only heighten his excitement. Brute force is rarely necessary because intimidation works. Every rapist whom I have interviewed has committed other types of crimes.

People find it puzzling, as well as repulsive, that elderly women become rape victims. Why, they wonder, does the rapist not prey upon an attractive younger person? It is the conquest that is of primary importance. The criminal seeks an available and vulnerable target; who fits that description better than a frail, elderly person?

Monty provided exceptional detail as to the workings of his mind, which resulted in his assaulting a young woman with a rock and then attempting to rape her as she was innocently walking in a forested area.

Monty came from difficult family circumstances. He said his mother didn't want him around after she divorced his father. His mother told me that, actually, it was the other way around. Her son became increasingly secretive and walled her out of his life. Acknowledging that she could have been a better parent, she voiced frustration because "I didn't know how to be close to him." She noted that Monty never asked for much; when he was nine, she bought him a computer, which was "all he ever wanted." She was shocked by his arrest for the attempted rape. She volunteered that she wouldn't have been surprised had she received a call informing her that her son had broken into a computer in the U.S. president's office. "We had trouble with him, but that just didn't fit. I wouldn't have seen this coming for nothin'," his mother remarked.

Monty resisted spending time with his father because he resented all the rules that his dad imposed. Although he was far stricter than his ex-wife, Monty's dad acknowledged, "I fell down on the parent end of the deal. When he did lots of little things, I let them slide. The older he got, the less I knew him." As a teenager, Monty took pride in being able to size people up and tell them what they wanted to hear so they'd think highly of him. A close relative warned that, since Monty didn't seem to heed anyone's warnings, the boy would "have to hit that brick wall and it'd be an eye-opening experience."

Long before the attempted rape occurred (when he was twenty-two), Monty was a one-man walking crime wave. He had stolen from his parents, illegally driven their car, shoplifted, created homemade bombs, and broken into houses. At thirteen, he had run up a large bill for phone sex. Despite being capable academically, he frequently skipped school, got suspended numerous times for disrupting classes, and finally was expelled. Uninterested in school subjects, he was a computer fanatic and was hired as a computer systems analyst. He spent hours watching Internet pornography, sometimes by hacking into sites that required payment.

On the day of the offense, Monty had gone to the woods as he often did, taking along a murder mystery that had a sexual theme. He quickly became bored with the book and began watching a young woman. He followed as she turned onto a path. Picking up a rock, he struck her on the head and knocked her to the ground. Holding her down, he yanked her clothes off, assumed a position to have intercourse, then ceased and assured her he wasn't going to hurt or kill her, whereupon he gave her his jacket to stem the bleeding and let her go. She went home and reported the crime; shortly after, Monty was arrested.

For nearly five years, Monty had fantasized accosting an attractive girl and raping her. He found tremendously exciting the idea of finding a young girl and being her first sexual partner. He masturbated daily while thinking about raping a virgin. The book he was reading that very day contained scenes of rape. Monty was not sexually deprived, having had sex recently with a number of consenting partners. But consensual sex was too commonplace. "Once I have something, I don't want it anymore," he remarked. Asked about the impact of what he did, Monty said merely that the victim might not desire sex for a while and "she may not want to go out in the woods." Such a statement is typical of criminals in that it reflects minimal cognizance of any damage that they inflict.

While awaiting trial, Monty wrote what he termed his "sexual history." In that document, he indicated that the attempted rape was not an out-of-character or impulsive act. His sex play began at age nine with an older sibling. He discovered his stepfather's pornographic films when he was ten and started masturbating. For two years, he engaged in sex with the family dog. At fifteen, he had sexual intercourse with a female, the first of a number of sexual encounters during his teenage years. He described himself operating as "a peeping Tom," which he thought might have been the prelude to thoughts about rape. Monty wrote, "It got so bad that I would get up before school while it was still dark and go looking in windows." Finally, he broke into a home and "jumped on [a girl] while she was sleeping. I don't think I stopped and ran because I thought it was wrong. I think I left because I was scared. I started spending more and more time alone out in the woods. I would go out where I thought no one would be, strip naked, and masturbate while fantasizing about rape."

When Monty discovered online pornography, there was an explosion of fantasy. "I began using my computer skills to break into pay porno sites. I also started finding rape videos I could watch and started masturbating to child porn a lot. Sometimes, I'd spend all night on the computer. I even had an artificial intelligence computer-generated girlfriend that would do whatever you told her to do. I was a different person behind the computer. I was in control and what I told the computer to do, it did. I didn't have to worry about the computer falling in love with somebody else or cheating on me or hurting me. The computer would always love me. Even before the rape fantasies, I used to fantasize that I had special powers and that I could make any girl I wanted have sex with me." All of this was a mental rehearsal priming him to take advantage of the opportunity that presented itself in the form of a young woman out for a walk on a lovely day.

I've mentioned previously that perpetrators of crime blame their victims. This is often the case with rape. At eighteen, Dewayne was charged with assault and attempted rape. Not the least remorseful, this young man lashed out, blaming a twelve-year-old girl. "She was a fast girl. Some young girls carry themselves like they're older. She was interested in me. That's why I was interested. You know how men is. When you get the chance to try something, you try to do it. I didn't believe she'd take it that route. She was scared of the punishment she'd get from her mother. If I was raping her, why didn't she scream to her aunt? That peeved me off. I don't care nothin' about what she say. I know what's true." Angry at his victim, Dewayne swore, "She'll get hers. I got the Lord. The Lord will make something happen to her. The Lord will give it right to her."

Sexual Exploitation in Adult Relationships

Criminals take advantage of the authority and trust that are inherent in the jobs they hold. A police officer stops a woman for a traffic violation but offers to let her go if she will have sex with him. A corrections officer capitalizes on the power he wields over inmates, promising extra food from the kitchen in exchange for sex. A minister cultivates a relationship with a lonely widow parishioner in order to have sex.

Among the most frequent ethics violations that are filed against psychologists are those having to do with sex between therapist and patient. Carolyn Bates and Annette Brodsky, authors of *Sex in the Therapy Hour,*[4] mention young, inexperienced therapists who use poor judgment and cross a boundary by falling in love with a patient. Once they recognize the potential harm, they desire to remedy the situation. In contrast, however, are "therapists with a personality disorder, which may be classified as an antisocial personality." Bates and Brodsky point out, "They are the last people in the world whom patients should trust; they have only their own needs in mind."

These exploitative relationships arise out of mental processes that are similar to those involved in a criminal's plot to embezzle funds from his job. He focuses on an objective. Then he ferrets out weakness and vulnerability in an individual or organization. Through misrepresentation and outright lies, he conceals his motives. However long it takes, he ingratiates himself, establishes a trusting relationship, and acquires a good reputation. He develops a modus operandi to achieve what he desires, exploiting the legitimate authority and power that has been vested in him by the very nature of his position. Then he strikes. If he is unmasked, he declares his good intentions, denies wrongdoing, and blames the victim.

Sexual Activity with Children in One's Own Family

Terry was not in love with his wife but was "having a love affair" with their seven-year-old son, Bobby. When his wife was not home, Terry and his son fondled each other and Terry would then masturbate to orgasm. He told me that Bobby "really enjoyed it and wanted to do it, but he sensed it was wrong." Terry reassured Bobby that "it's our love alone," meaning that what they did was to remain a secret. Terry saw nothing wrong with what he was doing, and asserted that Bobby often initiated the sexual activity. Asked what he thought Bobby got out of it, Terry replied, "A closeness to his father. I don't know if he derived any sexual pleasure. Sucking a boy's penis feels good, I'm sure. He never looked scared." Terry explained that this all occurred within the context of "a deep, loving relationship."

Terry's sexual contact with a minor did not stop with Bobby. He was able to lure other boys into the house by having his son invite them to play war games. "We'd wrestle, and pants would come off," he said. When Terry directed those boys to take down their pants, they did just that. Mutual touching occurred. Terry acknowledged that these other boys "looked scared, like I was intimidating them." He thought Bobby "enjoyed watching me do that. He wanted to look at the other boys too."

Terry had done pretty much whatever he felt like doing in all areas of his life. In college, he used illegal drugs, including LSD and marijuana. He dropped out of one school and enrolled in another. He continued to smoke marijuana and consume alcohol, reaching the point where he downed as many as a half dozen mixed drinks in an evening. Undisciplined financially, he said he was "living the good life" until he filed for bankruptcy. When he spoke of his dislike for his wife, Sally, I asked why he married her. "We got married real quickly," he commented, explaining that this was after they'd had a child out of wedlock. Apparently, having Bobby was also unplanned. When

Sally gained a lot of weight and "sex got boring," Terry engaged Bobby in sexual activity.

"I never cared about consequences. I went ahead and did it," said Terry, the "it" referring to whatever he desired. He had no idea as to how sexual activity with his son could have a negative impact. He speculated, "Down the road, I wonder what he'll think on his first date when he's trying to score with a girl." This comment revealed a great deal about Terry. One is that he never considered or cared about whether Bobby would suffer any adverse effects. His chilling thought about Bobby trying to "score" on a first date indicated that he sees people as objects. Terry was insensitive even to the immediate consequences as Bobby struggled to cope with the breakup of his family. Because of what his dad had done to other boys, Bobby and his mother had to move from the neighborhood, resulting in Bobby losing his playmates and having to change schools. Terry had no awareness of the emotional devastation that Sally experienced after his sexual activities with Bobby and the other young boys came to light. Terry even seemed indifferent to what would be an indefinite interruption to his relationship with his son. Given that Terry anticipated being sentenced to prison, it would be a long time, if ever, until he would be permitted contact with Bobby.

Sally's marriage to Terry had been an emotional roller coaster. Until the sexual activity with Bobby came to light, his drinking posed the greatest problem. When Terry became intoxicated, "he'd be difficult, argumentative, right on everything." Sally recalled how one night he'd refused to let her go to sleep, keeping her up for hours after she objected to his coming home late and not calling her. Terry treated Sally like a slave, making unrealistic demands, such as insisting that she vacuum the entire house twice each day. When he wanted to sleep late, she had to tiptoe around and keep Bobby quiet. Sally said that Terry would frequently "blow up about things that shouldn't be a big deal." With Terry going to prison, Sally had to begin her life all over, in debt and with a young son to raise. When I made reference to the tragedy that had unfolded for Terry's wife, son, and the neighborhood boys, Terry replied tersely, "I didn't realize it was a tragedy."

Pedophilia

Pedophilia has emerged dramatically into public awareness with the scandal among Catholic clergy and sensational stories like that of former Penn State coach Jerry Sandusky, convicted on forty-five counts of sexually abusing ten children over a fifteen-year period, among many other related offenses. These are not cases in which strangers forced themselves on children or enticed them with gifts. The culprits appeared to be responsible, caring adults who were entrusted with the care of children. Such individuals become influential in the lives of their young charges, for whom they assume responsibility as day care providers, scout-masters, camp counselors, and so forth. They are valued by their employers, admired by parents, and often adored by the children themselves. They have a stellar reputation because they are gifted in imparting skills, and at establishing rapport not only with children but also with parents and the community.

Connor's parents had separated, and his mother was gratified by Father Dan's attention to her eleven-year-old son. She enrolled Connor in church-sponsored activities, confident that he would be spending time in a wholesome environment. Father Dan showered the boy with attention and made him feel special by telling him how much he loved him. Father Dan's expressions of love did not stop with hugs and kisses. The priest fondled Connor through his clothes, then introduced the boy to oral sex and mutual masturbation. "I always tried to avoid him," Connor told me during my evaluation of him. Connor's efforts to pull away from Father Dan were met with nastiness and belligerence. On one occasion, the priest complained to Connor's mother that her son's rudeness had ruined a weekend outing. When his mother strongly admonished Connor, he abandoned hope that he would escape from the priest. He knew the priest was an esteemed family friend, and to report what was going on would be incredibly embarrassing, plus Connor knew no one would believe him. "He turned my life upside down and took away my youth," Connor proclaimed. Connor's faith in the Church and God was destroyed.

Adele reported a similar experience. She regularly attended Mass with her mother, and belonged to a church youth group led by Father Tom. Adele admired the young, handsome priest who took a strong liking to her. "I asked him to be my confessor," she said. Adele was seeing a lot of Father Tom because he was a family friend and visited her home. He would tell her she looked pretty and offer her rides home from church functions. "I was flattered. It was like I had a crush on him," Adele recalled, comparing herself to a twelve-year-old infatuated with a movie star. "It was confusing and flattering. Anyone would die for attention from him. My parents thought he walked on water. I was very religious. He thought I was special. He was like a blessing from God!" Adele wondered why, when all the girls were giddy around him, she was the one singled out for special attention. On her thirteenth birthday, the priest kissed her on the lips, drew her toward him, and confessed he was in love with her, declaring that their love was a gift from God. This was incredibly confusing to this young girl. "Of course, I believed him. Obviously, I couldn't talk to anyone. He said that others would not understand and not to tell anyone. This is so hard to explain. I completely trusted him and trusted God. I didn't think he was being a bad person. God never would have allowed this to happen if it was wrong."

Father Tom initiated Adele into a variety of sexual activities. Adele told me, "I never recoiled, because of the level of trust in him and in God and the fact that my parents trusted him, and everyone I knew trusted him." Adele grew even more confused when the priest acknowledged feeling guilty. She blamed herself for being the cause of his distress—"that I was doing something bad to make him feel guilty, that I was bad for existing. If I wasn't there, he wouldn't struggle and feel guilty about me having a crush on him." Nonetheless, Adele felt very fortunate that "this great godly man singled me out. It was from God unquestionably, but the world wouldn't understand." Adele reflected, "Priests carry a lot of power, like on a par with God. They can forgive your sins like God." Adele had always considered priests as infallible, "like God."

The sexual relationship between Adele and Father Tom lasted for years. If she resisted the priest's sexual overtures, he'd "get ugly and pushy" and she'd feel more guilty. Even though Adele was close to her parents, she could not imagine revealing what was going on. It did not make it any easier that Father Tom professed that her parents were his best friends. Father Tom had become like another parent. "He gave me guidance about friends, even about classes to take. He was considered a member of my family and was involved in everything, including birthdays and anniversaries." Adele explained, "The way my parents thought, I was special in God's eyes, and the priest recognized this."

Adele felt alienated from her peers, "different, like we didn't have anything in common." She felt badly that she could not bring herself to confide even in her closest friend. "If I did, I'd be betraying Father Tom." Once Adele left for college, she began suffering panic attacks. Father Tom was not far away. Uncertain what to do, she called him seeking reassurance. When she resolved to live a normal life and begin dating, Adele informed the priest, anticipating he would wish her well. Instead, he accused her of causing him such intense anxiety that he might have to enter therapy and eventually leave the priesthood. "It was a turning point. He didn't care about me," she realized. "I was devastated and got really depressed." Feeling abandoned and disillusioned, she suffered from anxiety and insomnia and experienced flashbacks of sexual encounters, leaving her feeling "dead inside." As she confided in a therapist, she began realizing she had been abused. Still she persisted in defending the priest, telling the therapist that what had happened was spiritual. After many months of psychotherapy and taking college classes, Adele ceased attending Mass and made friends outside the Church. "I put religion in perspective and saw things in a more realistic way," she commented. Adele filed a lawsuit against the diocese because she felt she had to "do something for myself and my self-respect."

A 1999 article in *Sports Illustrated* magazine titled "Nightmare" made the point that youth sports programs constitute "a ready-made resource pool for pedophiles."[5] The type of molester most common to youth sports victimizes on average nearly 120 children before being caught. The pattern of the pedophile coach is similar to that of the priests described above. Children admire their coaches. Parents perceive people who are so devoted to their children as role models. With the high incidence of divorce and two working parents, children spend considerable time supervised by coaches, circumstances that are conducive to forming close emotional relationships. Like Connor and Adele, children in sports programs do not report sexual activities with their coaches because they are too embarrassed and think that others won't believe them. And, most importantly, they do not want to get their coaches into trouble. As the "Nightmare" article reports, the children are the main victims. In addition, unsuspecting parents are devastated when they discover what has transpired, and lose confidence in their own judgment.

The dynamics described here apply to criminals in other positions who sexually exploit and abuse children. Ned moved from job to job, all of them positions in which he supervised children; he was a teacher, a choral group director, and a scout leader. Under questionable circumstances involving his behavior with young boys, Ned was allowed to resign from each position by promising to receive counseling. He'd then move to another state and take a new job working with children. Ned emphasized that he never cruised around looking to pick up kids who were total strangers. He explained that sexual activity evolved from a relationship that he formed over time with youngsters to whom he became emotionally attached. Under the pretext of offering guidance and instruction, he would show young boys photographs of naked children, some of which he had taken himself. He characterized what he was doing as teaching them about their bodies and sexual development. Talking to one boy about the genital changes he would someday experience, "I had him drop his pants. I touched him just enough to show him his testicles and let go. I was teaching him about himself. I showed him on myself. I had a warm feeling of being helpful."

Ned professed to love the boys with whom he became sexually involved. He asserted that the sexual aspect evolved naturally from a warm, emotional relationship and occurred always with the youngster's consent. He emphasized that sometimes it was the boy who initiated sex. To underscore his good intentions, he cited numerous instances in which he helped kids struggling with difficult family situations and who "needed care and affection." He stepped in and provided comfort, advice, and support. He spoke of one boy whose father was blatantly cheating on his mother. Having no one else to confide in, the child turned to Ned. "I gave him a massage with his clothes on," Ned recalled, then touched the boy's genitals. "It didn't feel inappropriate at the time," he stated. Ned went on a camping trip with another boy who had been physically abused by his father. "Sometimes we just lay together and talked," he said. At other times, while in a tent, they engaged in hugging, fellatio, and mutual masturbation. "I tried to be a teacher, parent, and a friend," Ned explained. He and this youngster made cuts on their wrists "and became blood brothers."

Ned also tutored boys who were having academic problems and assisted others in earning scout merit badges. He was extremely critical of a teacher who, in contrast to him, was "so blatant and enticed boys purely for sex." He pointed out, "If a boy resisted, I'd go no further." And, he constantly emphasized, "Everything I did was out of love."

Ned estimated that he had been sexually involved with nearly four dozen boys between the ages of twelve and fourteen. Ned's irresponsibility was not limited to having sex with boys. He bounced from job to job. He frequently overdrew his checking account and incurred substantial debt while living beyond his means. He characterized himself as "a mild alcohol abuser." During some of his sexual episodes, he was drinking, and on occasion he'd supply a boy with alcohol prior to sex.

Individuals like Father Dan, Father Tom, and Ned are criminals in every sense of the term. Sexual involvement with children entails misrepresentation and secrecy. There is an imbalance of power when an adult cultivates a relationship with a vulnerable, often naive person, then converts it into a sexual relationship, warning the child against telling anyone about it. Pedophiles betray the trust of the juveniles whom they are in charge of, as well as that of the youngsters' families. In the process, the pedophile builds himself up as a good person. If he is ever apprehended, he believes he is the aggrieved party. Never thinking that he has done any harm by loving a child, he contends that the only damage resulted from the publicity surrounding his arrest, and the child being subjected to questioning by police officers and social workers.

If the pedophile is not apprehended, his interest in a child ceases when he or she reaches a particular stage of physical development. The pedophile then moves on to the next youth.

Child Pornography

Under U.S. federal law, child pornography is defined as "any visual depiction of sexually explicit conduct involving a minor."[6] It may include a picture that "is sufficiently sexually suggestive." Receiving such pornography, even if one does nothing with it but view it in one's own home, is illegal. Transmitting a pornographic image of a child is known as "distribution." Photographing a minor engaged in sexual activity is regarded as "production" of child pornography. Penalties for any type of involvement with child pornography are stiff. People who receive, distribute, or produce child pornography face minimum mandatory sentences under federal law and can be prosecuted under state law as well.

Unquestionably, production of child pornography entails exploitation and abuse of children. However, not all men (almost without exception, males are the offenders) who receive and view child pornography are the same. While it is true that pedophiles are likely to have had involvement in child pornography, not everyone who views child pornography is a pedophile. An analogy, referred to in an earlier chapter, is the playing of violent video games. Many people who commit extreme acts of violence are avid consumers of such games. However, the vast majority of people who play violent video games are not violent. In other words, most of us do not enact that which we watch. I have interviewed men who have received and collected child pornography but who do not ever attempt to establish sexual relationships with children.

Consider Ben, who was on Social Security retirement disability for multiple incapacitating physical problems. He was barely able to drive to the grocery store and run other routine, nearby errands. Except for contact with his wife and her relatives, Ben lived an isolated existence. Bored and lonely, he spent day after day confined to his house. Severe migraine headaches and intense pain from other medical conditions made it difficult for him to engage for long in any sustained activity, even reading or watching television. He did have a computer, which he used to follow the news and the stock market as well as for entertainment. He and his wife were having sexual relations infrequently. Ben began looking at images of young adult women in bathing suits. This progressed to watching adult pornography, then nude underage girls in sexually suggestive poses. Ben had no children of his own and had no contact with children of any age. As he did with adult pornography, he saved images of juveniles on a flash drive. Early one morning, Ben's wife responded to a knock on the door and found the house surrounded by federal agents who produced a search warrant and proceeded to confiscate all of the couple's electronic devices. For receipt of child pornography, Ben was sent to prison to serve a mandatory five-year sentence.

For Ben, viewing pornography, including child pornography, was a relief from boredom. Never did he pay for pornography or send images to another person. At no time did he as much as fantasize about actually contacting a stranger, either an adult or child, for sex. During my evaluation, Ben repeatedly expressed how ashamed he was over immersing himself in pornography while seeking a diversion from physical and mental pain.

Ben's situation is very different from that of men who not only view child pornography but also troll through chat rooms looking for children with whom to establish liaisons online and then meet to have sex. For these individuals, child pornography fuels fantasies that are a prelude to victimizing children. The problem is that it is extremely difficult to distinguish those who prey upon children from people who view child pornography but would never consider actually seeking out a child for sex. It would seem that little purpose was served by sentencing Ben to five years in the penitentiary. The cost to U.S. taxpayers of housing Ben and caring for his many physical special needs is exorbitant. Measures such as house arrest with GPS monitoring would more than suffice as punishment. Ben's case is not unique. There are others like him who do not buy, sell, or distribute child pornography. They look at it in the privacy of their own homes but never seek out children for sex. Dr. Fred Berlin of the Johns Hopkins University School of Medicine and his colleague Denise Sawyer have cited research demonstrating that "the vast majority of individuals who have downloaded child pornography, and who have had no prior convictions for a sexual offense against a child, do not subsequently go on to commit hands-on sexual offenses."[7]

Uniform sentencing for this and other offenses was instituted in large part to avoid wide disparities in sentencing for the same crime. The disadvantage to sentencing guidelines that judges in the federal system are expected to follow is that one loses sight of the individual. Every person who sells a drug to an undercover agent is not the same. One person may be a relative neophyte in the drug world looking to make a quick buck, and unfortunate enough to select the wrong buyer. Another may be a major drug dealer who does the same thing. And so it is with child pornography. There is a major difference between Ben and a man whose collection of child pornography is part of a pattern that eventuates in his victimizing children.

8

Simmering Anger Flaring into Rage

Criminals expect others to behave as they want them to behave. Since many times each day this does not happen, they are perpetually angry. Consider the likelihood of frustration and disappointment if you lived with the following expectations. Driving to work, fellow motorists should give way and allow you to move at your own pace. Arriving at work, everyone should be delighted to see you, and throughout the day your colleagues, customers, and supervisor should be agreeable. Going out to lunch, you should be seated immediately and enjoy great food and fast service. Returning to work, the remainder of the day should proceed without conflict. After work, if you arrive at the service station to pick up your car, dropped off earlier that day, it should be ready to drive home with a reasonable price assessed for repairs. Upon arriving home, your spouse should be in a cheerful mood with a great meal on the table, and after dinner your children should remain quietly occupied, allowing you to recline in an easy chair and watch television uninterrupted. Whatever you ask of family members, they should accommodate you.

This scenario reflects how many criminals think. Their self-image rises and falls based upon whether others meet their expectations. When a tiny pin punctures a balloon, the entire balloon bursts. The same thing occurs at the smallest setback with a criminal whose entire self-image is on the line. What most people would consider just a part of life, the criminal reacts to as if something catastrophic has transpired.

These uncompromising individuals harbor an enormous fear of being put down. By reacting with anger, they ward off a sense of total worthlessness. A diminishing of self-worth occurs only in a person's mind. While most of us may react to criticism, at least initially, in a defensive manner, we retain the ability to evaluate it. If the criticism has merit, we can benefit and improve. Otherwise, we can disregard it. Our entire self-image is not at stake unless we interpret the remark in a highly personal manner—which is what criminals do constantly. You may be looking off in the distance. But because a criminal thinks you are scrutinizing him critically, he becomes incensed. You accidentally knock into him in the grocery store. He takes it personally and is prepared to fight. Accounts of prison life illustrate this point very well. Prisoners in the general population are allowed to spend time in the recreation area, where tensions often run high. The slightest bump, inadvertent eye contact, or other display of seeming disrespect can instantly escalate into a brutal assault, a fatal stabbing, or all-out gang warfare.

A responsible person comes to recognize that he has very little control over other people. He grows accustomed to coping with "Murphy's Law": If anything can go wrong, it will. (There is also "Sullivan's Corollary" to Murphy's Law, namely that Murphy is an optimist.) In the life of a criminal, there is no room for Murphy. Although the criminal's anger may not be visible, it simmers within, then ignites when he encounters the slightest thing that eludes his control. Like a cancer, the anger may be localized but, without warning, can metastasize so that anyone or anything in the criminal's path can become a target.

Consider "road rage" and its source. A driver suddenly cuts in front of you without signaling. You have a choice as to how to react. A responsible, safe driver will drop back and keep his distance, perhaps muttering under his breath. The criminal interprets the situation as a personal affront. Resolved to even the score, he retaliates by pursuing, screaming, cutting in front of the offending driver, forcing him off the road, perhaps throwing something at him, or even shooting him. Describing his state of mind whenever he encounters a driver who impedes his progress, one criminal commented, "I get so angry, I want to strangle somebody."

The criminal has a thin skin. He will dish it out, but he won't take it. His insistence upon "respect" is another indicator of how his mentality differs from that of an individual who is basically responsible. A noncriminal person gains respect through achievement. Respect is earned. For a criminal, "respect" is shown by others submitting to him. When he thinks he is being "disrespected," he will do whatever he considers necessary to demonstrate that no one can push him around. Perceived put-downs may be so slight and occur so quickly that it may be impossible for an observer to identify what precipitated the rage. A criminal may be saving a seat for a friend, but if someone else occupies the chair, the interloper punctures the criminal's inflated ego. He seeks to re-inflate it by challenging the new occupant's right to sit there. The same dynamic occurs when someone speaks to him in a particular tone of voice. Sensing a put-down, he flies into a fury and lands a punch.

Helen completed her quick shopping blitz through the department store and was rushing with her cart to pay at the cash register. She ground to a quick halt when her progress was impeded by two women who were browsing in the aisle. Helen thought she heard one of the ladies mutter, "If that bitch doesn't slow down, she's going to hit us with her cart." Infuriated, Helen spun around, grabbed the woman, and assaulted her. The cashier quickly summoned a security officer who detained Helen. The entire encounter was recorded on the store's surveillance system. Helen had been convicted several times in the past for shoplifting. For this assault, which left her victim seriously injured, Helen was sentenced to three months in jail followed by a period of probation. When she recounted the incident to her counselor, she spoke as though she had been the injured party. She was still furious that the other shopper got in her way, then had the nerve to call her a name.

It is difficult to know when adversity will strike. To a criminal, anything that does not go his way is adversity, and he takes it extremely personally. Just having someone tell him to do something he finds disagreeable is considered a put-down. Working at a menial job is a put-down, and so he may not work at all. "I'd rather be dead than have my friends see me sweeping the floor," said a twenty-year-old man with no job experience or skills. Riding a bus is a put-down because it is not in line with the image he wants to project. "I ain't riding no bus. Only lowlife ride the bus," exclaimed one man, explaining why he could not go to work. If someone questions a criminal's decision or offers a suggestion, instead of mulling it over, he responds with anger. Just to acknowledge that someone else's opinion has merit threatens the criminal's sense of omniscience. If a person with whom he has disagreed turns out to be correct, the criminal will do his utmost to discredit him. He cannot bear to be wrong. "If I bend, I break," is the prevailing mentality.

Pride stems from an inner sense of satisfaction experienced by accomplishing something positive. Whether pride is a virtue or a flaw depends on its basis and on how it is manifested. A coach takes pride in his team's championship, or a student takes pride in making the honor roll. This is different from the criminal whose pride is expressed by an attitude of superiority, an unwillingness to yield to another's authority, and a refusal even to consider a point of view different from his own. The criminal's gloating over conquests is a far cry from the inner pride of quiet satisfaction when a goal is responsibly achieved.

To admit wrongdoing, to concede, or to compromise flies in the face of the criminal's sense of omnipotence. Criminal pride is an all-or-nothing matter. A criminal will adhere to a position even to his own detriment. One teenager warned his parents that they could ground him for a month, but he would not repair a door that he claimed he did not break. He had actually torn it off its hinges in a fury after his father confronted him with drugs he had discovered during a search of his son's room. Criminal pride involves more than just having an oversized ego. It has a rigid quality that permeates the criminal's life. He must maintain this pride for his own psychic survival.

A criminal's anger in response to a put-down may be thinly disguised in sullenness, silence, or feigned indifference. It may erupt in ridicule and sarcasm, or burst forth into screaming and cursing. Its most devastating form is physical violence. During 2010, according to a federal survey, 35.6 percent of women and 28.5 percent of men in the United States reported that, during their lifetime, they had experienced stalking, rape, or physical violence by an intimate partner.[1] By resorting to intimidation and violence, some criminals do not allow their partners to leave, and remain confident that they will not suffer major consequences for injuries they inflict. They are usually correct in this belief. Many victims of violence wish to remain in the relationship rather than be alone. Because they are embarrassed and fear a loss of privacy, some do not contact law enforcement authorities. They want to avoid further abuse by their partner, which they know will occur if they inform anyone.

Criminals have described experiencing an adrenaline rush when they fantasize about violence, talk about violence, or commit acts of violence. One gang member referred to physically harming others as "an addiction." The "rush," as he termed it, was the supercharged sense of power that he felt.

We will now consider Gary and Lenny, two teenagers, and Wally, an adult in his forties. All grew up in white, middle-class families. Lenny lived with his mother and had little contact with his father because he detested his stepmother. Gary lived with both of his parents in an upscale suburban community. Wally, who was single, lived like a millionaire even though he owed thousands of dollars in credit card debt. No one could tell them anything they did not want to hear without risking extreme repercussions. None of the three appeared menacing, and all were intelligent, well-mannered, and articulate. Each had committed scores of crimes but had never previously been arrested. Because of their pretensions and their unrealistic expectations, they experienced a sense of being put down many times every day.

Finally, we will consider Lucy, a grandmother who felt shoved aside by her little granddaughter. Her jealous rage had catastrophic results.

Gary

Gary, age sixteen, had been arrested for attempted murder. Eager to talk about how he enjoys fighting, Gary commented, "I'm quick to get my head pushed up. I'm hyped to get mad." He mentioned a classmate teasing him for being the only boy in a gym class wearing a green shirt. "I chased him and hit him for that," he said. After brutally beating the boy, Gary was expelled from school and confined for committing assault and battery. Justifying the assault, Gary exclaimed, "You show respect, give respect." When I evaluated him at a detention center, Gary reported that he had become infuriated when denied the use of a phone to call "my girl." In retaliation, he'd shoved a roll of toilet paper, bed sheets, and blankets into a toilet, resulting in a massive flood. On another occasion, he became enraged when another boy called his brother a bitch. "I hit him, busted his nose," Gary said, which resulted in being confined to his room for a day. Gary boasted that the worst injury he'd ever inflicted occurred when he grabbed a crutch lying in a yard and started beating a fellow, cracking his ribs and fracturing his skull. Because the victim did not show up for the court hearing, charges were dismissed.

Criminals like Gary have indicated that they will not tolerate insults, and relish putting anyone who tangles with them in their place. Gary declared, "I'm looking for a fight. It feels good to inflict pain." His desire for a fight did not spring from a random urge to attack just anyone. He explained, "The person must have an issue with me." Gary's mother was a prime target of his rage because she was vocal in expressing disapproval of much that he did, and she tried to discipline him. She told me, "Gary is extremely sensitive. Just a change in my tone of voice turns his hackles up. He's easily triggered when challenged." Gary pledged to cease his warfare only if there was "mutual disarmament." He demanded that his mother back off and cease questioning him about where he was going and what he was doing. He contended that she had no right to ask why he didn't come home until four in the morning, why his car got towed, or about any number of other incidents. Asked if he was concerned about the steadily deteriorating relationship with his mother, Gary said flippantly, "I haven't killed anyone." He followed this by saying, "I just like to go after people; I'm looking for a fight," which revealed his determination to establish his superiority. Gary commented that he wears "soft gloves with steel-plate knuckles," referring to launching a charm offensive, then settling matters forcibly if need be. With no sense of shame, he characterized himself as "arrogant, a badass, and prone to violence." Gary eagerly volunteered graphic details about fights he had engaged in. In one instance, he pursued a fellow student, beating him with a large stick, placing one foot on the boy's throat, then kicking him in the head. His parents had no idea that these fights had occurred. Gary made sure he was off school property so no staff member could witness what happened and intervene.

Gary had fantasies of going on a rampage by rigging gas tanks of cars so they'd explode, then shooting at police officers to keep them at bay. Acknowledging he was angry at "life in general," Gary compared himself to a volcano in that his mind was loaded with fantasies of retribution toward others as well as violence directed against himself. "All my friends are pissed at me. I have bad grades. My mom embarrasses me in front of other kids. Friends make fun of me. Teachers look at me in a bad sort of way." This teenager said that, although he had threatened his parents, he had also devised specific methods to kill himself. "I have nothing to look forward to. I'd be better off dead. After six months, nobody would know who I was." Gary's advice to the world was "don't bug me." Despite his blazing anger, Gary said in all seriousness that he hoped to have a wife and children and to become an architect. When I pointed out that to achieve these goals, he would have to do things that others tell him to do even if he finds them disagreeable, Gary replied, "You have to modify your plans second by second. I can suffer through life." I recommended to Gary's parents that they look into placing him in a residential therapeutic boarding school. Trying to treat him in outpatient counseling or therapy would be like trying to catch a tidal wave with a bucket.

Gary indicated that sometimes he thought dying would be preferable to putting up with the demands and rejections that he was enduring. Criminals have been known to kill themselves rather than to submit to others and be under someone else's control for the rest of their lives. More than one offender has told me that he fantasized going down in a blaze of glory rather than putting up with life as it is. He would have the upper hand right to the end.

Lenny

Sixteen-year-old Lenny had become a nearly intolerable burden to his family. Susan Hall, his mother, adored him but was at a loss as to how to discipline him or even keep him safe. Most of the time, she had to contend with Lenny's chronic negativism and anger. All too frequently, she suffered through his rages, which left her reeling and wondering what she could do to avoid triggering her son's explosions. Ms. Hall never knew when Lenny would take offense to a suggestion or an innocuous request. When things were going his way, Lenny could be helpful, charming, and considerate. During my psychological evaluation of him, Lenny warned, "If I have a mind-set and want to do something, I will. When I get told to do stuff, it's annoying." This boy expected to rule the household, to be in charge. Still a minor, he was subject to the authority of his mother. He demanded that others suit his requirements rather than that he fulfill the requirements of others. He reacted to his mother's pleas for help with household chores as though he were being attacked. He objected to his mother "asking a lot of questions" as she tried to gain information as to where he was going, what he was doing, or whether he had done his homework. Complaining about her yelling, Lenny said he preferred not to speak to her at all. He reacted to her questions and reprimands by yelling, screaming, cursing, and telling her what a horrible parent she was. Sometimes, Lenny became so enraged that he would rush into his room and start smashing furniture. During one of the worst flare-ups, Ms. Hall became so distraught after her son barricaded himself in a room and started banging his head against a wall that she summoned the police. "I still don't know why *I* was the one being taken away," Lenny told me.

Lenny prided himself on "giving people grief." He talked back to teachers, walked out of class, and skipped school. The fact that Lenny was constantly in trouble did not faze him. "I don't think anyone should expect happiness from me," he declared. Lenny had no close friends, was barely passing in school, and was waging war against his mother, the person who cared most about him. Feeling put down because the world did not treat him as he thought it should, Lenny was constantly angry.

Wally

Wally, forty-two years old, was extremely dispirited about life. During a psychological evaluation, he lamented, "It's always something. I'm getting a lot older. I'm tired of all the crap." The irony to his statement was that "all the crap" was mostly a result of Wally's own behavior. Although he had chosen to sever relations with his parents, he blamed them for the estrangement and said he harbored "homicidal anger" toward his mother. He denounced his brother, asserting he shared nothing in common with him. But Wally had created the breach in the relationship by messing up an opportunity while employed by his brother. He complained about losing friends and remarked, "I don't know why I attract these people." Wally's so-called friends were guys he met at bars and clubs and who he acknowledged were "in unstable situations." Wally became incensed that a credit card company had blocked further use of his card because he had exceeded its limit. This didn't stop his using nine other credit cards and amassing huge gambling and travel debts. Wally explained that he had to spend four thousand dollars on a vacation "in order to get away from all the stress"—stress that he mostly created for himself. Wally remarked, "I didn't think about the cost until afterwards. I never realized what the fun would amount to." After having a number of car accidents and being cited for numerous traffic violations, Wally declared, "I should be driving around in a Mercedes." Resentful of the consequences of his irresponsibility, Wally believed that he was entitled to do whatever he wanted. Life was full of disappointment and anger as he kept digging himself into holes, but he never considered changing his behavior.

Rejection by a friend, lover, partner, or spouse is traumatic for anyone. The criminal immediately becomes possessive of anyone with whom he becomes involved, and he expects that person to do his bidding. Anything less constitutes a complete rejection. Involved sexually with several men, Wally had become particularly attached to Earl, who was married. Wally expected Earl to be available anytime and anyplace. He became increasingly agitated as he sensed that Earl was pulling away. Wally said to me, "He's blowing me off. He wants his freedom. If I see him, I'll kill him." He confided that he was thinking of phoning Earl's wife to expose him. Wally observed, "There's a fine line between I really care and I really hate him."

Lucy

A fear of being powerless and unable to cope with a situation can result in a criminal deciding to eliminate the source of the put-down. Lucy was a mother of three children and a grandmother. Although she had good health, a devoted husband, financial security, and supportive relatives nearby, she suffered from bouts of depression. From her perspective, life was not treating her well at all. One night, she, her husband, daughter, and grandchild drove to a shopping mall and had dinner. As they were walking on an elevated bridge to reach the mall's parking lot, Lucy picked up the toddler and threw her over the railing. The child dropped the equivalent of six stories and did not survive. Lucy pled "not guilty by reason of insanity." This case made local headlines as people wondered what sort of person could commit such an "insane" act. This turned out to be a case mainly about a woman who suffered a series of what she experienced as rejections, but which she had brought on herself.

Lucy was married to Oscar, a federal employee, for nearly

thirty years. The couple had two children, Gilbert and Cindy. Lucy shifted among a variety of sales and cashier jobs, never quite finding her niche. She and her son had a stormy relationship from the time Gilbert was a young boy. Her husband, Oscar, who assumed the role of the family mediator, explained that he was "more compromising" while Lucy was "more opinionated." The boy felt that only his father listened to and understood him. The mother-son relationship deteriorated to the point that Gilbert recoiled from her and isolated himself in his room. Lucy resented the close father-son relationship and, on one notable occasion, threw a temper tantrum in which she screamed unmercifully at her son and physically pushed her husband. Lucy dismissed the incident as a small spat.

Nothing seemed to work out as Lucy expected. First it was her son who rejected her. Then she began fighting with Oscar. Their connection was fraying as Oscar discovered that he could not trust her. While he was working, Lucy was embarking on shopping binges, then hiding her purchases. As the bills came due, Oscar found that his wife was incurring an alarming amount of debt that imperiled their financial security. Lucy borrowed money from relatives and continued her wild spending, purchasing items that she did not need or use. Oscar came upon clothing hidden away in a closet with two-year-old original price tags. He was reluctant to confront Lucy and incur her wrath. Lucy started demanding that Oscar take time away from work to be at home with her. On one of those days, she pulled a knife and refused to give him his car keys. Sometimes, Lucy wanted Oscar with her. At other times, she wanted him out of the house. Occasionally, she thought it would be best if she left.

What nearly ended the marriage was Lucy's fury over her daughter's out-of-wedlock pregnancy. Lucy took this event as a personal insult, signifying the end of her dream for Cindy. She had envisioned her daughter graduating from college, traveling the world, and living the sort of independent life she had never enjoyed for herself. Lucy perceived Cindy's pregnancy as an indictment of herself as a parent and a devastating betrayal. When Lucy first learned of the pregnancy, she was furious and let Cindy know how intensely she despised the baby's father, whom she wanted to punch in the face. When Cindy married the baby's father, Lucy reacted as though her daughter had died. Meanwhile Oscar, although upset about the pregnancy, realized he needed to accept what had happened and did his utmost to be helpful to Cindy and her husband, which exacerbated his conflict with Lucy.

Lucy sought the services of a psychotherapist and was treated for depression. She approached therapy the way she did everything else. As long as the therapist provided a sympathetic sounding board, Lucy continued to meet with her. When she didn't think the therapist was supportive, she withdrew. The same was true of her relationship with a psychiatrist who prescribed medication. When Lucy felt better, she had no use for the medicine. Mental health treatment records documented Lucy's volatile relationships. She was in conflict with her son, her daughter, her son-in-law, her husband, and, sporadically, with relatives. She became so discontented that she told the therapist she might leave home to spend several months with her mother.

Lucy became so depressed and angry that she made suicidal gestures, but then expressed relief that she was still alive. (She rejected a recommendation for hospitalization after one of her suicide attempts.) In discussing her attempts at suicide, Lucy focused on what *she* would be spared if she had succeeded, even though she was the source of most of her own difficulties. Lucy's therapist cited her "all or nothing" thought process. If she could not have things her way, she sought to rid herself of the source of her frustration and disappointment. At times, she ceased speaking to her son, her daughter, and her son-in-law. She refused to attend family celebrations. Instead of finding ways to address the problems she had created herself, she blamed others.

On the fateful night, the family had dinner at a nearby shopping mall. During the interview by detectives after the toddler was thrown over the railing, Lucy acknowledged being angry at everybody. She told the detectives that her husband loved the baby more than he loved her, and said that her son and daughter "had no more love for me." Lucy acknowledged harboring anger at the child for many months, "because everybody loves her." During the interview, Lucy never asked whether the child had survived the fall. The baby represented all that was wrong with her life. As a person who sought to eliminate whatever she disliked, she ridded her family of what had become the embodiment of her problem, her granddaughter. Lucy acknowledged that she had thought about doing what she did *while in the mall*. Walking to the parking lot, she arranged it so that her daughter and husband were walking ahead while she ambled behind holding the child. Cindy and Oscar never knew what happened until after the child was hurled over the railing.

A Note on the Limitations of Anger Management

Judges and counselors often recommend "anger management" to men and women whose anger has resulted in physical or psychological abuse. Anger management courses have become an expanding industry. These classes espouse various objectives, such as distinguishing between "rage vs. normal anger," "taking charge of anger," "toning anger down," "channeling anger," and "harnessing anger and frustration as vehicles for change." A basic principle is that anger is a normal emotion and that "constructive anger" can have a positive impact on relationships. One publication on understanding anger stated, "Anger has its advantages."

While anger management may help some clients in counseling, it is doomed to fail if applied to criminals for whom anger is as much a part of them as a finger is part of the hand. Noncriminals get angry but their anger is generally focused and does not get transformed into criminality. The implication of the term "anger management" suggests that it is acceptable—perhaps inevitable—for a person to get angry, provided that he contains the anger and expresses it constructively. For a criminal, anger can take a huge destructive toll when he perceives a put-down as a threat to his ego and even to his psychological survival.

Anger usually does not solve problems, and certainly not for the criminal. When the criminal is angry, he does not think clearly, and anger impairs his performance at almost any task. Because of his anger, he antagonizes and alienates other people. Anger results in emotional and physical injury. Expressing anger does not diminish a criminal's anger; it has an opposite effect. By ventilating it, he becomes even more incensed and determined to compel others to recognize the correctness of his position.

The options are not limited to suppressing anger or exploding. For a criminal to become a less angry human being, it is essential that he become aware of thinking patterns that fuel anger. If he becomes realistic in his expectations and stops trying to control other people, the criminal will experience far less anger.

For example, Kyle is furious because his dinner isn't ready when he arrives home from work. He goes on a tirade about how hard he works, accuses his wife of laziness, then blasts her for not appreciating all that he does. Kyle does not ask his wife how her day has been. He shows no interest in her other than that she serve him in the manner and at the time he expects. Kyle reacts to his wife's failure to fulfill his expectations as a challenge to his manhood. To "teach her a lesson" (an expression that is nearly always about control), he unleashes a torrent of abuse as he reprimands her and warns that he expects better treatment in the future.

Instead of learning to manage anger, the objective in working with such individuals is to aim toward *cessation* of anger.

This can be accomplished with some by helping them identify thinking errors, understand the ramifications of those errors, then learn and implement corrective thinking processes. If Kyle were to participate in such an endeavor, he would understand that circumstances beyond his control determine the outcome of innumerable situations. Instead of berating his wife, Kyle could inquire her about day, perhaps issue a compliment, then offer to help make dinner. If he learns to think realistically, there will be no anger that requires managing.

9

Criminality Is Primary, Drugs Secondary

The 1963 *Final Report* of the President's Advisory Commission on Narcotic and Drug Abuse stated that drugs "can turn . . . normal young men and women to crime."[1] This belief is still widely held not just by professionals but also by offenders and their families. Again and again, during interviews, criminals have declared that drugs have altered their lives drastically, changing them into someone very different from who they were before. They contend that their *only* problem is involvement with alcohol or drugs. No matter how serious their crimes, they reject the notion that they are "criminals." Many offenders maintain that their substance abuse caused them to commit crimes. Speaking of a homicide, one man asserted, "I didn't kill him. The drugs did it." Family members and others who think they know the offender well also attribute his illegal activities entirely to drugs or alcohol. Said one spouse, "Tony is an entirely different person when he drinks. Then, he is not the man I married." Strapped to Ohio's lethal injection gurney, convicted murderer and former cocaine addict Frederick Treesh said in a final statement, "This is where drugs lead you."[2]

Criminality does not reside in the bottle, the pill, the powder, or in any other substance. Drugs bring out and intensify what already resides within a person. They do not transform a responsible person into a criminal. If ten men get drunk, all ten will not rape, rob, or kill. They may fall asleep, become rowdy, or act belligerent; their behavior depends on their personality *before* they took the first sip.

Everything imaginable has been blamed for causing crime, and the same is true as to why people become frequent drug users. Many sociologists characterize drug use as a normal response to bleak conditions. Or they direct attention to a culture that values instant gratification. Psychologists cite poor examples set by role models—the fact that Dad drinks or Mom takes pills to calm her nerves. Citing peer pressure, the user contends that his buddies turned him on to drugs, that "everybody does it." Social critics lament the glamorization of drugs in film and on television, and assert that teenagers use drugs because they watch athletes and other celebrities indulging. Psychologist Neil Bernstein observed, "[Teenagers] see movies . . . which glorify the substance-soaked nightlife of bars and clubs."[3] The litany of reasons as to why people use drugs is endless. These explanations are seized upon by users to justify their conduct although they already have enough excuses of their own.

The man or woman with a criminal personality is likely to say that he or she uses drugs to escape. Many professionals concur, explaining that drugs offer escape from harsh realities of life, boredom, or hopelessness. If you ask the user what he is escaping from, he may respond by complaining about the squalid conditions in which he lives. Yet others, including family and neighbors, residing in the same bleak environment do not use drugs. If you press a criminal on the escape theme, he may cite specific distressing situations, some of which he created or compounded by his own irresponsibility. He is out of work, bill collectors are closing in, he can't afford to repair his car, and his wife is fed up and threatening to leave. What it boils down to is that the drug-using criminal wants to avoid the requirements to live responsibly that others impose. Far more important than escape is the excitement that drugs facilitate.

Michael, a convicted felon, said that he used drugs to escape, then paused to ask rhetorically, "What am I escaping from?" He replied to his own question: "I had a pretty good life. I rejected that. There were people who had horrible things happen, and they weren't doing this. It was the excitement, the adrenaline rush. I hate boredom. Paying the bills; it's mind-numbing. I prefer excitement over mind-numbing." His reference to paying bills symbolized what he considered the humdrum life of an ordinary, responsible person, which was definitely not for him.

The media bombard the public with reports dramatizing youthful drug use. Statistics are often misleading. Whereas curiosity prompts millions of people to experiment with drugs, for most, that experimentation is short-lived. Lumped together in statistics about drug use are individuals who experimented once or a few times and people who have been regular users for years. For example, in a 2011 report, Columbia University's National Center on Addiction and Substance Abuse found that 75 percent of all high school students "have used alcohol, tobacco or either legal or illicit drugs."[4] The word "used" could refer to one occasion or daily.

Drug counselors and drug users claim that drugs are used to "self-medicate." Dr. Edward J. Khantzian of the Harvard Medical School, widely credited with setting forth the self-medication explanation, stated that suffering is "at the heart of" addictive disorders.[5] Most of this "suffering," however, is usually nothing more than life's ordinary pressures and annoyances—living from one payday to the next, dealing with an occasional marital spat, being reprimanded at work, or changing a flat tire on a hot July day. The professional literature contains references to people turning to drugs to cope with almost any form of psychological distress imaginable—abuse, trauma, anger, depression, and low self-esteem. Despite the self-medication theory, no set of statistics indicates that most people turn to illegal drugs or misuse prescription drugs in order to cope with disagreeable situations. Quite the contrary is true. Responsible people cope with crisis in a responsible manner. Confronting illness, family conflicts, problems at work, or financial setbacks, they do not inject heroin, snort cocaine, or use other illegal drugs, nor abuse legal ones.

The criminal who regularly abuses mind-altering substances or prescription drugs is perpetually dissatisfied, restless, irritable, and bored. Before drugs ever came into the picture, he was a controller, a liar, a person who promoted himself at the expense of others. In every case that I have encountered, the criminal was immersed in crime *before* he smoked his first joint, popped his first pill, or first injected heroin. Criminals use drugs even when they are healthy, well-educated, hold well-paying jobs, and have devoted families. From their standpoint, life is an unending series of discrete events in which they struggle to control everyone and every situation. One offender explained, "I had seen my life as a chain of events without connection. In some sense, at any given time, I was always seeking power and control, creating the opportunity to file away war stories. The desire to live on the edge spilled over into my moral life. I always perceived myself to be on the edge of things. Let's push the limits, experience exhilaration, and feel that adrenaline."

Availability is key to the criminal's choice of a mind-altering substance. Alcohol is legal, and the most abundant. Conditions in the drug marketplace change in that what is available today may be scarce tomorrow. The quality of substances may also be a consideration, because drugs can contain contaminants. New mind-altering substances constantly appear on the market and are easily procurable online. "Bath salts," which can be injected or snorted, are a case in point. Not manufactured for use in bathwater, the product, according to the Substance Abuse and Mental Health Services Administration, "refers to a new group of drugs that contain one or more chemicals related to cathinone, an amphetamine-like stimulant."[6] According to the National Institute on Drug Abuse (NIDA), bath salts are in the form of "a synthetic powder sold legally online and in drug paraphernalia stores under a variety of names."[7] Glen Hanson, a NIDA-funded researcher, remarked about users of bath salts and the way they behave, "They do things that really don't make a lot of sense to the rest of us so we just kind of scratch our heads."[8] If one understands the criminal mind, the behavior makes a great deal of sense

The sophisticated user prefers particular drugs for specific purposes, and is well informed about the advantages and disadvantages of each. Amphetamines provide a quick infusion of energy but a severe letdown following cessation of use. Opiates knock out fear and sharpen thinking (given optimal dosage), but there is risk of dependency. Sedative-hypnotic drugs help the criminal assume an "I don't care" attitude, but dosage is difficult to regulate, and risk of physical dependence is high. Marijuana is a desirable party drug, relatively easy to obtain, but not powerful enough to be of much help by itself if a user is looking to lessen his fear of committing high-risk crimes. Some speak of the "courage" that alcohol gives them to approach and seduce a prospective partner. Others abjure the use of alcohol because it interferes with coordination and clouds their thinking.

With respect to marijuana, the pendulum has swung from the "reefer madness" scares during the first half of the twentieth century to legalization of the substance for medical use in eighteen states and Washington, D.C. In November 2012, residents of Colorado and Washington voted to allow any person who is twenty-one or older to legally purchase as much as an ounce of marijuana for personal use. The first commercial legal sale of marijuana to the public occurred on January 1, 2014, in Colorado. The state of Washington issued its first legal marijuana license on March 5, 2014. The June 2013 edition of the *Washington Lawyer* reported that members of Congress have introduced bills to legalize marijuana on the federal level.[9]

The public is in danger of being fooled into believing that marijuana is harmless. This opinion is not shared by parents who have watched a child become a regular marijuana user, or by counselors and therapists who treat adolescent users. There is evidence that long-term heavy use of the drug damages the lungs and reproductive system. NIDA reported that users who began smoking marijuana heavily during adolescence showed "lost cognitive abilities [that] were not restored in those who quit smoking as adults."[10] NIDA also cited data from several studies showing, "Marijuana use more than doubles a driver's risk of being in an accident." (According to a Reuters news report, in the state of Washington, more drivers stopped by police were testing positive for marijuana's psychoactive ingredient, THC, than before the drug was legalized for "recreational use.")[11] Most frightening to witness is the psychological damage—the so-called amotivational syndrome—as the frequent user retreats from his family, school, and responsible peers.

Marijuana has formed the cornerstone of some offenders' lives. One man, arrested for soliciting underage girls, told me that he considered marijuana "a vitamin for my happiness." He noted, "It makes me more upbeat and interested in things." Jack, a teenager, was extremely graphic in describing how central the drug had become. "After I tried [pot] a couple of times, it became an everyday thing. My life started revolving around pot. My mind was always filled with when I should go smoke, how I could get it, and actually being high. So, basically, if I wasn't high, I was talking about it, thinking about it, or trying to get it. I also would like to date people not because I liked them but because of what I would get out of it, which means 'weed.' Even if I didn't like a person, if I got drugs out of the situation, I would go be their friend." This adolescent began using marijuana early in the morning and would smoke it intermittently throughout the day and into the night.

For some youthful users, once marijuana loses its allure, it becomes a "gateway" drug to the use of other substances. Without question, regular users like Jack can develop dependence. Treatment is seldom successful, as indicated by NIDA's statement, "Even with the most effective treatment for adults, only about 50 percent of enrollees achieve an initial 2-week period of abstinence, and among those who do, approximately half will resume use within a year."[12]

For the individual with a criminal personality, drug use primarily facilitates bigger and more risky crimes, sexual conquests, and an enhanced sense of power and control. If the user seeks a religious encounter, he may experience that. If he is depressed and thinking of ending his life, drugs may facilitate suicidal thinking and behavior. Jack confided that he was often sad. Usually, marijuana lifted him out of his sadness. However, there were times when he became increasingly gloomy. It was on marijuana that he made several suicide attempts.

Criminals know the occupational hazards of crime: getting caught, convicted, and imprisoned. They also know that they could be injured or killed during the commission of a crime. For many, drugs give them the "heart" to do what they otherwise fear. Bob often fantasized about using a gun to rob a convenience store, but was "too chicken." With heroin coursing through his veins, he became emboldened, procured a pistol, and did just that. Heroin did not *cause* Bob to obtain the gun; use of the drug simply made it easier to eliminate fears temporarily in order to act upon what he had previously only considered. "Drugs knock off my caution," acknowledged another user, who took unusual risks by breaking into homes in broad daylight, something that he would have been afraid to do were he not on drugs.

Manny, twenty-three years old, tried nearly every drug available, cocaine being his favorite: "Cocaine makes me feel like I'm a success. I just love it. I have an obsession with it." Manny was no stranger to crime before he used drugs. He began stealing from his mother when he was twelve, made prank calls, egged houses, let air out of tires, stole a bicycle, broke a windshield with a BB gun, drove without a license, and shoplifted. He started using alcohol, followed by marijuana, then cocaine and other drugs. Once he became a regular cocaine user, the number of crimes skyrocketed. He grew far more extravagant, spending money at bars and fancy restaurants, on designer clothes, and on lavish gifts for his girlfriend. To obtain the funds, Manny helped himself to his mother's checkbook, forged her name, and cashed the checks. He also committed many burglaries and acts of grand larceny. He marveled that everything about his life was better with cocaine, including sex, which seemed more intense because he "lasted longer." The greatest excitement, however, revolved around the drug—obtaining it, snorting it, and selling it. Just riding around while thinking about where he'd buy it gave him a high. When I interviewed Manny, he had been arrested and charged with the check forgeries as well as other crimes. In jail and sober, he admitted to being so irritable without drugs that he felt "like getting in a fight and ripping someone's head off." He commented that the "next best thing to getting high" was talking with other inmates about drugs. Then he became calmer and was able to go to sleep more quickly, often dreaming about drugs. Manny reflected, "It amazes me how I could fool myself by thinking that my life was worthwhile. I thought I was a really good person. I thought I was intelligent and sensitive." He added, "I would be a fairly decent person if I wasn't using drugs." He was anything but. Never did he consider the grief he caused his victims, chief among them his mother.

Like Manny, criminals want to be number one sexually, just as they do in other aspects of their lives. Because drugs knock out fear of rejection, they are bolder about approaching a partner. A man remarked, "Without drugs, I had a fifty-fifty chance with a woman, but on drugs, she was a sure thing." He said that before he went on a date "it was essential to use—it was the only way to settle myself." By "settle," he meant eliminate his fears. On drugs, a criminal may be less choosy in selecting a partner. One man commented, "I didn't care if she was deaf, dumb, and blind. All I wanted was her torso." Not only does the drug user have sex with people whom he otherwise might not even consider, but he also subjects himself and his partner to greater danger. Being robbed, assaulted, or contracting sexually transmitted diseases are possibilities. Worries about sexual performance vanish under drugs, whether the anxiety is over genital size, impotence, or premature ejaculation. The urgency for sexual pursuit varies with the particular choice and amount of the drug. Many boast of their prowess when on heroin, but when their use of the drug escalates they lose interest.

Some criminals would not consider using drugs to commit crimes or to pursue sexual conquests. They know that drugs will interfere by rendering them less vigilant, thus more vulnerable to arrest. They use drugs while socializing, losing their shyness and becoming more outgoing at a party. One young man told me that he hid in a social shell but, when he used drugs, "I'd feel like I came alive." He remarked that if he was in a room with seven people and drug-free, he'd remain silent. However, if he was using drugs, "I'd talk to every one of them."

As long ago as 1945, the psychoanalyst Otto Fenichel cited "the extraordinary elevation in self-esteem" experienced by addicts as they inject or ingest drugs.[13] Ask a user what he means by "getting high." After expressing incredulity over your naïveté, he'll supply a vague response about feeling good, or perhaps say he becomes "euphoric." If you continue probing, you will hear statements like, "On drugs, I felt ten feet tall. On drugs, I felt I could do anything." The user is describing a heightened sense of being in control and an ability to surmount or totally eliminate any barrier to what he wants to do.

Criminals may use psychedelic or "mind-expanding" drugs such as peyote or hallucinogenic mushrooms. Naturally occurring psychedelic substances in plants were commonly used in ancient societies, and still are in some contemporary cultures, to induce religious experiences. Criminals use these substances in addition to contemporary synthetic hallucinogenics such as LSD ("acid") or the newer MDMA (known in the streets as "ecstasy" or "Molly"). In quest of a religious experience, criminals report acquiring unique insights into the nature of the universe and the meaning of life. But rather than being in touch with God, they experience themselves as godlike in their omnipotence and omniscience.

If a criminal has become despondent to the point of entertaining suicidal thoughts, drugs may intensify those ideas. His despair is not about his own shortcomings. Rather, the injustices of life weigh upon him more heavily than ever. He despairs because the world does not recognize him in a way that is compatible with his inflated self-image. He therefore sees little point in continuing to live. If he is confined for a long period, he is most at risk because he has failed in crime and his opinion of himself as a powerful individual has collapsed, at least temporarily. Making a suicidal gesture has an enormous impact. Taking an overdose, cutting himself, or inflicting significant self-injury in other ways compels people to pay attention. They are more likely to protect the criminal, succumb to his wishes, and go out of their way to alleviate his distress. Because the criminal's judgment is impaired by drugs, he may miscalculate and inadvertently kill himself by overdosing or inflicting a mortal wound. Or he may summon the determination to end it all, which he could not bring himself to do when sober. A certain antidote to suicidal thoughts is to reassert himself, to regain control and assert his power—in short, to commit a crime.

Criminals who are regular users of mind-altering substances attribute much of their behavior to becoming addicted. The word "addiction" has been so overused that it has been robbed of its meaning. Almost anything a person likes or does in excess has been termed an addiction. The list is extremely lengthy. In addition to drug and alcohol addiction, the professional literature contains information on love addiction, sex addiction, Internet addiction, football addiction, shopping addiction, theft addiction, gambling addiction, connection addiction, video game addiction, approval addiction, and food addiction. Even the person who says he needs a cup or two of coffee to start the day might be viewed as having a caffeine addiction. Some criminals require increasing amounts of a particular substance to provide the same impact they had experienced when using less. This is called the "tolerance effect," and physical dependence may develop.

There has long been a controversy over whether drug addiction is a disease. In its bulletin, *Mental Health Matters,* Centra Mental Health Services of Lynchburg, Virginia, states what now seems to be the consensus among professionals: "The person addicted to alcohol or other drugs is ill."[14] One thing is for sure. The individual chooses to inject, ingest, or snort a particular substance. He makes a series of decisions to obtain it, when and where to use it, and how much to use. A person cannot say no to cancer, but he can say no to drugs. The criminal latches onto the disease idea and uses it to explain his behavior: his "disease" was responsible. Apprehended for a crime, the criminal is effective in convincing others that he got hooked and lost control. His perspective is that he has been a victim of drugs, and that he is owed treatment and counseling and does not deserve incarceration. Law enforcement authorities and judges may not know the extent to which the criminal's life revolves around drugs. Furthermore, they may not realize that the criminal wants to maintain control and will avail himself of treatment only when forced to do so by the criminal justice system. In other cases, the criminal may hide the fact that, previously, he had walked out of a rehabilitation program or completed treatment but resumed drug use later.

The criminal's addiction is not just to a drug but to an entire way of life. There is excitement in every aspect of drug use, even before the criminal possesses the substance—fantasizing about drugs, talking about drugs, making one's way into dangerous areas where drugs are sold, the thrill of the deal. One young man said that he could not work because of an accumulation of traffic tickets resulting in the suspension of his driver's license. However, he had managed to travel any distance that was necessary to buy heroin. "I'd go into the city, not with my mom to go to the store, but to go sightseeing," he said. "Sightseeing" referred to entering dangerous areas where he could buy drugs. Meeting his connection, finding a safe place to execute the purchase, and bargaining the price while trying to ascertain the potency and purity of the drug were all part of the excitement. In addition to reaping profits from drug sales, the high voltage of searching out "customers" motivates drug dealers of any age. According to an Associated Press report, on October 8, 2013, an eighty-nine-year-old man pled guilty to interstate transportation of more than two hundred pounds of cocaine.[15] This was not a one-time offense, as the government had evidence that he had been involved for more than a decade in drug trafficking.

Consider the plight of Thomas, who spent a year in jail for a nonviolent crime. A judge suspended the remainder of his sentence and placed him in an intensive community corrections program. Thomas seemed to be doing well. He had a remunerative job cleaning upholstery, with a growing customer base. He enjoyed good health, freedom from incarceration, the benefits of money legitimately earned, and a devoted girlfriend. One day he arrived at a counseling session seething and said to me, "I thought if I gave up drugs, I'd have no problems. Now I have more problems than ever." He complained, "My truck breaks down. My customers are a pain. Bills pour in. I have the hassle of all these meetings to go to—probation, Narcotics Anonymous, counseling sessions. My girlfriend is on my case, wanting one thing or another. I have no time for myself. If this is life, it's a hell of a life." Thomas demanded to know, "What do you have that compares with cocaine?" To this stark challenge, I could only reply, "Nothing." I could not assure Thomas that working, paying bills, and attending meetings could possibly match the excitement that he had experienced in the drug world. Another offender, after six months of abstinence, asked, "Where's my reward?" He believed that, if he was not using drugs, life would be without problems. For both of these men, their "addiction" was not just to drugs, but to a criminal lifestyle.

ABUSE OF PRESCRIPTION drugs has risen dramatically in the United States since 2000. The American Psychological Association reported in 2013 that American teenagers were abusing prescription painkillers at a rate 40 percent higher than in previous generations.[16] After marijuana, prescription drugs were the most common type of illegal drug use. A Yale University study found that adolescents and young adults who abused prescription opioid pain medication had first been users of tobacco, alcohol, or marijuana.[17] Many men and women who abuse prescription drugs exhibit irresponsible, if not arrestable, behavior *before* getting "hooked."

A housewife and mother of two children, Nancy was apprehended by law enforcement authorities for falsifying prescriptions for narcotic drugs. (She never got arrested for stealing drugs out of medicine chests from the homes of relatives and neighbors, which she did regularly.) Nancy said that she became addicted to Percocet while being treated for migraine headaches. Her primary care physician stated that Nancy never acknowledged having any addiction. The doctor said, "We discussed the potential for addiction. We had a pain contract to prevent her from being addicted." This physician received a call from a pharmacy inquiring as to whether he had written a particular prescription, which he hadn't—a situation that led to Nancy's arrest. When I interviewed her, she was locked in a child custody battle with her husband, Sam, whom she described as extremely controlling and mean-spirited. Sam told me that his difficulties with Nancy did not begin with her drug abuse. She had always been controlling, perfectionistic, and generally difficult to get along with. The couple had separated before Sam was aware of her drug abuse. Sam told me, "She thinks I'm the root of every problem she has." He was seeking physical custody of their children because he wanted to ensure their safety. Nancy was not only abusing pain pills but also drinking heavily. A friend who knew her well stated that Nancy was remarkable for the front she put on. She said that, although Nancy might barely be functioning, on the phone she spoke coherently and in a normal manner. It was not until this lady went on a trip with Nancy and the children that she found her behavior troubling. "She has a really hard time focusing. She can do one task at a time slowly. With children, you have to do ten things at once, and she can't. It's almost like she is in a fog." Asked about her friend's observations, Nancy was shocked and asserted, "My mothering behavior is absolutely wonderful. I don't question my ability at all." Nancy was a consummate liar. Even while seeing a psychotherapist, she concealed her abuse of alcohol and drugs. Nancy vociferously objected to her ex-husband having more time with the children, and she spent more time and money on legal actions against him than on addressing her psychological and substance abuse problems.

Louise was another abuser of prescription drugs. She worked as a nurse in the office of a prominent physician. Stealing the doctor's prescription pad, she wrote herself prescriptions for Percocet. "I wasn't taking it because of pain. It was for the euphoric feeling. I knew it was wrong," she told me during an evaluation interview. When Louise was charged with multiple counts of prescription forgery, her nursing license was suspended. She acknowledged that she had been abusing other medications for years, including while working at a hospital. When she had to have surgery, she requested more painkillers than she needed. "I asked for them when plain Tylenol would have done the trick." Despite all the pills she took, Louise retained a stellar professional reputation. "My supervisor told me, 'You're one of the best nurses I ever had,'" she said with pride, referring to a job at a community clinic. Whenever she was questioned about her behavior, Louise blamed other people or circumstances. She hated being lied to, yet she lied to her husband and tried to make him feel guilty for not trusting her.

Deciding to be forthcoming during our interview, Louise acknowledged that she used drugs to alleviate boredom. She also felt a "need to be the center of attention. On Percocet, I thought everyone liked me. Everyone seemed to want to come to me." When she took the pills, Louse was energized, more talkative, and more confident. She said that the drug "made me feel like I was in control, like everything's going to be fine." And, she admitted, she was terribly wasteful, spending extravagantly. In addition to abusing prescription drugs, Louise acknowledged smoking marijuana and trying other illegal drugs.

Worried about her daughter and wanting to help, Louise's mother was candid in speaking with me. She commented, "Louise needs and wants a lot of attention and doesn't want anyone to be upset with her." This translated into Louise instantly disliking anyone trying to hold her accountable for any mistake or misjudgment. Her mother said that, at one point, Louise claimed to have had seizures. "I felt they were put on," her mother said and added, "She's a very good actress."

Tyler, Louise's husband, became suspicious when Louise was neglecting routine household tasks. Bills went unpaid. Ironing piled up. Louise seemed less energetic and was taking naps, which normally she seldom did. "Things just kept getting put off," Tyler remarked. Louise was risking her marriage, her infant son, and the career that she loved.

Louise volunteered, "I have a real addictive personality." Like others who abuse prescription drugs, she had developed a physical dependence. Consider Louise's circumstances. After having a stillborn child, she finally had a healthy baby girl. Her husband loved her, and she had devoted parents nearby eager to help. Although not wealthy, Louise and her husband were able to fulfill financial obligations. And Louise was venerated by everyone who employed her. Her problem might have been having "an addictive personality." Far more important, however, was her criminal personality. As her mother said, she excelled at acting. Louise lived a double life, stealing from her employers and deceiving those who loved and depended upon her.

To feed the "habits" of people like Nancy and Louise, there are physicians at clinics—sometimes called "pill mills"—who are ready to prescribe painkillers to almost anyone who walks through the door. William Eliot Hurwitz, MD, was convicted in 2007 of seventeen counts of drug trafficking. A sentencing brief of the United States Attorney stated that the doctor operated "a pain management practice that was simply out of control. . . . Hurwitz would regularly perform perfunctory exams, if at all, and rubber stamp and oftentimes encourage the patients' insatiable demand for excessive and obscene amounts (e.g., 1600 pills per day). . . . The patients would get their prescriptions filled by pharmacists, who were recommended by Hurwitz. . . . Dr. Hurwitz provided prescriptions for large quantities of controlled substances despite direct knowledge that his patients were abusing and/or selling the medications."[18] Note was made in the sentencing brief of the doctor prescribing "an obviously addicted and 'out of control' patient more than 1,800 OxyContin 80 mg tablets per month." The U.S. Attorney recommended imprisonment for life.

Research indicates that a predisposition to mind-altering substances runs in families. But even with a genetic or biological inclination toward addiction, people still are able to choose what they will or will not put in their bodies. If an individual is aware of a tendency toward addiction in his family, all the more reason to abstain from using mind-altering substances.

To further examine the notion of an "addictive personality," let's look at the case of Raymond, forty-two years old. Raymond maintained that he had been addicted to cocaine and to alcohol at different times in his life. He asserted that drugs were the source of his problems, especially inasmuch as they wrecked his promising career at a successful and growing technology company where he was earning more than $100,000 a year. As it turned out, Raymond had committed crimes before he ever used drugs and committed others during lengthy periods of abstinence. His criminal record listed convictions for burglary and grand larceny, numerous traffic infractions, and an arrest for driving on a suspended license. One might conjecture that Raymond was stealing to support his drug "habit." But, like nearly all other drug-using criminals whom I have interviewed, Raymond was stealing long *before* he had a habit. It can certainly be the case that once a user like Raymond becomes heavily immersed in drugs, he commits more crimes to keep pace with the growing expense of his usage. As mentioned earlier, his criminal output also increases because drugs help him shut off fears of being apprehended or injured.

If their motivation is sufficiently strong, criminals may go "cold turkey" on their own and abstain from the use of mind-altering substances. Their motives may not always be the purest. Aware that drugs interfere with their physical coordination and mental acuity, some have maintained sobriety in order to become more proficient at committing crimes. They want to be mentally sharper, their coordination better; or they desire to reinvigorate their sex drive. They know that their immersion in the drug world subjects them to increased risk of apprehension.

A 2011 article in the *Monitor on Psychology* discusses paying people to quit drugs.[19] Focusing on "contingency management," the article states that "even hardened criminals can change" using "psychology's fundamental laws of reinforcement," which can be in the form of "token gifts and pep talks from judges." If criminals are able to stop using drugs because they are paid, this suggests that the basic problem lies in the choices they make rather than their being in the grip of the "disease" of substance abuse.

Researchers are trying to develop a vaccination that will prevent drugs from entering the brain. During a 2013 television interview, Nora Volkow of the National Institute on Drug Abuse said, "A cure would be fantastic, and that means you get a medication like an antibiotic."[20] However, even if such a vaccine becomes available, abstinence from mind-altering substances does not address the main problem, which is the uncompromising, controlling personality of destructive individuals. Even if all criminals were to be drug-free, they still would have a lot more to change about themselves in order to become responsible human beings.

10

The Criminal as Terrorist

Normally, we think of terrorists as people who detonate explosive devices in public places, blow up airplanes, threaten people whose beliefs are contrary to their own, or engage in genocide against an ethnic group. Unlike many other violent offenders, terrorists justify their destruction by claiming that they are supporting a cause or religious belief.

Having spent decades interviewing and counseling men and women who have committed a variety of crimes, I began noting similarities between such individuals and heads of state who have committed atrocities against their own citizens. Thoroughly familiar with the thinking and behavior patterns of people with a criminal personality, I have observed what appear to be parallel patterns in perpetrators of political and international terrorism. No one knows when, where, or how these highly visible public figures will strike. They demonstrate the very criminal thinking I have been describing in this book. Although I have had no direct contact with these individuals, I have reason to surmise that features of the criminal personality apply to many of them.

The U.S. Code defines both domestic and international terrorism in terms of acts "intended to intimidate or coerce a civilian population."[1] Criminals operate as "terrorists" whether they target one person, a family, a community, or an entire country. A rapist, a car jacker, an arsonist, and a pair of snipers all commit acts of terror.

Perpetrators of domestic violence are terrorists. The marriage of Colin and Judy illustrates how an abusive spouse keeps the other in a perpetual state of subjugation and uncertainty through fear, threats, psychological abuse, and physical violence. Judy and Colin had come to the attention of the county's department of social services because one of their children told his teacher he was afraid when his parents fought. The marital relationship was so conflict-ridden that the court temporarily removed the couple's sons from the home and gave the paternal grandparents custody.

Colin had a criminal record that included forging checks, grand larceny, car theft, and repeatedly driving on a suspended license. He forced Judy to sign checks when he knew their bank account lacked sufficient funds to cover them.

Judy told her counselor that she had lost a part of herself, that she had no confidence, and that she was the one who had failed in the marriage. Whenever Judy tried to discuss anything with Colin, he responded in a manner that left her feeling "like I don't know anything." Deciding it was futile to fight him, she conceded to whatever he asked. Sex had become a major issue, in that her husband expected it on demand, marked the calendar on days they had sex, then recorded a rating on her performance. Colin humiliated his wife further by offering to pay her each time. One night, Colin walked out, yelling, "I'll just have to buy sex."

Day in and day out, Colin would wear Judy down. When

they walked along the street, he chastised her for walking too slowly. Colin criticized what Judy wore, became infuriated when she had her hair cut, and was caustically critical if she did not wear perfume. Even when Judy became engrossed in a book, Colin would fume, "You like the book more than you like me," and insist that she pay attention to him. If dinner wasn't ready exactly when Colin wanted, he would inform her precisely the number of minutes she had to get it on the table. Judy recalled an occasion when he screamed and threw things at her: "I ended up in the bedroom crying. He told me, 'If you say another word, I'll smack you in the face.'"

Judy was the financial mainstay of the family, but that did not stop Colin from invading their joint account to spend money on whatever he fancied. She and Colin had no friends as a couple, and she was not allowed to socialize outside of work. Judy's job was the one aspect of her existence that was not under her husband's control. Colin complained that Judy was letting her job go to her head and acting too self-important. For Judy, the job was a lifeline because she had people to talk to and was appreciated because of her competence.

The couple's altercations became increasingly physical. During a quarrel, Colin hurled a ring of keys and struck her on the neck. When Judy announced she was leaving, headed toward her car, and drove away, Colin pursued her in his car and rammed the rear of her vehicle. He then dismantled wires under the hood and warned that if she tried to leave again, he'd get a gun and "put her six feet under." On another occasion, when she retreated out of fear to the bathroom, he broke down the door. "He grabbed me, and I was cut where his nails dug into me, and he gave me a black eye." Judy was terrified to report the injuries she had suffered.

Judy professed to her counselor, "There's one thing I'd love to do, stand up to him and tell him how I feel." But she remained with Colin for several reasons. Despite Judy's income, they had incurred joint debt, and Judy could not imagine how she would survive financially on her own. She was certain that Colin would pursue her if she left. However, the critical factor keeping Judy in the marriage was her own insecurity. She told her counselor, "I expect too much from him," and criticized herself for being a poor housekeeper and for not desiring sex. Taking her marriage vows extremely seriously, Judy hoped that she and Colin would iron out their differences and regain custody of their children. Also sustaining her were periods when they got along well, during which Colin was affectionate, gave her gifts, and took her out to dinner.

Judy attended a court-sponsored group for victims of domestic violence. Emotionally worn down, she was suffering from fatigue, headaches, and anxiety. Finally, she resolved to leave and developed a plan. Conditions were as favorable as they would get. She had received a pay raise. The children were safe, she had a car, the support of her minister, and a place to go. She packed her belongings, drove to a friend's home, and made arrangements to move nearly a thousand miles away where she had family and good job prospects. Social services restored custody of the children to her because they would be living in a safer environment.

Judy was married to a domestic terrorist. Terrorists operate in different arenas. Under the cover of advancing a cause, a person can conceal his underlying criminal personality. I remember in the 1960s interviewing a college dropout who had joined civil rights marchers in Alabama. When he returned, we spoke about the events on his trip. With great excitement, he described brutal police tactics, dogs turned on demonstrators, fire hoses sprayed at protestors. I never heard a word about social justice and racial equality, causes which ostensibly prompted him to take the trip south. He was not a terrorist, but he was a liar, a thief, and a drug user. Students in the university community had to keep a close eye on their bicycles because he might make off with them if they were not securely locked. Although he espoused the rhetoric of civil rights, what mattered to him was being on the scene of the excitement, then returning as a big shot to impress others with his stories.

It is highly likely that most terrorists have a criminal mind. Perhaps some are pure and sincere in their motivations for embracing their cause. It is not a huge leap for one who understands the mental makeup of criminals to extrapolate the personalities of despots and tyrants. As they act in the name of a cause, these ruthless individuals terrorize and slaughter their adversaries.

Most men who become ruthless dictators were criminals long before they attained their positions of absolute authority. In his classic book *The Psychopathic God,* Robert G. L. Waite provides more than five hundred pages of analysis of Adolf Hitler.[2] His observations provide evidence that, from childhood, Adolf Hitler manifested thinking and behavior patterns common to criminals. Waite notes that temper tantrums were "the means little Adolf had used to frighten his doting mother into compliance with his demands." By age eleven, Hitler was "no longer the obedient star pupil of previous years." Rather he was "argumentative, self-opinionated, willful, arrogant and bad tempered." The young Hitler "demanded of his fellow pupils their unqualified subservience, fancying himself in the role of leader." According to Waite, Hitler's twelfth year was "unusually important in his personal development. The boy who had been the star pupil of village schools began to fail; the outwardly cocky, hyperactive ringleader of robust neighborhood games became the morose, self-absorbed, withdrawn preadolescent who talked to trees on lonely hills, orated to the winds, fought with his parents, caricatured his teachers, and hated the world." Hitler's academic performance deteriorated so that he had to leave one school and enter another, which he left before graduating. At sixteen, Hitler purchased a lottery ticket, not unusual in itself, but Waite writes, "What is striking about young Hitler is his absolute conviction that he would win." He planned how he'd spend the money. When he did not win, he went into "a blind fury." Hitler was both sentimental and brutal toward animals. A 1936 decree showed "particular solicitude about the suffering of lobsters and crabs" and specified how they should meet the most "humane death." And yet Hitler was observed "[turning] savagely on his own dog," whipping him "like a madman." At the time he was concerned about lobsters, Hitler was reported to have remarked to an associate, "Do I intend to eradicate whole races? Of course I do . . . . Cruelty and brute strength . . . . The masses want it. They need the thrill of terror to make them shudderingly submissive." The rest of the infamous story of Adolf Hitler is that of a criminal who amassed the power to terrorize, torture, and slaughter millions.

Modern terrorists show similar patterns in that, like Hitler, they were criminals before embracing causes that they exploited to assume power. The United States offered a $25 million reward for Abu Musab al-Zarqawi, the notorious jihadist. Writing in *The Atlantic* about his "short, violent life," Mary Anne Weaver characterized al-Zarqawi as a criminal before he joined any cause.[3] "As a teenager al-Zarqawi had been a bully and a thug, a bootlegger and a heavy drinker. . . . He was disruptive, constantly involved in brawls. . . . When he was fifteen, he participated in a robbery of a relative's home, during which the relative was killed." In 1994, at the age of twenty-eight, al-Zarqawi was sentenced to fifteen years in prison for possessing illegal weapons and belonging to an organization banned in Jordan. According to Ms. Weaver's account, al-Zarqawi "flourished" during his incarceration. "He was stern, tough, and unrelenting on anything that he considered to be an infraction of his rules, yet he was often seen in the prison courtyard crying as he read the Koran." Al-Zarqawi was said to have "sauntered through the prison ward like a peacock" and "organized prison life like a gang leader." After his release, he established camps to train fighters and was sought by the United States for masterminding bombings, suicide missions, and executions. It appeared that al-Zarqawi was more intent on creating mayhem and slaughter than on advancing a particular religion or ideology. Calling him a "fighter-superstar," *Time* magazine pointed out, "In his view, slaughtering fellow Arabs who followed different forms of Islam was as important as killing Westerners."[4] On June 7, 2006, al-Zarqawi was finally killed by United States forces.

Many observers have stated that perpetrators of terror, acting in the name of a holy war sanctioned by their religion, perverted the very teachings of that religion. Commentators like Stanley Bedlington in the *Washington Post* wrote that the late Osama bin Laden "defiled his own religion" and willingly transgressed "strict Koranic injunctions."[5] And, many years ago, a writer for *Time* pointed out, "The jihad [bin Laden] declared against the United States, in the eyes of most religious scholars, was never a holy war; it was a blatant fraud."[6]

In her assessment of Osama bin Laden, psychology professor Aubrey Immelman found the leader of al-Qaeda did not "fit the profile of the highly conscientious, closed-minded religious fundamentalist, nor that of the religious martyr."[7] Citing bin Laden's "blend of narcissistic and antisocial personality patterns," she characterized him as "adept at exploiting Islamic fundamentalism in the service of his own ambition and personal dreams of glory."

Late in 2013, the Central African Republic was on the verge of genocide. Muslim armed groups from the north, called the Séléka ("alliance") were killing, raping, and pillaging Christian communities. The *Washington Post* reported that "a conflict that had more to do with predation and power than with religion" took a turn for the worse as Christian militias began attacking Muslim communities, "slitting the throats of women and children and at times announcing that they wanted to exterminate all the Muslims."[8] *Aljazeera* reported that four hundred people had been killed during three days of violence.[9]

Terrorists can attach themselves to any cause, including environmental protection, animal rights, historical preservation, or any number of political movements. They later justify their criminal behavior by citing the cause that it purportedly served.

Consider the case of Florida native Paul Jennings Hill, an anti-abortion activist, seminary graduate, and ordained minister. On July 30, 1994, Hill approached The Ladies Center in Pensacola, Florida, an abortion clinic that he knew well. There he targeted Dr. John Britton, a clinic physician; and his bodyguard, a retired U.S. Air Force lieutenant colonel. Hill shot and killed both men and was quickly arrested. He was convicted of capital murder and executed by lethal injection at the Florida State Prison on September 3, 2003. There are thousands of citizens who are against abortion, some vehemently so. But it takes a particular type of individual to become such a zealot that he kills in the name of a cause.

According to newspaper accounts, in adolescence, Paul Hill "showed rebellious and even violent tendencies." He was arrested for assaulting his father, who tried to get him treatment for his abuse of marijuana and LSD. A neighbor who grew up two doors from him told the *Washington Post,* "I always felt that he was unconcerned about the consequences of things that he did."[10] This neighbor recalled that, when Mr. Hill was thirteen, he pried his dog's mouth open and spat in the dog's throat. Paul Hill was an absolutist with "no tolerance for gray." He was described as transforming himself from being a hellion to striving to be "a model Christian." However, according to a pastor quoted in the *Pensacola News Journal,* Paul Hill "had difficulties in all of his pastorates, because he was so intense, he couldn't live with people who didn't agree with him."[11] This killer, referred to in the press as a "domestic terrorist," was unrepentant until the end.

There has been a focus, especially in the wake of "home-grown terrorism," on how people become "radicalized" or persuaded to join a particular cause. Criminals searching for excitement are ripe for recruitment. They require little persuasion and need not travel far to obtain training. The *Washington Jewish Week* termed the Internet "a virtual library for terrorism," where individuals fuel one another's discontent.[12] The Internet publishes ideology and propaganda. It is an inexpensive tool for terrorist groups to employ for recruiting, raising funds, and ordering supplies. Representative Ed Royce, serving as chairman of the House Foreign Affairs Committee, commented that "cyber hate sites" provide "an infatuation to excitement" as well as "detailed instructions."[13]

A criminal does not have to attend a training camp in Afghanistan to learn how to construct bombs. In fact, the Boston Marathon bombers constructed their bombs based on an al Qaeda article, "How to Build a Bomb in the Kitchen of Your Mom." Professor of management information Marie Wright noted that both the Internet and the open environment of U.S. colleges and universities "provide forums for the presentation of radical messages" that appeal to certain young people.[14] And, she observed, "Individuals have a tendency to seek out other like-minded individuals." This last point is corroborated in a Central Intelligence Agency report that states, "Many terrorist groups depend on prison recruitment success to swell their ranks. Inmates recruit fellow inmates directly as well as spot and assess others for later recruitment upon their release."[15]

Al-Shabaab, the group claiming responsibility for the September 2013 massacre at a mall in Kenya, was endeavoring to lure American men to join their ranks. Later, Al-Shabaab emphasized that three of the jihadists came from Minnesota.

According to Washington, D.C.'s CBS News Affiliate, a leader of the organization made a pitch on a recruitment video by saying, "If you guys only knew how much fun we have over here, it's the real Disneyland."[16] Such language seems to constitute an appeal more to an appetite for criminal excitement than to a desire to serve a worthwhile cause.

Hackers perpetuate a reign of terror as they invade shopping systems that contain data for billions of dollars in transactions each day. During the 2013 Christmas shopping season, hackers breached the security of nearly 70 million customers of Target, one of the nation's largest retail stores. The theft of credit and debit card information potentially enabled criminals to make fraudulent purchases throughout the world. It was estimated that the company might have to spend $100 million to repair the damage and to pay for legal fees. Quoted in the *Washington Post,* Beth Givens, founder of the nonprofit Privacy Rights Clearinghouse, stated, "It's an arms race. And the crooks are almost always ahead of the game."[17]

General Michael Hayden, former director of the Central Intelligence Agency, warned about "layers of threats" as he told the *Washington Post,* "Nation-state actors are coming at us. They want your intellectual property.[18] They want your trade secrets, your negotiating position. There are some criminals out there who want your PIN number, your credit card number and so on." General Hayden continued that these individuals, who are insatiable, "will begin to acquire capacities we now associate with criminal gangs."

The most lethal act of domestic terrorism to date occurred in 1995 when Timothy McVeigh bombed the Alfred P. Murrah Federal Building in Oklahoma City, killing 168 people, among them 19 children. From descriptions in the voluminous press coverage, Mr. McVeigh appeared to have had many of the characteristics of the criminal personality. From the age of thirteen, he was not just a gun enthusiast but, according to a *Wash-*

ington Post report, was "obsessed" with guns to the point that he made drawings of them in school when he was bored, and brought guns to school to impress other students.[19] As a teenager, McVeigh was observed speeding at seventy miles an hour, yelling at slower drivers, and grasping his shotgun "like he was going to blow them away." Dropping out of community college, McVeigh drifted from job to job and, by gambling, amassed huge debts that he could not pay. At twenty years old, he was making and exploding bombs. While serving in the military, he met Terry Nichols, who later became his accomplice in the Oklahoma City attack. After resigning from the army, in part because he was unable to qualify to become a Green Beret, Mr. McVeigh wandered through forty states, buying and selling firearms at eighty gun shows. In temperament, he was described as "veering from passivity to volcanic anger." Convinced of the evils of government, he ranted about government as the enemy of the individual citizen, allegedly because it was seeking to curtail citizens' rights, especially the owning of firearms. Before the Oklahoma City bombing, Mr. McVeigh had considered a number of government officials as candidates for assassination.

On April 15, 2013, another act of domestic terrorism occurred when two bombs exploded near the finish line of the Boston Marathon, killing three people and wounding more than 260. Two brothers who had immigrated from Russia in 2002 with their parents were the alleged bombers. Tamerlan Tsarnaev died during a police shoot-out, but his nineteen-year-old brother Dzhokhar survived and was arrested and imprisoned. Considerable information became available about the older brother, but less about Dzhokhar, who pleaded not guilty to all charges while awaiting trial.

In a *New York Times* article titled "A Battered Dream, Then a Violent Path," Tamerlan Tsarnaev was characterized as a college dropout, a social isolate, and a violent young man.[20] Heavily involved in boxing and known as "a big puncher," Tamerlan did not adhere to the training regimen and totally stopped participating. On one occasion, he breached boxing etiquette by entering a locker room "to taunt not only the fighter he was about to face but also the fighter's trainer." He increasingly isolated himself and seldom worked, leaving his wife—who was on public assistance and food stamps—to support him and their young child. Before he was married, a girlfriend had dialed 911 to report that he was assaulting her. A young woman who fell in love with Tamerlan when she was seventeen told the *New York Post* how Tamerlan tried to control her through intimidation and violence (the dynamics were similar to those in the relationship between Colin and Judy mentioned earlier in this chapter).[21] "Tamerlan told me I should only talk to Muslim girls," she stated. The young woman recalled Tamerlan ripping a pair of her jeans and striking her in the face with them. "I was in love and scared he'd leave me if I didn't do what he said. Looking back, I had a lucky escape," she remarked. Early in 2012, Tamerlan went to Russia for six months, leaving his wife and child. Items from Tamerlan's Amazon account "wish list," which has been made public, include *How to Make Driver's Licenses and Other ID on Your Home Computer* and *The ID Forger*. Subsequent investigations have linked Tamerlan to drug dealing, and to participation in a triple murder sixteen months before the Boston Marathon attack.

With respect to Dzhokhar, the younger brother, people wondered how a smart, social, and athletic student at the University of Massachusetts, known to have "a heart of gold," participated in such a horrendous crime. In a *New York Times* article titled "The Dark Side, Carefully Masked," Dzhokhar was said to have been secretive about his personal life.[22] He described himself as "a heavy sleeper and a great liar." He drank and smoked "more marijuana than most high school or college students." As Dzhokhar bragged about skipping classes, his grades dropped. Although his brother prayed regularly, he never was particularly devout.

According to newspaper reports, FBI and local officials have continued trying to understand how these brothers were "radicalized," whether there was a single development or tipping point in their alleged "turn" to violence. It remains unclear how much influence ideology or religious belief had in their lives. According to a friend, "Tamerlan would throw out foreign words like 'jihad' and 'inshallah' without really understanding their meaning." Furthermore, he married a Christian wife. What is documented is that Tamerlan was a criminal well *before* he bombed the Boston Marathon. In the aftermath of that tragedy, an explanation for Dzhokhar's conduct has been put forth that is similar to an explanation of the behavior of Lee Boyd Malvo, the younger of the Washington, D.C., snipers—that Dzhokhar was brainwashed, in this case by his older brother. Yet people who knew Dzhokhar said that he was very much his own person.

The people whom I have described in this chapter are terrorists. Without question, they all have features of a criminal personality. If one wants to know whether to ascribe their criminality entirely to belief in a cause, consider who these individuals were *before* embracing a cause.

11

"Decent People"

During the early days of my research, in the 1970s, the feature of the criminal mind that I found most surprising was that *every* offender regarded himself as a good human being. The participants in the study acknowledged that, from society's point of view, they were "criminals," in that they broke the law. What I have found ever since is that every offender, male or female, juvenile or adult, believes he is, at heart, a good person.

"If I thought of myself as evil, I couldn't live," one offender told me. A man with a lengthy criminal record culminating in the murder of a policeman stated, "I've always been a caring individual. I was never really a violent person. I don't feel I've ever been self-centered. I try to help people whenever I can without expecting anything in return." Interviewed in the penitentiary, this man continued, "I'm happy with myself." A teenager who brandished a gun to rob restaurant employees of the day's cash receipts justified what he did by saying, "No one got hurt," completely oblivious to the aftermath that victims of violent crimes experience. So how is it that people who murder, rape, rob, molest children—in short, commit any crime imaginable—retain a good opinion of themselves?

Criminals know right from wrong, legal from illegal. They may be even more familiar with the laws than many responsible citizens. Despite this knowledge, they decide to make exceptions for themselves, just because it suits them at a particular time. As one man commented, "I can make anything wrong right. I can make anything right wrong. Right is what I want to do at the time." If a criminal regards something as wrong for himself, he will not do it. An act is wrong if it is too risky. An act is also considered wrong if the criminal deems it too petty and thus beneath him. A big-time operator may consider shoplifting wrong only because the proceeds are too paltry or he thinks that, with all the surveillance techniques that stores employ, it isn't worth taking a chance. If a criminal errs in judgment and is apprehended, he may admit that what he did was wrong and even express what appears to be remorse. However, his sense of wrongfulness and regret relates to getting caught, not to having committed the offense in the first place.

People who are basically responsible can be insensitive to the fact that they have hurt someone else. If their behavior is called to their attention, they apologize out of shame or embarrassment, and endeavor to make amends. Because the behavior in question is incompatible with their view of themselves, they sincerely regret what they have done, learn from the experience, and try not to behave in similar fashion again. Occasionally, responsible individuals have difficulty accepting the fact that they have harmed someone. They engage in denial, insisting their intentions were good. And an otherwise responsible individual may retaliate when he feels hurt. In general, however, responsible human beings try to take others into account. They are, in fact, "decent" and do not build themselves up by preying on the vulnerability of others and tearing them down.

Criminals have referred to heinous crimes that they have

committed as "mistakes." An adolescent told me, "I'm a regular teenager. I made a mistake, a bad mistake," referring to his grabbing a pistol and shooting his girlfriend during an argument. There was nothing "regular" about this boy nor was the homicide a "mistake." But this was his perspective; he thought of himself as a good guy, not a killer. Offended by my inquiry about his prior relationship with the deceased, he said indignantly, "You have only the bad stuff, not the good things. There's nothing bad in my life to talk about except this one thing." Meanwhile, an officer of the court had prepared a twenty-page report documenting his egregious violations of his parents' rules, habitual truancy, failing grades, and his affiliating with youths who committed burglaries, auto thefts, and grand larceny.

Criminals set themselves apart from those they consider to be the really bad guys, thereby preserving an image of themselves as good people. For example, criminals who attend school or hold a job, no matter how erratically, disparage those who do neither. Obtaining an education and bringing home a paycheck are badges of responsibility. Cloaking themselves in this mantle of respectability elevates their opinion of themselves while it enables them to get away with things on the side.

Many criminals are remarkably talented. Prison art-shows display the work of gifted painters who have little formal training. Having corresponded for fifteen years with serial killers and death row inmates, Anthony Meoli observed that nearly every serial killer is artistic. During an interview with psychologist Katherine Ramsland, Mr. Meoli commented, "Their ability to capture the subtle spatial nuances of imagery is an unusual trait."[1] Some criminals are musically gifted, performing their own compositions on instruments they learned to play totally by ear. Many who do not play an instrument are music aficionados. Some criminals are excellent craftsmen, fashioning stylish leather goods or constructing handsome, sturdy furniture. Others have a knack for repairing just about anything.

If a criminal receives accolades for his accomplishments, his sense of his own worth is enhanced. People familiar with his criminal record grow optimistic, hoping that he will direct his talents toward becoming a constructive citizen. Because he lacks self-discipline, however, the criminal is unlikely to develop those talents. He has little interest in training programs that entail drudgery and perseverance. Instead, he expects overnight to become a highly recognized artist, to turn out a polished product, or compose a masterpiece. Since immediate success is seldom possible, he loses interest. There are exceptions. Anticipating public admiration or financial gain, some criminals develop their skills, which makes it easier to conceal other, not so admirable behavior.

People who are not criminals also fail to make use of natural aptitudes or to cultivate their talents. They may set such unrealistically high standards for themselves that they quickly become discouraged and quit shortly after embarking on a new undertaking. Some talented individuals have such a neurotic fear of failing that they give up before facing evaluation by others.

The responsible person discovers meaning in the process of achievement. He may be prouder of his determination in persevering and surmounting obstacles than of the final product. Not so with the criminal. When he is not an immediate success, he asserts himself in criminal enterprises that are far more gratifying.

Another way in which many criminals maintain their good opinion of themselves is through religion. Schooled in religion as children, they took to heart what they learned. Their parents report that, while in elementary school, their offspring were superbly behaved, helpful at home, faithful in attending religious school, and protective of kids who were underdogs. As children, these individuals were critical of others who committed the slightest impropriety. They believed that to remain in God's good graces, they must strive to be better than good, purer than pure. Their determination, though sincere, did not last. In a manner typical of criminals, they shifted from one extreme to another.

As his world expands, the criminal as a child encounters increasing temptations, and his mind focuses on doing what is forbidden. The steady erosion of his intentions to remain pure is often difficult to observe. Those who think they know him well are astounded when this model child appears to suddenly explode into antisocial activity. Yet religion is not abandoned forever. Criminals return to religion out of nostalgia for childhood, or they seek religious sanctuary when they long for serenity or a soothing ritual. However, just as they exploit everything else, criminals also exploit religion. They pray for success at a criminal enterprise. If they are apprehended, they pray to get out of a jam. Criminals seek salvation after they are confined, then resolve to mend their ways. Many offenders turn to religion in prison. Faith-based programs have proliferated in correctional facilities. In some instances, criminals exploit clergymen, trying to win them over to gain special favors or enlist support for an early release. Some appear sincere as they occupy themselves with religious studies and attend services. It is likely, however, that many of these individuals would quickly jettison their pious ways if they were released.

Religion has little to do with how the criminal lives. As a child, he may serve as an altar boy at a morning service but that very afternoon embark on a shoplifting spree. As an adult he may pray in church but later rob a person at gunpoint. Members of organized crime profess to be religious. They build shrines in their homes, attend church, and donate to charity. But these acts do not stop them from murdering their adversaries. For criminals, religion and evil exist side by side, each compartmentalized from the other.

Clergymen often lament that worshippers fail to live by the teachings of their faith. Feeling virtuous after attending a service at a church, mosque, or synagogue, congregants may curse fellow drivers as they scramble to leave the parking lot. But most of these people, despite their flaws, retain a sense of social boundaries, obey laws, and fulfill obligations. The criminal, on the other hand, has a remarkable capacity to shut off considerations of responsibility or morality so completely that he freely commits murder, rape, or other atrocities. He perceives no contradiction between prayer and crime. Both are right for him, depending on what he wants at a particular time.

Ironically, the criminal's religiosity can foster crime, for, when genuine, it bolsters his opinion of himself as an upstanding citizen. It is as though by having prayed and confessed his sins, the criminal has emptied his cup of whatever evil it might have contained so that he has more latitude to do as he pleases.

Although the criminal may not accept what others consider to be moral standards, he claims to have his own. Other people are liars, scoundrels, perverts, and criminals; not he. He looks down on them as depraved because they do things he would not. For this reason, it is not surprising that prison cultures are so highly judgmental and some prisoners (especially those who exploit children or the elderly) are viewed as the lowest of the low and require protective custody. The criminal regards specific crimes as wrong and thus off-limits for him, simply because he personally finds them offensive. Criminals differ as to what limits they impose on their own conduct. One says that a child molester should be killed, while another advocates that a rapist be castrated. However, each offender considers whatever he himself does as beyond reproach. One tough teenager said that anyone who knocks a "little old lady" down on the street to grab her purse should be "strung up." However, this same youth broke into an elderly woman's apartment while she was still there, terrorized her, and made off with her jewelry. To his way of thinking, this was perfectly acceptable because he did not physically attack her. A white-collar criminal may siphon hundreds of thousands of dollars into his own bank account, forcing the closure of a small business and the loss of jobs for dozens of innocent employees. Yet this serial embezzler is horrified at the thought of physically assaulting somebody.

Noncriminals have a tendency to resist seeing the criminal as he is. Many people have difficulty thinking of another human being as gratuitously and maliciously injuring others. They cling to the view that everyone is good at heart, that extenuating circumstances explain even the most vicious crimes. Throughout his life, the criminal exploits this tendency of others to see him as basically good. Noncriminals recognize his talents, witness him doing good deeds, and hear him espouse noble ideals. Those who interact with him, whether family, friends, or strangers, frequently fail to penetrate the thicket of his lies, vagueness, and self-serving statements. They want to believe in him and are reluctant to judge him harshly unless he has committed a violent crime or compiled a lengthy police record. Even then, they may provide their own justifications for his behavior. The case of Irene illustrates this instinct.

Irene appeared to be a devoted wife and stay-at-home mother for her two daughters. With her bubbly personality, she had many friends. But behind the facade of a highly educated, responsible, and emotionally stable woman was an entirely different human being. Irene had shoplifted from so many stores that she had stacks of new clothes piled in the trunk of her car and hanging in her closet. Several arrests did not deter her, and the stealing continued. In addition, she engaged in extramarital affairs. Her husband claimed that she had trumped up false charges of domestic abuse, resulting in a court-issued protective order forcing him to leave the marital home. After Irene left the girls alone in the house at night so she could rendezvous with a man at a nearby hotel, Child Protective Services intervened, and she was charged with child neglect. The court vacated the protective order, and granted her husband exclusive use of the marital residence as well as custody of their daughters. Irene was not permitted to see the children until she received therapy and completed a parenting course.

Irene presented herself to me as the aggrieved party, wronged by her husband and the court. She contended that her husband traveled constantly, did little to help around the house, and constantly belittled and humiliated her even in front of the children. Irene maintained that, because she had an incompetent lawyer, the judge had failed to understand her circumstances. Now her aggressor was back in the house employing a nanny to care for the children. Irene had a rationalization for everything. She explained that, when she was stealing, she was under such enormous stress that she was unaware of what she was doing. She claimed that medication impaired her judgment. Irene was outraged at the assault upon her character, for she genuinely believed that she was a good mother and an honest person. She asserted that whatever had gone wrong was not her fault, and that she should be restored to her rightful position as the custodial parent.

I interviewed Irene's parents, who were hanging onto the image of Irene that they had held since she was a young girl. Despite her arrests and the court-imposed ban on visiting the children, Irene's parents were convinced that any misconduct was an aberration and did not reflect the true personality of their daughter, whom they practically idolized. They did not defend Irene as much as endeavor to inform me about her generosity, popularity, conscientiousness, and superb moral character. Two of Irene's friends did the same thing. They had not known about her involvement with Child Protective Services and the court. When they heard from other sources about what had transpired, they were incredulous.

Like Irene, a criminal may appear to have much going for him in terms of personality, talents, and accomplishments. If an incident occurs that is discordant with the positive view that others hold of the offender, they refuse to believe it. Irene certainly was not going to volunteer information about her arrests, or about the circumstances under which she left her children alone at night. Friends who had visited her at home, observed her with the children, and entrusted their own children to her were certain that Irene had been set up by her husband, then received unfair treatment by the court. One lady, shocked that a judge would form such a negative opinion of Irene, commented, "[Irene] is a wonderful person. That's not her. They must be talking about someone else."

I HAVE CONDUCTED independent child custody evaluations for the past thirty years. Occasionally, I encounter a situation in which one of the parents has a criminal personality. He spares nothing in building himself up while tearing his spouse down. He lies and deploys power and control tactics to defeat his spouse, as if gaining custody is a trophy. The battle is less about the child and more about winning. While threatening to bankrupt his spouse and take away that which is most precious to her—the children—the warring parent truly believes that he is the better parent and a far more honorable human being.

Marcia told me that her husband Lance had mounted a ferocious campaign to win custody of their three children. He threatened to reduce child support, impoverish her, and make life so miserable that, eventually, the children would beg to live with him. He warned that if he failed to obtain sole custody, he would withdraw from the children's lives. He predicted that after he had done so, the kids would quickly come crawling back. Although Lance had loved Marcia enough to marry her and have three children, he no longer had one positive observation to make about her. Spewing contempt, he characterized her as selfish, psychologically unstable, and impossible to deal with. Moreover, he maligned anyone Marcia associated with, especially members of her own family. Even activities that were positive, he cast in the most negative light. For example, Lance portrayed Marcia's establishing a swim team at their country club as an example of self-aggrandizement. While the couple lived together, she was the primary caretaker, and he was mainly an absentee father, spending an inordinate amount of time at the office, participating in golf outings with his buddies, and pursuing a variety of other interests. Lance gambled, drank, and used illegal drugs. Even when he was home, he'd often demand that Marcia hire a babysitter to take care of the children if she went out.

During the custody evaluation, Marcia did not spend nearly as much time tearing her husband down as he did in castigating her. Sometimes, Lance frightened her when he made remarks such as "You heard of O.J. [a reference to O. J. Simpson, acquitted of the murder of his wife]." Or he'd announce, "I'm going out to get laid and get a blow job."

Ironically, after the marital separation and while the custody litigation dragged on, Lance began doing what his wife had begged him to do, namely assume a more active role in the children's lives. Lance's strategy was to do whatever was necessary to win. Accordingly, the breakup of the marriage resulted in the children receiving more attention from Lance than they ever had, and their attachment to him increased. After I issued my report, Lance was livid about being denied sole custody (I had recommended joint custody but with the children living primarily with their mother). He informed Marcia that he would not visit the children anymore. He also told her that he had destroyed all of the children's pictures and photographs. By renouncing the children, Lance had shown his true colors. Eventually, he started spending time with them again, but only for brief periods.

Lance truly believed that he had been an excellent husband and devoted father. He claimed that Marcia married him because she was "attracted to the prosperity" his career would bring them. He told me that Marcia had "declared war" by asking him to leave. Lance said, "I tried everything to make this marriage work," including being home every night by five o'clock and becoming increasingly communicative and open.

On a personality inventory, Lance's responses to questions were extremely self-favorable. The test report stated, "He would cover over his shortcomings and act as though people should conform to his stereotypes and social expectations much more than they do." During the custody evaluation, Lance presented himself as concerned more about his children than about anything else, asserting, "I've been a model father in the last ten months. She hasn't been a model mother." While conceiving of himself as a "model father," Lance was continuing to harm his children by drawing them into the middle of the marital fray, then abandoning them. Lance was not merely posturing. He sincerely believed that he was the better parent and that his character was morally superior to that of his wife.

Criminals proclaim that they value their family and desire to be fully accepted, no matter what they do. Yet their caring words do not match their harsh actions, as they tend to treat family members like personal possessions. Over and over, they demand, intimidate, threaten, betray, disappoint, frustrate, and exhaust their families. When the criminal's parents don't do what he wants, he tries to make them feel guilty. If they express disapproval of the choices and decisions he has made, he accuses them of attempting to control his life.

OVER MANY YEARS, Troy's family had established what had become a highly prosperous real estate development company. His parents groomed him for taking over the firm as they prepared for retirement. As he was granted increasing responsibility, Troy complained that the job had turned into a nightmare requiring him to be available around the clock. He said that his father would not surrender the reins of authority and was controlling and irritable. Troy thought that he bore the brunt of his father's anger when any problem arose. "He'd never compliment me. It became apparent he never fully trusted me to run the company." It turned out that his father had good reason to distrust him. Troy began not showing up for work, then used a company credit card for personal expenses. Eventually, Troy's parents discovered that large sums of money were not accounted for. Over time, millions of dollars disappeared. It turned out that Troy had been the culprit, purchasing expensive electronic devices, buying luxury cars, and sustaining huge losses while gambling on the Internet and at casinos. In addition, he invested impulsively in businesses that eventually became defunct. From time to time, he replaced some of the stolen funds from temporary gains in investments. Troy was able to conceal his embezzling mainly because his family trusted him enough to grant him considerable autonomy.

Troy thought of himself as fundamentally a good guy who had made mistakes. He was proud of his generosity. Without authorization, he loaned money from the family business to others who were going through tough times. "I'd never let anyone else pay," he said, referring to his frequent dinners at restaurants. And he covered hotel and meal expenses for groups of friends who accompanied him on what he called "bigger than life" trips to Las Vegas. Troy said that toward his wife he was "affectionate, always giving, always generous." All he desired for himself, now that he had turned forty, was to "have an easygoing life with no worries; to retire and sit back on a beach," and never have to work again.

Asked to make a list of what he considered positive and negative features of his personality, Troy complied. He characterized himself as "reliable, loyal, self-motivated, doesn't require supervision, and a take-charge kind of guy." Among the negatives, he said that he drinks too much, does not share emotions, "tries to please everybody," "pretends to be smart," "lies some-times," and "gambles badly." Unshaken in his perception of him-self as a dutiful son and a generous man, he was incarcerated for destroying in several years what it had taken his family decades to build. Even after all this, his mother and father visited him in jail, and he characterized them as "supportive."

I have encountered numerous cases, similar to the above, in which a criminal has ruthlessly exploited his family's trust and support. Among them was Morgan, a young man who had a penchant for living beyond his means, flying first-class to resort destinations, staying in luxury hotels, and running up huge tabs at posh restaurants, paying for it all with a credit card he stole from his parents. He amassed tens of thousands of dollars in credit card charges before he was caught. His parents chose not to prosecute him but expected him to work and gradually repay the money, and to learn from the experience. Affirming that he was remorseful and promising to reform, Morgan appeared to be living a modest, disciplined life in which he had no money unless he earned it by working. He seemed to be functioning re-sponsibly until he quit his job and came to live with his parents. At that particular time, his father was sick and unemployed. Always interested in the stock market, Morgan invested $500 of his savings and made a modest profit. His appetite whetted, Morgan was certain he could make "huge gains" if he had more money to invest. Impersonating his father (he had the necessary identifying information, including Social Security number), Morgan authorized nearly one hundred thousand dollars to be wired into his own bank account, after which he embarked on a stock buying binge. He turned out not to be the financial wizard that he thought. Believing that he had achieved his fantasized "huge gains," it turned out that Morgan had miscalculated and incurred enormous losses. Meanwhile, his father had phoned his own bank to have funds wired from his account to another at a different institution. To his dismay, he was informed that far less was in that account than his last bank statement showed. Morgan's parents were devastated by the financial loss, but far more distraught over their son's reversion to old patterns; he had again taken advantage of them in a premeditated, calculating manner. Morgan explained that this time he had a far different motive than in the past, when he'd been driven by pure greed. His aim was not to become rich but to make money to help his family during a rough time in their lives. "This money wasn't for me; it was my intention to make money for Dad," he explained. Rather than disown their son or put him out of the house, Morgan's parents took the attitude that the losses they incurred would be worth it if it opened their son's eyes. His father told me, "I do believe he wanted to help the family. That is key in evaluating his motive. [Morgan] can be dead wrong and not know it." And he concluded, "[Morgan] is a good person. It's the wrong thinking and part of his search for self-esteem."

Frequently, parents and others close to a criminal offer justifications for his behavior. Doubting that he was even capable of being malevolent, they explain his behavior in terms of extenuating circumstances or deep-seated psychological problems. Morgan knew precisely what he was doing; his actions were intentional. His parents could never bring themselves to believe that their son could ever be so heartless.

CRIMINALS ARE SKILLED at ferreting out weakness and vulnerability. Senior citizens can be particularly tempting targets. The American Association of Retired Persons (AARP) reported, "Americans 50-plus accounted for about half of the nearly $11 million in losses from intimidation schemes reported to the Internet Crime Complaint Center."[2] According to AARP, criminals intimidate seniors in a variety of ways. They threaten violence unless the person targeted pays a supposedly overdue bill. They send someone directly to the house to shake the person down for money that he purportedly owes. Another ruse is to claim that their victim must immediately pay to them a fine owed to a court or other government entity. Threats to murder senior citizens are made to scare them into paying off a hit man. (In 2012, 1,354 people reported being extorted to the tune of $2 million by criminals threatening to kill them unless they paid up.) AARP noted that these statistics are likely underestimates, because victims are intimidated into silence or are embarrassed to acknowledge that they were duped. Seniors are also frequent victims of medical identity theft, which occurs when criminals acquire personal information so that they are able to buy prescription drugs or obtain medical treatment.

An arena in which criminals can operate with little risk is when they are entrusted with the care of impaired elderly men and women, especially those suffering from dementia. With personal financial information available on the premises, caretakers invade bank accounts, forge checks, and gain access to credit cards. In one case, a caretaker for a wealthy lady in South Florida was able to use the woman's credit card and pay a casino a small service charge to obtain large cash advances that went into his own pocket. When this lady received her long-term-care checks, the caretaker would forge her signature, deposit only a portion of the amount into her account, then appropriate the remainder in cash for himself. More than $300,000 in cash and property disappeared from the lady's estate before her family members, who lived more than a thousand miles away, became aware that funds were missing.

Interestingly, criminals who prey upon elderly people often express great sentiment toward their own grandparents and senior citizens in their neighborhood, and they go out of their way to help them. They carry groceries, shovel snow, help them cross the street, and run errands. These offenders are extremely protective if they think someone is preparing to take advantage of seniors whom they know. The criminal's affection for older men and women of his immediate acquaintance contributes to his view that he is a good person.

Criminals differ greatly as to where their sentiments lie. Some are so fond of animals that they will bring home an abandoned, injured animal and treat it more tenderly than their own children. One murderer refused to squash a bug because he didn't "want to kill a living thing." These animal lovers will interfere with and even assault a person whom they see mistreating an animal. Other criminals abuse animals or are indifferent to them. Similarly, some love babies, any baby. It tears them up to hear an infant cry, and they rush to soothe a baby. But then there is also the criminal who doesn't care for babies at all, not even his own. A wailing, implacable infant may evoke murderous thoughts or even a physically brutal response.

CRIMINALS WHO HAVE sex with minors are no exception to the theme of this chapter; they too believe that they are good human beings. Even though their victims are children and they are aware of the illegality, they do not see themselves as "criminals." These offenders are quick to point out that they do not use force, and assert that those with whom they have sex enter into such activity eagerly.

As he faced sentencing for production of child pornography, I interviewed Henry, a diplomat who had been stationed in a war-torn country. Henry came from a poor family and was the first to attend college. He went on to graduate school, after which he rose quickly in the agency by which he was employed. Polite, charming, and gregarious, Henry mingled with the local people and showed appreciation for their culture. He was invited to homes where he befriended a number of young girls, whose parents were delighted by the interest this handsome, well-to-do American expressed in their daughters. Henry had sex with these acquaintances, some of whom were as young as fourteen. He explained that, in that society, girls physically develop at an early age and, in some instances, he thought they were older than they turned out to be. Moreover, he commented, they are not considered children, because they assume adult responsibilities at an early age. Henry was emphatic that sex was easily available, that he never used coercion. He filmed his activities—all of which, he maintained, were consensual.

A different picture was presented by the prosecution, based on interviews with some of these women—that Henry had groomed these females for sex by leading some to think he would give money to them or their families. He also intimated to some of them that he might marry them, which gave hope to their parents, who were struggling just to survive each day. The judge in his case did not agree that what Henry did was acceptable because of the customs of that particular culture. Rather, Henry was a predator who used his diplomatic status to gain entrée into local homes, then with false promises lured underage girls into sexual activity at his residence—which was technically on United States soil.

Henry was outraged at being charged with crimes when he thought of himself as a hardworking, patriotic American who had been doing an outstanding job representing the United States. He saw himself as uniquely able to identify with the local people in a way that none of his fellow diplomats could. He vehemently denied exploiting minors in order to have sex with them. He said that, because of his own background, he was able to identify with people who worried about the source of their next meal. Citing his own struggles, he expressed gratitude to the United States government for the wonderful professional opportunity afforded him, and he patted himself on the shoulder for serving the public rather than entering a more lucrative field in the private sector. As for filming the sexual activity, Henry said unapologetically that he had long been accustomed to filming all aspects of his life, and that his sex partners saw the camera and did not object to being filmed. With the judge seeing the situation quite differently, Henry received a lengthy penitentiary sentence.

WELL-INTENTIONED PROFESSIONALS, SUCH as counselors and social workers who want to help criminals, often think that a major issue is low self-esteem. They see that a criminal has failed in so many ways: in his family, at school, at work, in interpersonal relationships, at developing his talents. Because they encounter him in a situation where he appears despondent, they may diagnose his core problem as depression and having an inferior self-image. And indeed the criminal may look depressed, because he is in a situation that he desperately wants to escape. Understanding that criminals see themselves as good people should help well-meaning individuals avoid wasting time in a fruitless effort to boost the criminal's already gigantic ego.

Law enforcement officers know that criminals believe they are good human beings, and incorporate this information into their interrogation strategies. They tell an offender that they understand he has a good heart and perhaps did not intend to harm someone. This comes across not only as less abrasive, but also as more sympathetic, than coming at the individual as though he is totally evil. A detective was interviewing a thirty-five-year-old man just after he had been apprehended as the main suspect for murdering his friend in the heat of an argument. In a comforting tone, the officer said to him, "It's been a tough few hours here, but you seem like a really nice kid. I know you're not a bad guy. You're a good guy, you know, and sometimes bad things happen to good people. We just want to know the truth about what happened. We're all in this situation. We want to help you get through this but you have to, you know, be willing to work with us, to be honest with us." The idea behind such an approach is that a suspect may be more forthcoming once he is assured that his interrogator considers him to be a good human being.

12

Mental Illness, or a Criminal Personality?

Misdiagnosis of a Dangerous Person

I received a telephone call from a criminal defense attorney asking me to evaluate Clay, thirty-two years old, who had been arrested for burglary. Little did I know that this would begin a tumultuous four-year relationship of working with one of the most difficult to manage and dangerous individuals that I had encountered. Clay was a veteran of psychiatric outpatient and inpatient programs, emergency crisis centers, day treatment programs, and stints in the county jail. Although he had ceased living with his frazzled and distraught parents, they always supported his getting treatment. They had been put through the wringer since he was a young child, and had first sought mental health treatment for their son when he was nine years old. They had one other adult son, who had posed no particular difficulties and was functioning independently and responsibly.

Always strong-willed, Clay started to resist attending

school in fourth grade, turned most parental requests into a battleground, began using a variety of drugs as a teenager, and flew into rages during which he punched holes in walls at home and physically lashed out at his parents. A high school graduate, Clay was intelligent and creative, but disorganized and easily distracted, seldom following through on any project, hobby, or interest. He worked at many jobs but either quit out of boredom or was fired because he was irritable, intimidating, and generally resistant to doing things on others' terms.

Because Clay was disinclined to seek treatment, mental health professionals encountered him mainly during crises when he was brought to them by a parent or through the legal process. There were occasions when he agreed to treatment because life seemed hopeless. During the sporadic course of his mental health treatment, psychiatrists and psychologists diagnosed Clay with a variety of conditions, and doctors prescribed nearly two dozen medications in line with their assessments. Clay's records document that, at different times, he was homicidal, suicidal, psychotic, anxious, paranoid, and a substance abuser. In short, he seemed to be a walking textbook of psychopathology.

Clay spent as long as two straight months in residential psychiatric facilities. That rarely happens unless a person pays out of his own pocket or has unusually good insurance. His diagnoses ranged from schizophrenia, a potentially crippling chronic disease, to an anxiety disorder that sometimes lends itself to mild medication and brief outpatient treatment. Although Clay had been diagnosed with an array of mental disorders, some hospital staff members who observed him during eight-hour shifts realized that his conduct stemmed from deliberate choices rather than from a mental illness. Not surprisingly, Clay was a manipulator who frequently left inpatient facilities against medical advice. Here is a summary of his hospitalization and treatment.

» Two weeks in a hospital at age seventeen for anxiety and insomnia.

DIAGNOSIS: ANXIETY REACTION, PASSIVE DEPENDENT PERSONALITY

• "Excessive dependence and reluctance to take responsibility
for his own life."
• Clay was urged to take steps toward independence, e.g., look
for a job; his response was to get angry and leave the hospital
against medical advice.

» Three years later. Two weeks in a hospital after a physical altercation with his mother (whom he described as "flaky" but
"a good person"), then overdosing on sleeping pills. Delusions
of a religious nature reported.

DIAGNOSIS: SCHIZOPHRENIA, PARANOID TYPE

• Described as withdrawn, cynical, refused to answer
questions; became irritable when questions were repeated; said
that people were following him and stealing his money.
• Social worker reported that he was "somewhat of a game
player and is able to manipulate people."
• Recommended long-term hospitalization "for his own
protection and in view of his inability to cope."
• Transferred to another hospital for an involuntary admission
and three-month stay.

» One year later. Two and a half months in a hospital. Admitted after police were called because of a physical altercation
with his father (whom he referred to as "straightlaced but a
good person"). Father bailed him out of jail so he could be
hospitalized.

DIAGNOSIS: ACUTE UNDIFFERENTIATED SCHIZOPHRENIA,
BORDERLINE PERSONALITY ORGANIZATION

- There is a note that Clay displayed signs of "autism," but no details were provided.

» Three years later. Hospital admission: complained of auditory hallucinations, confusion, and suicidal ideation.

DIAGNOSIS: SCHIZOPHRENIA, CHRONIC UNDIFFERENTIATED

- Clay left the hospital against medical advice.

» Later that same year. Hospital admission: taking excessive medication, drinking, depressed, thought he was dying; complained of hallucinations and delusions.

DIAGNOSIS: SCHIZOAFFECTIVE DISORDER

- Clay left the hospital against medical advice.

» Later that year. Hospital admission (voluntary) for three weeks.

DIAGNOSIS: ACUTE DEPRESSIVE REACTION, INADEQUATE PERSONALITY DISORDER

» One year later. Hospital admission for depression; overdosed on prescription medication and alcohol.

DIAGNOSIS: MAJOR DEPRESSION RECURRENT

- Clay said he was no longer suicidal and signed himself out against medical advice.

» One year later. A two-day involuntary detention at a mental health facility after having thoughts about murdering his ex-fiancée.

DIAGNOSIS: CHARACTER DISORDER, RULE OUT PASSIVE/DEPENDENT

- "He was cooperative and oriented in all spheres. He denied hallucinations, delusions, and ideas of reference. His insight and social judgment were good."
- Again, he left against medical advice.

» Four years later. Admitted to the hospital through emergency services complaining of depression and vague suicidal ideation. Three weeks in the hospital.

DIAGNOSIS: ADJUSTMENT REACTION WITH MIXED FEATURES

- Problem identified as "ineffective coping."
- Said, "I wanted to buy a gun and kill myself." The hospital chart then states that [Clay] "denied emphatically having any suicidal thoughts."
- Complained about premature ejaculation.

It is very challenging for mental health professionals to figure out what is going on with a person who, like Clay, presents such a complicated picture, especially when those who are trying to help him have little opportunity to interact with him long-term while he is living outside of a residential facility. I had that opportunity. After I evaluated Clay, I was asked to treat him as an outpatient.

Clay was coherent, lucid, and restrained in his emotional expression. I never saw him in a psychotic state. At our first meeting, he acknowledged, "I've always been difficult to live with. There are times I choose to be selfish." Clay disclosed almost immediately a nearly lifelong pattern of destructive and illegal behavior that included almost every type of crime—theft, forgery, arson, substance abuse, drug distribution, abuse of animals, assault, driving infractions, disorderly conduct, and destruction of property. He also acknowledged sexual arousal at physical contact with the child of a girlfriend. At times, Clay grew despondent enough to contemplate how he might kill himself, and also angry enough to think about killing the woman who'd broken their engagement. With respect to the former, Clay assured me, "Killing myself is something I'd never do. I'm afraid of the hereafter."

"Ideas that I manufacture become real," Clay volunteered. He explained that he formulated ideas about how specific situations ought to turn out, then acted on that basis. This was not an indicator of a psychotic thought process, but rather evidence of Clay's unrealistic expectations that people were to do whatever he wanted. His mother told me, "All he thinks of is himself. The poor thing. He can't get out of himself."

Clay demonstrated extremes of patterns described in this book. If he didn't like a job, a person, an activity, or something about a hospital stay, he'd get angry and walk away. He said about Alcoholics Anonymous, "I just get angry at A.A. I don't like what I hear. I leave there feeling like drinking." He denounced a day treatment program as "bullshit" and a "frivolous waste of time" because the participants were worse off than he was. The one plus was that he found it to be "a nice place to flirt." Clay got along well with people as long as they did what he wanted. Otherwise, they quickly became adversaries to whom he felt no obligation. Asked what he thought about his parents financially supporting him well into adulthood, Clay said cavalierly, "It doesn't bother me at all. I put on a show that it does." His ex-fiancée had told me, before ending their engagement, about their relationship deteriorating as Clay was unresponsive to her emotional needs. Having been attacked during one of Clay's rages, this young woman was frightened about extricating herself from their relationship. "I don't have the love I once did," she commented, adding, "He says he doesn't belong to me. He just uses my body. I ought to go my own way. I'm scared he'll want to retaliate because he'll want to hang on."

Clay acknowledged that his rages constituted his biggest problem. He said they sometimes occurred several times in a day, leaving him exhausted. His anger would surge to the point that he'd fantasize about killing people. He mentioned stopping at a grocery store where he sighted a correctional officer whom he remembered from jail. Driving to my office, he savored ideas of torturing and killing "that smart-ass punk."

Clay often complained of boredom. One day, he declared, "I'm bored. I'd like to do something illegal." And so he cruised through an area known as a hangout for prostitutes. At other times, he grew despondent, lamenting, "I have this condition for which there is no cure. I'll die in a mental institution or prison if I'm lucky." He felt "trapped in my own empty, meaningless existence."

Clay vacillated in his opinion as to the value of medication. Usually, he deemed it worthless, "not the answer." Occasionally he acknowledged that it helped him sleep and calmed homicidal thoughts. Clay intensely disliked the side effects of some medicines and asserted that it was absurd to issue prescriptions to a "drug addict," a term he applied to himself. Eventually, Clay conceded that he needed to take medication "for the county." This was a reference to his probation officer requiring that he comply with his psychiatrist's decisions regarding medication.

Clay's psychiatrist wrote in a brief report that Clay "presents a chronic danger." He cited the extreme shifts in Clay's moods and behavior, which seemed to occur without warning. He referred to Clay experiencing "manic phases" accompanied by grandiose thinking, and dark depressive episodes that resulted in suicidal thoughts. Having spent dozens of hours with Clay, I disagreed with that assessment. When Clay's unrealistic expectations were unfulfilled, he was downcast sometimes to the point of thinking that it would be best not to live. At other times, he thought he could master any task and be a colossal success. Neither view was realistic.

Antisocial people like Clay shift from unbridled optimism and a sense of invulnerability to unmitigated pessimism and despair. Their changes in outlook and demeanor may be visible to others. The oscillation does not signify the presence of a mental illness, such as the currently common diagnosis of "bipolar disorder." The highs and lows stem from the criminal's inflated sense of importance and his intense distress when his unrealistic expectations go unfulfilled.

My job was to help Clay become aware of his errors in thinking, and to bear in mind past and present consequences of that thinking. One might conjecture that a man like Clay would be indifferent to consequences. Having experienced many disagreeable results of his behavior, Clay learned to gain control of his thoughts and the accompanying extreme moods.

Clay practiced mentally pouncing on criminal thinking, considering its potentially harsh outcome, then deterring it. While discussing his thinking, Clay was very candid and specific. For example, he acknowledged, "I see little kids barely out of diapers, and I think about having sex with them." About his ex-fiancée, he said, "I'm glad she has to live in constant fear and has to sleep with one eye open." He also reported thoughts like "I'm just another burnout, a loser. I'm going to be like this for the rest of my life." Statements like these signaled danger, as they arose from self-pity and anger. Clay vowed that he would try to live like other people. Although he asserted, "I don't like to be told what to do," he obtained a job stocking shelves in a store.

We talked about how his failure to deter criminal thoughts and acts would guarantee the very outcomes he feared the most—lifelong institutionalization, homelessness, no friends, more anger and despondency. Clay's psychiatrist grew more positive and wrote, "Clay is appropriately concerned about controlling homicidal and sexual feelings so that he doesn't hurt anybody."

Clay was making a beginning at living responsibly. There was no quick fix. He had run-ins at work and was on the verge of quitting several times. Some days he struggled to make himself get out of bed. He learned to talk to himself constructively so that he would persevere. With satisfaction, he noted that he had hung onto his job for more than a year, a contrast to the three dozen jobs he had held during the last ten years. Clay exclaimed, "Working has done me some good, just the idea I can put in a forty-hour workweek and get a paycheck."

Clay observed, "I have a charismatic way about me. I have an obsession that other people must like me." On the surface, he had an engaging personality. This was a negative attribute in that Clay readily attracted people whom he manipulated and controlled, eventually alienating them. The result was he felt empty and resentful. Despite setbacks, Clay became more reasonable in his expectations of other people as he learned to be empathetic rather than doing whatever he pleased.

Progress was evident but erratic. With another bout of insomnia, Clay began to brood. He said he was fine when the sun was shining and he was out among people. But home at night, feeling lonely and unloved, Clay was asking himself, "What's it all for?" Despite all pillars of his support remaining accessible, Clay's progress was unraveling. He received a speeding ticket and then continued driving "to run away from myself." When I met with him, Clay declared, "I'm never going to be anything more than I am right now." Having been "preoccupied with death," he was starting to read obituaries. Calling himself a parasite, Clay then asserted, "I don't think I should have to work." He questioned the point of any job "where you have to be pleasant when you feel like shit," and said that he had been living life to little avail "the county's way." Clay mentioned experiencing "a few thunderstorms inside my head," a reference to bouts of intense anger. We again discussed his options—crime and its inevitable consequences, suicide, or change. As discouraged as Clay was, he did not want to end his life nor did he want to spend it in the penitentiary. Finding meetings with his probation officer helpful, he commented, "She laid it on the line. I heard every word. She's very good at what she does." Realizing that it had taken tremendous effort to progress, Clay was stunned at how quickly his gains could vanish. He indicated that he had regained perspective when he said that, overall, he had just experienced one of his best years. He remarked that even his brother was impressed by the "new, nice" Clay.

Clay commented about a critically important factor in avoiding a psychological collapse when he got discouraged. He stated, "I've got these people I can turn to in the middle of the night. There are a lot of people who truly care; it's not just what I can do for them." Clay said that, had it not been for his parents sticking with him, "I'd have been in a state hospital or jail. You and I would never have met. Possibly, I'd be on the streets." In an optimistic vein, Clay commented, "There's something good out there for me somewhere." He was struggling to push "bad thoughts" out of his mind. "I don't let them torment me," he asserted. Clay acknowledged that the threat of being sentenced to the state penitentiary if he committed another crime helped keep him out of trouble.

What continued to upset Clay was the idea of being an ordinary person. "Society expects me to present myself as an average person when I'm not. I'm above a lot of that." Then he articulated a sobering realization, "I've had opportunities all my life, but I've always gone for the instant reward. It's been a lifetime of making bad choices." But Clay did not consistently maintain this perspective. He continued to despair. He reported wanting to "throw in the towel." Through the probation officer's efforts, Clay gained admission to a residential mental health center. Surprisingly, he was positive about the facility, characterizing it as "where the thinking patients are—not just a warehouse," and compared it to a family with a caring staff. Clay became eligible for day treatment, where he progressed. My work with Clay ceased, as he was to remain in the day treatment program.

Many years later, I learned that Clay still had a strong support group of professionals as well as friends. Although his parents were supporting him, he was living on his own. He had not been arrested again, and his relationships had improved.

It is essential to identify the source of depression. Antidepressant medication will not alter the unrealistic expectations of a criminal. For a person like Clay, both anxiety and depression may be alleviated if he recognizes his thinking errors and applies correctives. There is no pill and no traditional form of treatment that will effectively address the core of the criminal personality. Once that personality is recognized, it requires a dedicated, trained, synchronized team to work with the person when he is in the community, focusing on the most salient issue—"errors in thinking." A strong commitment of resources is essential. And, of course, there is no guarantee of success. However, it is almost certain that the cost of not making the effort will be catastrophic.

The Myth of the "Out of Character" Crime

Some people with no prior criminal record commit serious crimes. Such was the case with Bernard Madoff, who embezzled millions of dollars from his hedge fund clients. You often read about such people, as they seem to have been good human beings who, quite unexpectedly, did something horrific. Friends, family, and coworkers describe them in a positive manner. These offenders are known to be accomplished in their professions, good neighbors, contributors to the community, devoted to their church, and ready to help anyone in need. It appears that something must have happened so that they "snapped" and committed a crime that was "out of character."

It is impossible to commit a crime that is out of character. It would be like asking a building to fly; it is not within the building's nature to do so. You cannot be other than who you are. A crime that appears out of character can be understood only by discerning what the character of the individual truly is. Madoff, as it turned out, was also an adulterer, a prevaricator, and sexual harasser. His chronic thievery spanned decades before an economic downturn finally exposed his massive Ponzi scheme.

I have evaluated many defendants who had fine reputations before committing heinous offenses. People who thought they knew these perpetrators well had no way of knowing what had been brewing in their minds, sometimes for years. In some instances, these individuals had committed other crimes but had been clever enough not to get caught, whereas others had long fantasized about engaging in certain behavior before finally doing so. Not surprisingly, when these "out of character" offenders are finally apprehended and held accountable, their main objective usually is to minimize their culpability (and prison sentences) by emphasizing their past exemplary conduct.

From the moment I meet a defendant, two evaluations are occurring. I am evaluating him, but he is also evaluating me. The criminal seeks to gain my sympathy by offering mitigating factors for what he has done. By claiming mental instability of one sort or another, he'll deny or minimize his culpability and hope to minimize the penalty. If he has a genuine but temporary mental disorder, this may become the focus of treatment, and he may improve. But the criminal personality remains untouched, and more injury to others is a certain result.

The defendant is likely to unleash a barrage of tactics to prevent my getting to know him. He may relate what he thinks I want to hear. He may blame other people. He may remain totally silent and refuse to cooperate. He may envelop me in a fog of vagueness, as he appears to answer questions while leaving a lot unsaid.

Sometimes these singular offenses are regarded as "crimes of passion." The person appears to lose control and commits an isolated, unplanned crime. These crimes frequently occur within families, as when, in the heat of an argument, a husband grabs a nearby item and, using it as a weapon, murders his wife. The perpetrator has not been a killer in the past and, according to statistics, is unlikely to kill again. But the person who commits a crime of passion and the calculating, cold-blooded murderer often have similar mentalities. Blustery, inflexible, and impatient, each demands that others do what he wants. They flare up at even minor slights. Instead of coping constructively with unpleasant situations, they compound their problems. When frustrated or disappointed, they angrily blame others. Vowing inwardly to even the score, thoughts enter their minds as to how to destroy a real or perceived adversary. The "out of character" crime may be preceded by a long series of threats or assaults that were hushed up or disregarded by the family. Despite appearances, when the homicide is finally committed, it is by a person to whom violence is no stranger. In the perpetrator's mind, he has already annihilated the source of his distress many times. In a sense, one could say he was programmed to murder his wife—programmed not by someone else, but by his own habitual pattern of thinking.

In December 2012, twenty-year-old Adam Lanza killed twenty-six people, twenty of them students at Sandy Hook Elementary School in Newtown, Connecticut. He had no criminal record. A former classmate told a television interviewer that Mr. Lanza "was not a troublemaker, not antisocial, not suggesting in any way that he could erupt like this."[1] However, detectives discovered that, when he was just ten years old, Mr. Lanza wrote "The Big Book of Granny," a chilling compilation of episodes in which "Granny" and her son carried a bag of weapons similar to those Mr. Lanza used ten years later in the Sandy Hook massacre. The ten-year-old described Granny threatening to shoot and kill children in their classroom. A character, Dora the Berserker, suggests, "Let's hurt children." So, for at least a decade, Mr. Lanza had entertained thoughts of killing children before he took action.

In a case that I know well, since I evaluated the perpetrator,

Nicholas, age twenty-seven, pursued a teenage girl as she got off the school bus, then followed her into her home and committed a brutal rape. Having watched her for a number of days, he had determined that she was alone until her parents arrived home early in the evening. People who had known Nicholas his entire life thought it impossible that he was capable of even thinking of such a crime. His attorney obtained glowing character references attesting to how conscientious, honest, and accomplished he was. As a little kid, he'd pulled his wagon through the neighborhood offering vegetables from the family garden. However, when the police searched his home, they found hidden away a stack of written, detailed, graphic sexual scenes that Nicholas had spent years composing. The fantasies were laden with cruelty and violence as he envisioned forcing himself upon males and females, children and teenagers. Nicholas especially relished the idea of being the first to have sex with inexperienced teenage girls. This young man had followed women whom he worked with at his evening job. He sat outside their homes in his car, fantasizing and masturbating. However, he took no action until he stalked the girl whom he raped. The crime Nicholas committed was very much "in character," but there was no way anyone could have divined the thoughts that he'd had over many years.

Stella was stopped by a security guard as she left a department store with expensive items of clothing concealed under her coat. Her arrest came as a total shock to her mother, brother, and three sisters. Although family members found her difficult to get along with, they never suspected she was a thief. Stella worked hard and was extremely devoted to her mother, who had cancer. As it turned out, committing grand larceny was very much in character. For years, Stella had engaged in massive amounts of shoplifting without getting caught.

My job in conducting a psychological evaluation is to place the crime in context, to make sense of what, on the surface, seems to make no sense. It is difficult to get to know a person well, and it can be accomplished only over time. One can imagine the challenge of understanding an individual's character in a short period under less than ideal circumstances. The person has been arrested, and I may be seeing him in jail. Because gaining an understanding of his background, personality, and legal status cannot be done quickly, I usually spend many hours interviewing him. To enhance my understanding of how these individuals have functioned in different aspects of life, I interview family members, friends, work colleagues, and counselors. In addition, I review employment records, financial documents, police reports, school files, and records of any mental health treatment.

It may seem that a person has committed an "out of character" crime because he "snapped." That is to say, he was enduring such intense stress that, finally, he reached a breaking point. Let's look closely at what this really means. Consider a man who gets laid off from work during a company-wide reduction in force. Infuriated at the injustice and seeking revenge, he obtains a gun, returns to his workplace, and starts shooting. A person's reaction to adversity depends on his personality. In this example, the perpetrator's colleagues who were also laid off did not seek revenge, even though they too may have been treated unfairly. Some may have become depressed and reclusive. Others may have turned to heavy drinking. No doubt, some became fiercely determined to search the Internet and go door-to-door seeking a new job. Unexpected and tragic events occur. The critical question is how the person deals with what happens. The key to understanding a person's behavior is to know that person's character. Unfortunately, the criminal personality of some people may be hidden even from close friends and family members, until it is too late.

"Senseless" Crimes

In August 2012, an Australian student was gunned down while jogging in the Oklahoma town of Duncan. News reports stated that the suspects who confessed to the homicide did not know their victim and selected him at random.[2] The reason they gave was that they were "bored." To relieve their boredom, they pursued him in their car and shot him in the back. In the aftermath of the shooting, people tried to make sense of what seemed to be a senseless crime. Some attributed a racial motive but there was insufficient evidence for that explanation.

How could boredom explain killing a total stranger? If one understands the workings of the criminal mind, it is feasible to grasp that boredom can indeed be the motive. Earlier in this chapter, I mentioned that Clay said he wanted to do something illegal to relieve boredom. What he and others like him find intolerable is to live within the constraints of the law and of society. Crime is an antidote to boredom. As discussed previously, there is excitement in every phase of a crime.

Seemingly senseless crimes make sense if one understands the mentality of the offender. The common motive behind many crimes that seem senseless is the thrill of doing what is forbidden. Thomas, age twenty-six, discussed what was on his mind as a young teenager: "I thought I'd be a serial killer." Increasingly fascinated by serial killers, he thought about "how they kill, the pleasurable, even sexual evil. I idolized Charles Manson." Thomas mused over how great it would be "to be worshipped and have people kill for me." He commented, "I like guns. It's powerful to hold one in your hand." Although he was incarcerated before he killed anyone, Thomas harmed people just for the thrill. He said he enjoyed "ruining a relationship on purpose, breaking people down, picking on them, putting them in situations where they'd get rejected, reminding them they're a piece of shit." He would single out an "easy target" just to entertain himself and, without provocation, make that person miserable. Thomas recalled targeting a boy whom he didn't even know. "Daily I'd see him, take his money, beat him up, and torment him." Thomas could not conceive of living like responsible people do. Crime was the oxygen of his life.

On April 2, 2014, at Ft. Hood, Texas, Ivan Lopez killed three people and injured sixteen. He was said to have suffered from anxiety, depression, and possibly post-traumatic stress. After this and every other mass shooting, there is a lot of head scratching and "what if" conversations. Were there recent warning signs? Could the person have been identified as "at risk" for such behavior before the calamity? If the perpetrator was already in treatment, what went unaddressed? Will additional funding for mental health services prevent such disasters? Can potential mass murderers be identified when they are children?

At this point, we know that perpetrators usually do not announce their intentions to commit crimes. In those few instances when they do, they do not supply the specifics. No one knows if, when, or where they will strike. We may be able to identify individuals who already have a history of making threats or engaging in violence. That does not mean that, under current laws, we have the ability to detain them, much less force them into intensive treatment. And, in those instances when we can compel them to receive treatment, there is no way to assure their cooperation. At first, the least restrictive approach must be tried, which usually means outpatient treatment. If a potential mass shooter is in treatment, it is likely to be once or twice a week, which is totally inadequate. It is hardly surprising that criminals do not bare their souls to strangers. They deploy tactics to keep adversaries (which is how most criminals regard therapists and counselors) at bay, often by lulling them into believing they know more than they do. Criminals spend their lives deceiving others about who they are. A therapist is just another person to conquer. Many treatment "graduates" have gone on to commit shocking crimes.

Eccentrics, loners, and scary people inhabit our free society. Very few will become mass shooters. Absent their being identified and adjudicated as a threat to others or themselves, there is no way to engage them in treatment and be sure they will remain there. All of the above does not mean we should throw up our hands and abandon the effort to improve mental health services. But it does mean that society's expectations of mental health professionals needs to be realistic. In the meantime, we must accept that these people whom we cannot identify or intensively treat will surface and wreak havoc until our laws change and our science improves.

"Impulse Disorder" Crimes

To some observers, it appears that offenders repeatedly commit crimes because they are at the mercy of impulses over which they lack control. A child steals from his parents, from classmates, from neighbors, from stores, and from construction sites. It seems that no matter where he goes, he returns with something that does not belong to him. He may be labeled a kleptomaniac because he appears unable to resist impulses to steal. But behind the appearance of an uncontrollable impulse lies the stark reality of the offender's calculating and proficient method of operating. Wherever he is, the thief habitually scans the environment to take advantage of opportunities. He does not have to develop an elaborate scheme for every theft. He devotes about the same degree of thought to his stealing as most people give to driving. Both acts become matters of habit, and for each, vigilance is necessary.

What is habitual is not necessarily compulsive and beyond one's control. To say that a person has a habit of doing something does not signify that he lacks responsibility for his actions. Just as a person can adapt his driving to icy pavement, so a thief adapts his pilfering to current conditions—what kind of surveillance he thinks there is, the accessibility of the merchandise, the location of exits, the number of people between him and the closest exit. This type of thinking is calculating, not compulsive. If the thief is apprehended, he may claim that he was compelled by an irresistible inner force to steal. By throwing the case into the bailiwick of the psychologist, he hopes to be evaluated as not responsible.

Sandra was a pro at shoplifting. Half-jokingly, she said that she might as well be called a "customer sales representative," because she was so accomplished at taking "orders" from "customers," locating items at bargain prices, and then "filling" these orders by pilfering the requested merchandise, which she then sold. For years, she was skillful enough to avoid detection. On one of her sprees, she became careless and was finally caught. Sandra stole so frequently that a mental health professional might conclude that she was in the grip of a compulsion. That was far from the case. Instead, she was highly skilled at what she considered her "job."

A person who frequently sets fires may be referred to as a pyromaniac, especially if readily discernible motives such as revenge or jealousy seem to be absent. Like "kleptomania," "pyromania" refers to a recurrent failure to resist impulses. I have found that a pyromaniac is a calculating person who is very much in control of what he does. He chooses the time and place to set a fire, then takes precautions to avoid detection. By setting fires, he wields enormous power over human life and property. He can terrorize a community and inflict enormous damage. Then he can smugly sit back, enjoying his triumph as a building becomes engulfed in flames. As he watches the fire department struggling to contain the blaze, he is reasonably certain that he will not be caught. A 2012 article in the *Journal of the American*

Academy of Psychiatry and the Law reports, "Individuals whose pyromania goes into remission often engage in other impulsive or compulsive behaviors (e.g., gambling, substance abuse).[3] This observation illustrates a point made throughout this book. If an individual with a criminal personality ceases committing a particular type of crime, he likely will engage in others.

From my clinical interviews, I have concluded that so-called compulsive thieves and arsonists are simply people who enjoy what they do. They are as much in control of their behavior as the bank robber or offender who commits arson for profit. Any criminal activity, repetitive or not, could be considered abnormal in that it is socially proscribed, and most people do not engage in it. But this does not automatically make it a sign of illness or thereby exonerate the offender from responsibility. For behind such crimes is a person who deliberates and acts with the knowledge of possible consequences, and this information makes him more calculating as he pursues his objectives.

Although some delight in the chase, criminals exercise extreme caution to avoid actually being caught. Usually they are successful, but sometimes even a pro can get overconfident. When an offender errs in his assessment of risk or makes an obvious gaffe, a psychiatrist or psychologist may conclude that he really wanted to get caught, instead of seeing the offender as a person who is overconfident and slips up. They may even go a step further and claim that his behavior represented a cry for help. I have never found this to be the case.

Insanity

The insanity defense is seldom used, and it rarely succeeds. (Idaho, Montana, Kansas, and Utah have abolished it. In each of those states, except for Kansas, a defendant can be found guilty and mentally ill.) To convince psychiatrists, psychologists, and the court that he is insane, a criminal must satisfy one of several legal definitions of insanity, depending on the legal test used in a particular jurisdiction. Does he know right from wrong (1843 M'Naghten Rule)? Is the crime the product of a mental disease or defect (1954 Durham Rule)? Does the defendant lack substantial capacity to appreciate the criminality of his conduct or to conform to the requirements of the law (1972 American Law Institute Penal Code)? Twenty-five states use M'Naghten, twenty states and the District of Columbia use the American Law Institute Penal Code, and only New Hampshire uses the Durham Rule. In some states, the burden of proof of insanity is on the defendant; in others, it's on the state.

It is possible for a person who commits two similar crimes within a very short time period to be found guilty in one state and not guilty by reason of insanity in another, depending upon the legal standard. In *Kier Sanders v. State of Mississippi,* a defendant was found to be insane for the killing of one grandparent and guilty of murder for killing the other, even though he shot each of them, one right after the other, with the same weapon.[4] The judge sentenced Sanders to life in prison with the provision that if the law changed to allow him to be released on parole, Mr. Sanders would then be committed to the state hospital.

Just as his crimes have been rational and deliberate acts, so is the criminal's scheming of the insanity defense. A person who is accused of a crime may attempt to fake mental illness, using behavior that ranges from the subtle to the bizarre, depending on what tactic he surmises will be most convincing. He may pretend to be at the mercy of voices that direct him. He may proclaim that he acted as a messenger from God. He may feign delusions of persecution, asserting that people are plotting against him. A suicidal gesture may help accomplish what the criminal wants. He notifies a cell mate as to when he will hang himself and requests that a correctional officer be summoned to cut him down. He figures that if he is considered a suicide risk, he will be shipped to a hospital. Claiming amnesia is a strategy that may stymie expert evaluators and tie the hands of a jury.

Displays of symptoms of mental illness may be dramatic in jail, during courtroom proceedings, or at a hospital where the criminal is sent for observation. One murderer brought the court proceedings to a halt when, after a recess of the trial, he refused to emerge from his cell. No amount of persuasion could budge him. The judge then ordered correctional officers to use force to return him to his seat in the courtroom so he would be present at his own trial. This man had been lucid and cooperative while in jail and during his psychological evaluation. Thus, his belligerent conduct was seen for what it was, although his defense attorney tried to argue that the man's conduct provided evidence of mental illness.

Rarely does a criminal believe that he is mentally ill, and he is likely to be offended if anyone calls him crazy. But he is willing to be called just about anything if it can help him beat a charge. Some crimes are so sordid that it would seem they could originate only in a mind that was sick. What is crucial, however, is not how sordid or bizarre the crime is but whether the perpetrator knew right from wrong (or satisfied whatever legal standard for insanity was in force in the jurisdiction where the crime occurred).

Dan killed his aunt with a hatchet, severing her head. The crime was so grizzly that one would likely think the perpetrator had to have been mentally ill. The defense attorney filed an insanity plea. Before the homicide, Dan, age twenty-four, was no stranger to violence. He acknowledged having had a fascination with weapons since he was twelve years old. His history of criminal behavior began early in adolescence when he destroyed property in his family's home, used illegal drugs, and engaged in assaultive conduct and domestic violence. With respect to the homicide, Dan said he was masturbating in his room when he heard his aunt coming up the stairs. Putting on underwear, he grabbed a belt and met her on the stairway, wrapped the belt around her head tightly, then strangled her. Thinking that she was still breathing, Dan dragged her to the basement and hacked off her head. He told me, "I thought if I cut her head off, no way in hell can she be breathing." While being interrogated by the police, Dan claimed that the woman's death was accidental. When I inquired whether severing her head to ensure she was not breathing was an accident, he replied, "No." Dan wanted to be certain that his aunt did not survive to summon the police or to testify in court. Dan had no history of mental illness, but claimed insanity. The jury found him guilty of first-degree murder.

Having a mental illness does not mean that a person loses the ability to make choices, or that he loses the capacity to distinguish between right and wrong. However, some cases certainly can be confusing. Shortly after Norman pointed a gun at a bank teller and escaped with cash, he was apprehended and charged with armed robbery. The court ordered an evaluation to determine his state of mind at the time of the offense. Norman maintained that the "insect god" who was his father ordered him to hold up the bank, and he was obeying that order. He had a prior history of mental illness, including hospitalizations.

Norman had experienced long periods of unemployment, but he was able to live on his own because his parents helped him financially. Before he robbed the bank, Norman was running out of money, and debts were mounting. With a few hundred dollars, he went to Atlantic City, New Jersey, to gamble. He lost money but went there again and wagered what little money he had left. This time, he had better luck. Nonetheless, he did not use his winnings to pay his debts, and bill collectors continued to hound him. He said that as the son of the insect god, he turned to his "father" for guidance and was told that he could improve his situation by robbing a bank. He used the gambling proceeds to purchase a gun, and committed the crime.

I could never determine whether Norman concocted the "insect god" to help his legal case or whether the "insect god" was a manifestation of occasional psychotic episodes. As I examined the sequence of events, it became clear that Norman had made deliberate choices at critical junctures. His crime had to do with obtaining money that he desperately needed. Norman selected a location where gambling was legal. He was able to purchase a bus ticket and successfully got himself there and back. Having lost money on the first trip, Norman decided to try again and was more successful. He could have spent that money in many ways. However, his choice was to purchase a gun to gain access to even more money. He didn't go to a playground or to a butcher, but to a bank where he committed the robbery. Like Norman, a person may be mentally ill but still retain the ability to plan and execute a complex crime.

I have interviewed criminal defendants who claimed that voices instructed them to kill. Rick maintained that he heard voices directing him to kill himself or to kill others. Yet, until he finally killed someone, Rick spent more than a decade ignoring the voices, disobeying their commands. He had made no suicidal efforts, nor had he become involved in any physical altercation. The reason Rick gave for killing a friend was that voices told him the friend intended to kill him. It turned out that he and the friend had a history of arguments that became quite heated. So the homicide occurred within the context of a volatile relationship. Rick acknowledged that during the actual killing, he did not hear voices at all. After he murdered his friend, Rick initially concocted a story about being robbed and threatened. When the police apprehended him, Rick was rational enough to immediately comply with their instructions and submit to being arrested. A person can have cancer and chicken pox at the same time; one doesn't cause the other. And so a person can have a mental illness but still know right from wrong and make rational choices.

During three weeks in the fall of 2002, John Muhammad and Lee Boyd Malvo terrorized the Washington, D.C., region, killing ten people while wounding three others. Mr. Malvo, seventeen years old when he committed the crimes, was convicted of capital murder for gunning down FBI analyst Linda Franklin outside a store in Virginia. His attorneys entered an insanity defense. They maintained that, as a father figure, John Muhammad dominated and indoctrinated the youthful, impressionable Lee Malvo. Experts for the defense found Malvo to be suffering from a "dissociative disorder." According to the American Psychiatric Association, "[Its] essential feature . . . is a disruption in the usually integrated functions of consciousness, memory, identity, or perception."[5] The APA states that this disorder may manifest itself in people who have been "subjected to periods of prolonged and intensive coercive persuasion," such as that which occurs in brainwashing.

The heart of the defense's case was that Mr. Malvo was not himself because he was under "the spell of the charismatic but devious" John Muhammad. The *Washington Post* summarized the task of the defense as "trying to convince a jury that the Persian Gulf War veteran (i.e., Mr. Muhammad) transformed Malvo into an acolyte, a killer protégé who lost his capacity for sound judgment and free will as he succumbed to the psychological grip of his older companion."[6] A cult expert and a child soldier expert testified in Mr. Malvo's behalf. In addition to the defendant's lawyers, many analysts and commentators were convinced that Mr. Malvo suffered from a mental illness. The cover story of the November 6, 2002, issue of *Newsweek* was titled "The Sick World of the Snipers."[7]

I served as an expert for the prosecution during the mental health phase of the trial. My testimony is a matter of public record. I spent thirty-four hours interviewing Lee Boyd Malvo and did not find him to be this allegedly malleable youth who was led astray by an adult killer. In fact, Malvo told me in no uncertain terms that he was "not impressionable, not weak-minded." As a young boy, Malvo was strong-willed and had a quick temper that others feared. He told me about beating a fellow student with a garbage can after identifying him as the boy who had been stealing his lunches. He recalled wishing he had a machete to cut off the boy's hands. Before he ever met John Muhammad, Mr. Malvo stole from his mother, repeatedly shoplifted, and killed more than a dozen feral cats with a slingshot and metal bearings. Another psychologist who testified for the prosecution observed that Mr. Malvo changed his story in order to accommodate his attorney's depiction of him as a naive and needy boy, ripe for indoctrination. It was clear to both me and the other psychologist that Lee Boyd Malvo eagerly embraced Mr. Muhammad and shared much of his view of the world. The jury convicted Lee Boyd Malvo of capital murder and sentenced him to life in prison.*

I HAVE BEEN depicted as a person who does "not believe in" the insanity defense. This is not accurate. I have certainly observed criminals malingering in order to be found legally insane and thereby avoid a prison sentence. However, every case is new, and my work is not guided by what I "believe" but by the evidence. In the past several years, I have found two defendants to qualify as legally insane under the laws of the Commonwealth of Virginia. In one instance, the jury disagreed and found the defendant sane. In the other, I was selected by the prosecution to evaluate a woman who was charged with assault on a police officer, reckless driving, and destruction of property.

Ariele awakened one morning hearing voices loudly proclaiming that the world was coming to an end. The voices di-

---

* I discuss this case at greater length in my book *The Myth of the "Out of Character" Crime.*

rected her to go grocery shopping, obtain what she needed, and not worry about paying. When she arrived at the store, she was surprised and confused when she saw customers paying as usual. "I was upset because I thought everything was free," she recalled. Ariele encountered a store employee whom she perceived as advancing toward her in a menacing way. She responded by shoving the woman, knocking her down, after which she left the store empty-handed. Ariele saw a police cruiser pull up, but didn't suspect it had anything to do with her. She jumped into her car and took off for home. The police clocked her traveling at speeds up to eighty miles an hour in a congested area. Drivers got out of her way, and pedestrians froze in their tracks. Siren blaring, a squad car pursued her. Ariele did not have far to drive before she pulled into the alley leading to her apartment. She remembered seeing a police car in front of her. She had slowed down considerably but then plowed into the vehicle. She remembered the police officers directing her to get out of her car. However, she did not obey the command. She recalled that she felt no harm would befall her if she remained in her own automobile. The police tried to pull her out but encountered resistance. They used a Taser on Ariele, then dragged her out by her feet, handcuffed her, and called an ambulance.

The question was whether this woman was mentally ill, and if so, whether the mental illness impaired her to the extent that she did not know right from wrong. The police report indicated that Ariele drove skillfully, maneuvering at high speeds through traffic and arriving at her intended destination without incident—at least until she drove into the police car. Her purposeful driving seemed to indicate that perhaps her judgment was not so impaired. However, the route that she traveled she could follow by rote, so many times had she driven from her residence to the grocery store.

I spent many hours interviewing Ariele, members of her family, her psychiatrist, and her current social worker, and reviewed extensive medical records. The voices began bothering her during adolescence, but she didn't want anyone to know about them. As a young adult, she experienced the voices appearing and vanishing in line with her seesawing moods. After barely graduating from high school, she had several failed relationships with men. Because she thought she attracted only "bad men," Ariele purposefully gained nearly one hundred pounds so "I wouldn't attract them anymore." Ariele attempted suicide after being married less than half a year. When her husband found her locked in their bedroom, he summoned the police. Ariele recalled, "I wanted to lie in my bed and die peacefully." She was hospitalized and given electroshock treatments after she failed to respond to earlier attempts to help her.

After her release, Ariele held a series of jobs, performing well at each until she started hearing voices and behaving erratically. Ariele's brother commented, "She is the most loving, compassionate person when she's on her meds. Off her meds, it's scary to be around her. She's a person you don't know."

Ariele was treated by psychiatrists who prescribed medication, which she took depending on how she felt. A few months before her arrest, she stopped treatment and ceased taking all medication. Her psychiatrist considered her "totally psychotic" when he last met with her. When Ariele did not keep her next appointment, the doctor tried unsuccessfully to contact her, then called her brother. She had reached the point of withdrawing from everyone, including family, and secluded herself in her apartment. She remembered hearing "numerous voices, male and female, that were almost demonic." Ariele commented, "I thought they were real. They'd come in and talk to me day and night." Her brother was so alarmed that he called the police. At the crisis center, she impressed the intake worker as being in good enough condition for him to record in his notes that Ariele's responses were "logical, responsive, and cogent." Consequently, she did not meet the criteria for hospitalization. Ariele explained to me that she had held herself together long enough to get through the interview because she feared being locked up for the rest of her life in a psychiatric hospital.

After her arrest, Ariele ended up confined in an adult detention center, where she continued to hear voices. "I just put the covers over my head," she recalled. She refused to speak to her attorney and rebuffed her mother the first several times she came to visit. "I thought I wasn't safe," she recalled. "I was still hearing voices and seeing things."

Ariele was transferred to a state hospital where she could be evaluated around the clock and given appropriate medication. She recalled thinking, "This place is wonderful. They talk to me like a real person, not like I am a nut. I wasn't locked up in a cage and was getting all my medicine." While a patient at the hospital, Ariele did not want to plead insanity, because she was terrified that she would be locked away indefinitely. Because of this fear, she would have had no reason to feign mental illness.

Not only did Ariele have a long history of psychotic behavior, but at the time of the offense she was confused, disorganized, and unresponsive even to the police officers who had to drag her out of her car. In my report to the prosecutor I stated that, at the time of the offense, Ariele was sufficiently impaired by a mental illness to an extent that she could not appreciate the nature, character, and consequences of her actions. The case was not prosecuted. Ariele remained in the community, supported by her family, and closely monitored by mental health treatment providers.

The insanity defense remains controversial. There are several caveats for those who undertake these evaluations. One is that it takes many hours of probing to penetrate the defendant's self-serving statements and to understand his thinking processes. Second, it should not be assumed that because a person is psychotic at the time of the evaluation, he was psychotic at the time of the crime. Finally, even if it can be ascertained that the person was mentally ill when he committed the crime, it does not necessarily follow that he did not know right from wrong.

Psychiatric hospitalization can give a criminal an excuse for more crimes. Each time he is treated at a psychiatric facility, there is additional documentation of instability. Whenever he is arrested, he will be regarded as an offender with a psychiatric condition. Consequently, for a new offense he may wind up again in a hospital rather than a prison. If he thinks that he can get a better deal, perhaps a softer life, in a hospital than in a prison, he will continue trying to outfox the "shrinks."

13

Locked Up

In mid-1982, when the first edition of this book was being written, there were 394,380 inmates in prison in the United States. At the end of 2011, 2,266,800 adults were incarcerated in federal and state prisons or county jails.[1] In addition, 4,814,200 were on probation or parole. In 2012, approximately one in every thirty-five adults in the United States was incarcerated or on probation or parole.

Prisons are said to serve four functions. The first is deterrence: people obey the laws and do not commit crimes because they wish to avoid losing their freedom. The second function is retribution: society wants to "get even with" and punish those who have committed crimes. A third function is incapacitation: criminals cannot harm law-abiding citizens if they are locked up. Finally, prison is supposed to provide opportunities for rehabilitation. That is why most prison systems use the term "corrections" in their official agency titles. Prisons, however, do not usually contribute to the rehabilitation of criminals, as you will see in this chapter.

Movements to reform prisons are accelerating in strength and scope. One reason is the skyrocketing expense of incarceration. It has been estimated that the cost of housing an inmate in a New York City jail is $167,000 per year, the same as the cost of a four-year Ivy League education. At the end of 2011, a year at Princeton University cost $37,000, versus $44,000 for a year of confinement in a New Jersey state prison. Critics of current sentencing practices hold that, with new developments in technology, punishment of nonviolent, low-risk offenders can be imposed without incarceration and without sacrifice of the public's safety. GPS monitoring and the use of electronic leg "bracelets" are already widely used to provide close supervision.

Reformers have also been turning their attention to improving conditions inside correctional facilities. Because of overcrowding, some states have been ordered by courts to release inmates before their sentences end. Another focus of reform efforts has been to address the frequent incidence of sexual assault in prison. In 2003, the Prison Rape Elimination Act was passed with the objective of eliminating rape in adult and juvenile correctional institutions.[2] Another area singled out by reform activists is the use of lengthy periods of isolation in so-called supermax (short for "super-maximum security") prisons. These facilities, purportedly designed to hold the most violent and dangerous offenders, have been under attack for violating the Constitution's Eighth Amendment, which prohibits cruel and unusual punishment.

A fallacy perpetuated for decades has been that prisons, jails, and juvenile detention centers serve as schools for crime; that they transform people into worse human beings than they were before they were incarcerated. Prison is a breeding ground for crime only insofar as criminals expand their associations and find support for their own antisocial patterns of thought and behavior. Although a criminal is likely to hear almost nonstop conversations about crime, drugs, and sex, he chooses whether to participate or ignore them. He is not a hapless victim who is corrupted by fellow inmates. He has made choices in the past, and he continues to make choices as to whether to continue his life of crime, either within the institution or when he returns to society.

A related fallacy is that it is impossible for an incarcerated criminal to change because of the corrosive influence of the prison culture. In one of its publications, the Michigan Family Impact Seminars stated, "Social survival involves evasive and deceitful behaviors and aggression and violence. A prison environment discourages the behaviors required to be a responsible [person] or even a caring and compassionate adult."[3] Whereas it is true that most inmates have little interest in change, they do not interfere with the small number who do. I have spoken at length with inmates who indicated that they would make time serve them while they served their time. This meant that they would work at self-improvement so they could live a more responsible and thus a better life upon release. As long as they stayed out of the action in prison, remained sociable, and did not hold themselves up as better than others, their fellow inmates did not interfere.

An offender serving a sentence for a homicide made the following observations about the effects of prison on inmates. "A prison can be a school for anything that you want to study, whether it be a vocation, a GED, a second language, or crime. It is all on the individual, what they choose to focus on, if they decide to focus on anything. If they do choose crime, there is no lack of instructors. Many prisoners find someone who can be an asset to them, to talk and learn about crime and plan future crimes together. This is all in the attempt to commit the perfect crime without getting caught and make lots of money. I know of prisoners who deliberate hours per day for years on future criminalistic endeavors." This inmate wanted no part of those discussions. Instead, he was diligently working on physical conditioning; reading a variety of books, including those on self-improvement; studying religion; and attending classes. He remained on civil terms with other prisoners and cooperated with the prison staff, but mostly kept to himself.

In prison or on the street, criminals have the same patterns of thinking. Once they adjust to their surroundings, most are determined to establish themselves in the inmate hierarchy. Inmates have different methods of getting what they want in prison, just as they did outside. Some wage open warfare individually or in gangs, challenge staff at every turn, and brazenly defy regulations. An inmate may conclude that direct confrontations with staff or fellow prisoners are futile, that there is wisdom in restraint. The model inmate may be the consummate actor. Contemptuous of everyone from the warden to the correctional officers, he plays up to them. By lining up allies, he expects to make life easier. Even the toughest con may decide that—in order to score brownie points—it is worthwhile to scrub his cell, buff the floors each morning until they gleam, and work diligently at his institutional job.

One inmate, who never had an infraction during years of a penitentiary sentence for second-degree murder, expressed a view that is prevalent among inmates. He stated, "I have developed such a contempt for the officers it's almost indescribable. I don't even think of them as people. It'd be hard to distinguish between us and them if they weren't wearing uniforms. They are criminals who joined the force before they could be arrested. I do think of myself as superior to many people I meet here— inmates, guards and staff. It's hard not to."

Another inmate's parents asked me to evaluate their twenty-seven-year-old son, Devon, while he was in jail. His parents thought they detected a genuine desire on his part to change. They wanted to know if I agreed with their assessment, and to learn how they might help their son while he was confined and upon his release. It was not difficult to understand why Devon's parents were hopeful. From what they could discern, their son had a new attitude toward them and toward life in general. During visits to the jail, they heard Devon speak about returning home and restarting his life under their guidance. However, Devon presented a decidedly mixed picture to me. He professed to want to change, and pointed to the fact that he had behaved himself while in jail; he'd received no write-ups for infraction of the rules. Nonetheless, as we spoke, it was clear that his idea of change was to conform in order to avoid hassles with the staff, but still do whatever he pleased.

Devon said that he "caught a charge" for selling drugs and possessing an unregistered gun. Starting in childhood, he had engaged in burglary, grand larceny, destruction of property and, later, numerous probation violations. Devon was unusually specific in recalling his thought processes. He spoke graphically of his attitude toward his cell mate. "I see weaknesses, and fuck with his self-esteem. He's overweight and eats and eats. I make him feel like he's fat and lazy. I make fun of the photo of his girlfriend. I torment him. I piss on his blanket and spit on him and piss in his cup. I slashed him on the arm with a razor. I abuse him. He looks for my acceptance. As he becomes more and more appeasing to me, the more and more I abuse the power I have over him. He was very annoying in his weakness, and the gutless way he carried himself made him easier to prey on." Devon, a white man, revealed another aspect of his personality as he spoke of his attitude toward African American inmates. "I took the dice they gambled with when they weren't paying attention and flushed them down the toilet. I tend to look down on blacks and am frequently angered by them. I've come to have a lot of contempt for them." Priding himself on being sort of a master manipulator, Devon bragged, "I've learned to carry myself without being seen as a troublemaker. I instigate problems between others for my enjoyment. I even instigate others to do the instigating." Devon managed to change just enough to stay out of trouble, all the while continuing his criminal patterns.

The deputies at the facility had to deal with the mayhem Devon created, often without knowing its source.

Good behavior has its rewards in the achievement of special status or privileges and, in some instances, the possibility of early release. In some systems, an inmate can earn "good time" credit. Federal Sentencing Guidelines provide for up to a 15 percent reduction in time served for good behavior. Some states have even more liberal early release provisions. A prisoner may have one day of his sentence lopped off in return for a certain number of days of good behavior. But good behavior "inside the walls" is not necessarily a harbinger of good behavior after a prisoner is released. David Carpenter, the California "Trailside Killer," was so trusted by the prison staff that he was running counseling groups. A parole officer predicted that his days of lawlessness were over. This was during his incarceration for a brutal assault, *before* he was paroled and then killed innocent hikers in California parks.

The criminal believes that confinement is the last in a string of injustices that started with his arrest. Laws and others' rights meant little in the past, but now that he is confined, he becomes highly legalistic about asserting his own rights. Criminals who wind up in prison facing lengthy sentences or a death sentence frequently offer a litany of excuses for their predicament: the police were out to get them, turncoat accomplices who bargained for leniency were the real culprits, their defense attorneys were incompetent, the judge was biased, and the jurors already had their minds made up before they fully considered the evidence.

Long after he has begun serving time, a criminal may seek to overturn a verdict or have his sentence reduced. Some spend hours in the prison library poring over law books and composing appeals. Some criminals make a career as jailhouse lawyers, conducting legal research and preparing documents for themselves and other inmates, collecting money, property, and personal favors as a fee.

The assertion of rights continues throughout confinement and extends far beyond a preoccupation with legal statutes and procedures. As the criminal demands protection of his rights, he tries to intimidate members of the staff, who fear lawsuits and violence. He insists on his right to join an activity if it appeals to him, or asserts the right not to participate if he finds it distasteful. At different times he may assume opposite stands on the very same issue. He may demand psychological treatment and threaten to sue to get it, or he may invoke his right to refuse treatment.

When the doors of prison first lock behind them, some criminals are temporarily frightened, remorseful, and depressed. These emotions are not alien; criminals experience them occasionally on the street when they tire of the daily grind of looking over their shoulder, or when they regret disappointing people who care about them. Behind bars, they have plenty of time to think. The present is grim, and the future looks bleak. Some immerse themselves in prayer and reading religious books. Others ponder how to end it all. The turmoil and fear experienced by these criminals do not last. The man who trembles upon entry to prison may, in time, revert to what he was before—tough as nails. Although even some of the most seasoned criminals begin their sentences in despair, others enter prison hardboiled. If a man has committed crimes but never before served time, going to prison gives him status. Now that he has made the "pen," he is in the big leagues.

The behavior of an inmate may be geared initially to what he has heard about an institution before he enters it. Prisons gain reputation among their "alumni" and among other criminals who hear about life at a particular institution. Some are maximum-security institutions, notorious for being the end of the road for unmanageable convicts. These are often formidable fortresses with fences encased with multiple layers of razor wire, tall watchtowers monitored by armed guards, electronically controlled gates, and interior surveillance with closed-circuit television. But elaborate and costly security measures do not prevent highly volatile inmates from stabbing, raping, engaging in gang warfare, and rioting. The highest priority of an inmate is to survive. A new inmate knows that he must demonstrate from the outset that he is as tough as the next guy. In institutions housing violent offenders, the staff struggles to prevent inmates from taking over. Inmates occasionally win out and have the staff so intimidated that it depends on prisoners to maintain order.

At the opposite extreme are minimum-security facilities, known in the federal system as "camps." These institutions house the least dangerous offenders. Lacking foreboding towers and razor wire, some resemble college campuses. Inmates may wear and launder their own clothing, enjoy relatively liberal visiting hours, and have the opportunity to participate in a variety of academic and vocational training classes. The camps offer intramural sports and community-sponsored social activities.

Super-maximum security prisons have been constructed in more than two-thirds of the states. A federal supermax facility in Florence, Colorado, houses high-profile prisoners such as "Unabomber" Ted Kaczynski and Oklahoma City Federal Building bomber Terry Nichols, as well as terrorists who have endangered national security. Supermax institutions are intended for "the worst of the worst"—inmates so dangerous that they cannot be safely housed within the general population of other correctional institutions. These prisoners have been violent in society and have continued to be violent in confinement, assaulting and even killing staff and other inmates. Some have incited riots or are gang leaders. As mentioned, supermax prisons have become targets of lawsuits for violating the Eighth Amendment. Plaintiffs contend that inmates suffer from prolonged isolation and severe sensory deprivation in a harsh, psychologically traumatizing environment.

For example, Trent was serving a life sentence for first-degree murder. While incarcerated in different prisons, he amassed more than fifty conduct reports, some for extremely serious infractions. Trent was found in possession of a shank assembled from a nail and wood. There were numerous incidents in which he attacked inmates, punching, choking, knocking them to the floor and stomping on them. On one occasion, he punched an inmate in the head and continued beating him until two inmates intervened. Trent was constantly abusive to correctional officers. On one occasion, he wiped his rear end and threw the paper at a deputy. Trent screamed at one female officer, "Give me some motherfucking coffee you bitch. If you don't, I'll spit on you." Eventually, Trent was placed in a supermax prison. In protest, he composed a lengthy statement alleging violations of his due process.

While serving a life sentence for first-degree murder, armed robbery, and battery, Rodney received more than two dozen reports for misconduct. Upon being ordered to empty his pockets, he refused, then struck an officer in the face and threatened to "get" him when released. Indignant when he was placed in isolation, he screamed, "You're putting me in control just for hitting an officer. What are you going to do when I stick one of these motherfuckers?" While standing in a cafeteria line and glaring at an officer, Rodney "lowered his hand to his groin and started shaking his penis and scrotum area" and laughing. He told the officer, "If you ever say another fucking word to me again, I will get you." At another prison, when Rodney was directed to go to the segregation unit, he grabbed an officer and began to assault him, for which he was charged with attempted battery. On yet another occasion, he suddenly attacked a staff member, beating him with his closed fist. He then threatened to kill the officer after he was released from prison. Repeatedly, Rodney refused to do what he was told and terrorized both staff and inmates. He informed one officer that he must have a private cell and warned, "You try and put anybody in this cell, and I will fuck him up good." A more minor infraction, but an infraction nonetheless, occurred when, without authorization, he took a law book from the library, ripped out a page, then inscribed his name, indicating he had appropriated it for himself.

Inmates and staff have far less to fear when men like Trent and Rodney are removed from their institutions. In a supermax prison, such inmates spend nearly the entire day alone in a single cell. When they are moved to take a shower or exercise, they are usually restrained with leg irons and handcuffs and accompanied by at least two staff members. Just as they "earned" their way into a supermax by their violent behavior, there is also a system of phases by which they can earn their way out. Educational and self-improvement programming is available to those willing to participate. Professor Daniel Mears of Florida State University cited both positive and negative "unintended effects" of supermax prisons.[4] An example of the former is "improving living conditions and outcomes for general population inmates"; and of the latter, "increased mental illness." At present, supermaximum security prisons remain lightning rods of controversy as to how well they achieve their goals.

THE CRIMINAL IS quick to detect dissension among staff members and exploit it. In many institutions, racial tensions run high. Fully aware of this, the inmate will invoke race where it is completely irrelevant to the issue but expedient for him. He cries discrimination to shift attention from what he has done wrong to consideration of whether the staff is prejudiced. He injects race if he loses a privilege, is spoken to harshly, is ordered to do something that he finds disagreeable, or has been caught for a violation and is about to be punished.

In prison, just as on the street, the dilemma of whom to trust hangs heavily in the air. Criminals don't know what trust is. If they use the word and say they "trust" someone, they usually mean that the person won't betray them. "Don't snitch" is a code among inmates. The price of squealing on another con may be a beating or, possibly, death. Even so, the inmate realizes that every man is out for himself and that even his closest friend may turn informant to save his own skin or to acquire privileges. Although convicts have a shared understanding about "no snitching," the dominant ethos in prison is the same as it was on the outside, "fuck everybody else but me." Writing thirty-four years ago in *Corrections* magazine, Stephen Gettinger made an observation that still holds. He reported, "Some prison observers say that the inmate code's prohibitions against informing are more honored in the breach than in the observance. The trading of information is as common, and as necessary to the daily life of any prison as taking the count."[5]

As he serves time, the criminal experiences psychological changes. There are periods of profound depression, similar to that which overwhelmed some upon arrival. As the days, weeks, and months drag on, prison life grates upon the inmate. Outside, the criminal expected the world to suit him, and in prison he's no different. His complaints resound with righteous indignation as he ignores the fact that he is where he is as a consequence of the choices he has made.

Besides complaints, there can be genuine regrets. In contrast to the bleakness of prison existence, inmates glimpse life outside through radio, television, letters, periodicals, and occasional visitors. They may lament the fact that they are aging, and life is passing them by. They have much to regret—not just their incarceration but their previous indifference or opposition to many opportunities to live a different kind of life. There is plenty of time to look in the mirror and reflect.

Ernie told me that he was sick of being in and out of jail and hurting his family. While espousing intentions to turn his life around, he confessed that other thoughts plagued him incessantly. "I think about dealing with unsettled scores with those who still owe me money or who have been saying bad things about me. I fantasize about how I'm going to get back at them and get away with it. Most of my daydreams consist of settling scores and making illegal money. My nightmares consist of me getting into trouble or running from the law." Ernie thought he had found a solution when he said, "My hope for the future is that I can use my skills in a legitimate and professional setting. Although I want to quit committing crimes, I do still want to manipulate, scheme, and deceive. The alternative—working hard just to eke my way through life, is overwhelming and boring. I negotiate with myself on how to cruise the gray area with minimal risk. I can't help but know that I will be fighting this inner battle my entire life. I wonder where I'd be at right now if I had not gotten in trouble with the law." Turning away from self-reflection, Ernie did what he had always done, fault circumstances including the ones he had created by his own irresponsibility. "Penitentiaries are not a place for the penitent. It's more like a university for criminals," he asserted. Then he criticized his father because "his work consumed him. He was supposed to teach me to be a man." The bottom line was that, no matter whom Ernie faulted, he still found the very idea of living without crime totally repugnant. He remarked, "I get overwhelmed when I think about getting out of jail and having to start all over again."

An alternative to change is suicide. Some criminals had suicidal thoughts on the street when things weren't working out. In confinement, an inmate may grow despondent over the meaningless of his life, yet he continues raging at a world that he thinks never gave him a fair shake. One inmate who was contemplating suicide said, "I wouldn't have to put up with shit anymore."

In federal and state prisons, 185 inmates committed suicide during 2011. During the preceding decade, the rate of suicide by prisoners nationally was 15 incidents per 100,000 inmates.

(Thirty years ago, the rate was double that amount.)[6] Suicidal gestures dramatizing the inmate's plight are more common than actual suicides. A heavy but not lethal dose of drugs, a wrist slashing with a crude, handmade knife, or an inept job of hanging oneself compels others to take notice. The inmate may wind up in a less harsh environment, such as a prison hospital or psychiatric facility.

The despondent inmate may seek salvation in religion. Some criminals study the Bible or Koran, applying its passages to their own lives. They flock to religion classes and discussion groups, sing in choirs, share in readings or the liturgy, and participate in other religious programs. Some experience a sudden flood of religious inspiration and overnight become converts to a particular faith. Zealously, they impart their insights to others. The institutional life of these inmates becomes pervaded by religion. They infuse their artwork with religious motifs. Their poetry, letters, and other writings resound with religious themes. Some inmates, less public about their preoccupation with religion, withdraw and quietly devote hours to reading and prayer.

Prison Fellowship is perhaps the most well-known religious organization in prisons throughout the world. It was founded in 1976 by the late Chuck Colson, Special Counsel to President Nixon, who served a federal sentence in the aftermath of the Watergate Scandal. In prison, Mr. Colson experienced a religious transformation. During 2012, Prison Fellowship was active in 334 prisons and reported that 3,520 inmates made decisions to commit their lives to Christ.[7] Another example of extensive religious programming can be seen in the "in-house seminary" at the state penitentiary in Angola, Louisiana. Participants can earn a two-year associate degree in Pastoral Ministries and a four-year bachelor's degree in Theology.[8]

Institution staff members have no way of knowing whether the depression, spirituality, or attempts at reformation are genuine or whether the criminal is up to his old tricks. When genuine, these phases may last for months at a time. Anecdotal reports attest to improved prison conduct on the part of inmates who are practicing their religion. For most, it is a phase. When it ends, the criminal emerges with his basic outlook intact.

A criminal's absorption with crime does not necessarily diminish just because he is locked up. Despite the restrictive environment, he schemes, talks about, and continues to engage in illicit activities. Any external stimulus, such as a television crime show, a detective novel, or a lurid crime story in the paper, feeds an already busy mind—as do his daily conversations with other inmates. Through letters and visitors, the criminal hangs onto old ties, in addition to establishing new ones in prison. To some, confinement poses a greater challenge than ever to get away with violations. Theft is rampant in prisons. Anything that a man wants to hold onto must be kept on his person or surrendered to a trustworthy staff member. An inmate may be robbed by his cellmate when he sleeps, takes a shower, or at any other moment when he relaxes his guard. Inmates not only steal from one another, but also swipe personal belongings from the staff and food and other supplies from the institution.

Just as the criminal made sexual conquests outside confinement, he may attempt to do the same within. Sex is a powerful weapon to control and obligate others. A transaction may occur between two inmates in which sex is bartered for food, personal possessions, or money. Each criminal gets what he wants from the other and gives up little of importance. But sex in prison is often brutal.

The threat of rape can command respect and breed fear among inmates. Many pairs of eyes rove up and down the body of each new young man who enters the institution, especially if he is of slight build and physically attractive. In his bed at night, a new inmate may be beset by a gang of inmates who threaten him with far worse than rape or sodomy if he resists or informs. It is a jungle in which the strong subjugate the weak. To obtain protection, an inmate may submit to become the lackey and sexual slave of one of the most feared inmates.

Rape in prison often goes unnoticed or ignored by staff. It has, until recently, been regarded merely as a risk of life in prison, almost a routine occurrence. The 2003 Prison Rape Elimination Act included provisions for adequate numbers of prison employees, ensuring ways to report sexual abuse privately, and training staff to prevent sexual abuse. The 2013 website of the American Correctional Association indicates that "Preventing Sexual Misconduct" is among the organization's most requested workshops. Despite all the attention that this problem is receiving, a 2012 article in *USA Today* reported that "nearly one in 10 prisoners report having been raped or sexually assaulted by other inmates, staff, or both."[9]

Gambling is a way of life in correctional facilities. Like sex, it is a means by which criminals obligate others and build themselves up. Bets are placed on card games, board games, outside sports events, and almost any other activity in which the outcome is unknown. The gambling may be organized, as in daily numbers games linked to a downtown connection by a staff member. In most facilities, regulations prohibit inmates from having money on their person. Yet there are inmates who are flush with cash they have acquired by gambling, from visitors, or by doing favors for staff. If cash is not available, anything that is valued can be currency in a wager, including canteen items, personal possessions, or drugs. Many a fight in prison has erupted over an unpaid debt. When the inmate wins, he may insist upon payment that is higher than the actual amount bet. In lieu of demanding immediate total payment or charging losers usurious rates, he may cancel debts—if, say, the debtor happens to be a staff member who can close his eyes to particular violations or help the inmate gain privileges.

Correctional institutions take precautions to prevent contraband from being brought in, but criminals are ingenious.

A shakedown of a correctional facility may yield a variety of contraband items, especially handmade weapons. In prison industries, inmates are in regular contact with sharp, heavy, and breakable objects that they can turn into weapons. Even without access to such materials, inmates can fashion weapons from anything in the environment. A mop can be transformed into a club. While flooding his cell with water from the sink, one inmate brandished a toothbrush and screamed, "I am going to get someone when they come in." Another kicked over a table in the dayroom, broke a leg off of it, and then threatened a deputy. In another episode of misconduct, an inmate created a spear out of nail clippers, a rolled up newspaper, and a ballpoint pen.

Illicit drugs often float around prisons and psychiatric hospitals housing criminal offenders. Drugs are plentiful in prisons nationwide, not just in the vast prison systems of large states. Drugs find their way to inmates concealed in packages or in what appear to be legal documents that are not subject to the same security procedures as is the regular mail. An innocent-looking apple may have a drug injected into its core. A tempting chocolate cake may have drugs baked between its layers. A sugary powder surrounding hard candy may be heroin. Visiting at many institutions occurs through inmates and visitors communicating via a telephone receiver while seeing each other through a pane of glass. However, institutions that allow contact visits may experience an influx of drugs. A long kiss may not be an expression of love, but it can be a means of transmitting capsules. Inmates returning from work-release may import drugs, concealing them in body cavities. Prison employees may bring in contraband from outside. A staff member realizes that he has a permanent market and an easy way to make money. Instead of selling directly to inmates, the staff dealer identifies one whom he can trust to serve as distributor, and who will conceal the source of the supply. For a job reliably done, the distributor is well compensated. He too stays behind the scenes, lining up other prisoners who will actually make the sales. Everyone gets a piece of the action, and the staff member remains insulated by others fronting for him.

It is impossible to ascertain the frequency of staff collusion with inmates. Whereas most employees in corrections are conscientious and responsible, some desire to work with or near criminals because they identify with them and find them exciting. Such individuals relish listening to inmates' accounts of their exploits, and they sometimes join the endless bantering about crime, drugs, and sex. Such staff members would abhor working with the physically impaired or senior citizens; it would be far too tedious. Criminals intuitively sense which employees are very much like themselves, and carefully test the waters to determine who can be compromised. The criminal expects to gain a potential ally who will not turn him in for infractions and who will help bail him out of trouble. If such expectations are not met, the inmate has the goods on the staff member for potential extortion.

Gang operations have made conditions in prison increasingly unsafe for the general inmate population. According to a report in the *Washington Times* in 2010, gang-related drug activity was the leading cause of prison violence.[10] The advent of the cell phone, although regarded as contraband, has facilitated drug trafficking. Gang leaders are able to maintain contacts outside prison walls as well as with other prisoners to coordinate deliveries and sales. During 2009, in California prisons, five thousand contraband cell phones were confiscated.[11] The gang problem constituted such a threat to security at corrections facilities that institutions embarked on a policy of isolating inmates with such affiliations. In 2012, Ohio developed a plan to institute a three-tiered structure with nine "levels of freedom."[12] Gang members would be isolated in either maximum or supermax facilities, but could earn more freedom through good conduct and by completing programs oriented toward "rehabilitation."

A prison gang leader, known as a "shot-caller," already has established his reputation in the streets. He is literally the person who calls the shots or gives orders to subordinates who are expected to do as they are told. This individual knows the correctional facility inside and out and has been described as comparable to the general of an army. He exerts considerable influence over events both in prison and outside. He can command that a hit be put out to assault or kill someone inside the institution or in the community. His subordinates are subject to his demands even after they are released from prison. *USA Today* reported that, following the 2013 homicide of the director of the Colorado prison system, the state's governor launched an investigation into whether other public officials were being targeted by prison gangs.[13]

Shot-callers have amassed such power that prison staff may rely on them to help maintain order. Government authorities and prison staffs in other countries, faced with gangs controlling prisons, have negotiated with shot-callers. According to a press report, homicides in El Salvador dropped in half when shot-callers and government officials worked out a "quid pro quo" approach. By granting gang leaders better accommodations in prison and making other concessions, "a fragile accord" was reached resulting in shot-callers instructing "their underlings to stand down."[14]

All the above is intended to underscore the point that criminals are criminals, no matter where they are. In prison, their personalities remain as they were. What may vary is the degree of risk they will take and the methods by which they operate. Those abstaining from crime still miss it, but they content themselves with fantasy and conversation about crime.

Contrary to what many people believe, most criminals can and do learn from experience. But not what society wants them to learn. In prison, criminals have ample time and opportunity to sharpen their skills for future crimes and to think about how to avoid mistakes from the past. Some resolve that upon release they will lie low, limit themselves to small crimes, and forgo the big-time ventures. Or they will mastermind a crime but remain behind the scenes rather than participate directly. Such intentions are short-lived. Once inmates step outside prison doors, their appetite becomes voracious for the excitement of the old life. Some do in fact become more successful criminals, immersing themselves in crime but being slick enough to avoid apprehension. Others avoid arrest for a long time but eventually land back in the slammer. One man declared that, in the future, he would be "a misdemeanor criminal." He said he'd be satisfied with using a few "soft" drugs, visiting prostitutes, and trying to avoid fights unless someone messed with him. A year later, he was back in prison for a series of armed robberies. Some inmates plan their next crime before release from confinement. The prison gate has hardly closed behind them before they slip up, get caught, and are charged with a new offense.

It is widely believed that criminals outgrow crime or "burn out." The burnout theory may be based on the fact that some older criminals cease to get arrested for street crimes, and so they don't return to prison. In his book *Making Good: How Ex-Convicts Reform and Rebuild Their Lives*, Shadd Maruna, a professor of criminal justice, observed, "A person can, apparently, burn out, hit rock bottom, and yet carry on with criminal behavior."[15] It is true that as a street criminal ages, he is not as agile and literally cannot run as fast as he used to. He may have mellowed, but only in that he takes fewer big risks and his offenses may be less serious. But his criminal personality remains unchanged, and people still suffer at his hands.

14

"Rehabilitation" Revisited

The pendulum has swung back and forth as to whether it is worthwhile to expend funds to help criminals change. Disenchantment with "rehabilitation" began during the 1970s and early 1980s. A well-known gloomy assessment of rehabilitative programs by sociologist Robert Martinson, published during 1974, led many to the conclusion "Nothing works."[1] With funding for rehabilitation drying up, the emphasis shifted to punishment. Although this resulted in getting criminals off the street for lengthier periods of time, statistics indicate that approximately four out of ten people were rearrested and reconvicted after being released back into the community. Some estimates provide an even grimmer picture. With the recidivism rate remaining stubbornly high, it became time to take another look at possibilities for rehabilitation.

There are two major reasons for the ineffectiveness of rehabilitation efforts. One has to do with underestimating how difficult it is to effect enduring character change. It is an especially formidable task to work with criminals, many of whom share the perspective of a felon who declared, "If you take my crime away, you take my world away." Like him, many offenders reject any opportunity to change. Yet another reason for the poor track record of rehabilitation programs is that the criminal justice community and the community at large believe that the criminal has the same needs as most people, but that he does not know how to fulfill them in a socially acceptable manner. They fail to understand that criminals think differently from responsible people. Mistakenly, they believe that programs that succeed in helping people with other types of problems will have similar results with criminals. Countless millions of dollars are dumped into myriad educational, vocational, social skills, and artistic enrichment programs, most of which have not been empirically tested for their effectiveness. That is, we have no proof that socially trendy "rehabilitative" programs such as yoga, gardening, money management, diary writing, theater production, and poetry composition offer any hope of changing the way the criminal mind works.

The very concept of criminal rehabilitation is flawed. If one looks up "rehabilitation" in the dictionary, the definition is "to restore to a former capacity."[2] An architect conceives of a plan to rehabilitate an old cathedral, to restore it to its former grandeur. A stroke victim undergoes rehabilitation to help her regain functions she once had. There is nothing to which to "re-habilitate" most criminals. From childhood, they rejected the basic principles of how to live responsibly in society. The scope of the task of change entails helping a criminal to "habilitate" himself, which exceeds the scope of "re-habilitation." Helping a criminal become a responsible human being requires a far-reaching change in thinking. Anything short of undertaking that objective is like pouring a delectable sauce over a slice of burned, rancid meat.

Never has there been complete abandonment of the rehabilitative ideal, even under presidential administrations known for conservatism on social issues. When federal and state budgets were lean, private and community organizations stepped in and offered programming. America remains especially reluctant to give up on its youth, to write off any youngster as an incorrigible delinquent or criminal. In fact, the emphasis in juvenile justice is on rehabilitation. The California Division of Juvenile Justice makes this clear in the first sentence of its website statement: "The Division of Juvenile Justice provides education and treatment to California's youthful offenders up to the age of 25 who have the most serious criminal backgrounds and most intense treatment needs."[3]

Belief in the viability of rehabilitating adult offenders has not vanished even during times of diminishing financial resources and public indifference. The thousands of correctional counselors, case workers, educators, vocational teachers, and mental health professionals employed by adult correctional institutions consider themselves to be more than custodians of a warehouse. Most prisons and psychiatric facilities for criminals offer inmates a variety of programs. While some are time fillers designed to occupy inmates productively, most claim to prepare the criminal to reenter society. Let's look at what is being done currently in the name of "rehabilitation."

Integral to a philosophy of rehabilitation is helping inmates acquire skills so that they can make their way in society without resorting to crime. This is based on the flawed premise that people turn to crime because they lack certain skills. During 2010, ten percent of GED (General Equivalency Diploma) testing in the United States occurred in correctional centers.[4] Nearly 75,000 inmates took the test, and 75.1 percent passed. The GED Testing Service reported that "personal satisfaction" motivated 63 percent of the incarcerated test takers, whereas 38 percent named seeking a better job as their reason for desiring to earn the equivalent of a high school diploma. With respect to the latter, recent studies indicate that few GED test takers in the general population go on to earn a higher degree and, overall, most fare no better in the job market than dropouts who did not pass the exam.[5]

The high rate of success in passing the GED is telling. When they were in school, many criminals rejected the dedicated efforts of their teachers. With time on their hands and little to do in confinement, inmates surprise instructors by how rapidly they learn to read. With a year of instruction, while incarcerated, a criminal may achieve more than he did during all his years in school. Some who have never read an entire book turn into avid readers as they discover that immersion in a book alleviates the tedium of life in prison. Some offenders are able to enroll in college classes by mail. Goucher College, Bard College, Wesleyan University, and Cornell University are among select institutions of higher learning that offer courses for credit inside prisons.

Receiving a high school diploma or its equivalent, or any other academic achievement, is certainly a plus and reflects constructive use of an inmate's time. Not only is the individual able to locate job notices and seek out other opportunities, but the self-discipline of learning to read in and of itself is, of course, worthwhile. However, reading and other academic accomplishments do not transform a criminal's character and change the thinking patterns of a lifetime. There is the possibility that an outcome of literacy programs is criminals who can read rather than criminals who are illiterate.

Vocational training remains a top priority in corrections. The thinking is that if a criminal equips himself for a skilled job, he will be able to support himself legitimately and thus be less likely to prey upon society. Prison industries provide opportunities to earn a small wage while learning a trade. The National Correctional Industry Association described these enterprises as providing "real work experience to inmates, teaching them transferable job skills and work ethic to help prepare them for post-release re-entry and employment."[6] Inmates turn out a wide variety of products such as mattresses, furniture, signs, janitorial supplies, and picture frames. The program is self-supporting, as income is derived from the sale of the goods that are produced. Equipping a criminal with job skills makes sense. However, many criminals had professions or trades before they entered prison, and they still committed crimes. The end result of vocational training is often a criminal with job skills rather than a criminal without job skills. The criminality remains. To what avail is it to have, for example, a highly skilled carpenter if he shows up late, steals from the job, overcharges for materials, or fails to stand behind his work if a problem arises? And there is always the possibility that the offender will apply his new skills to gain access to homes or commercial establishments where he will commit more crimes.

Some correctional facilities provide opportunity for inmates to acquire money management skills. "Financial literacy" will ostensibly help offenders remain debt-free, live within a budget, pay bills on time, develop habits of saving, and keep track of expenditures. Many criminals see no reason to budget. If they want something, they consider themselves entitled to it and will appropriate it in whatever manner they choose. Although they scheme far ahead into the future, they do not plan long-range in responsible endeavors. Setting aside funds for a child's education or establishing an investment portfolio that can be used in retirement are ideas from another planet for most criminals. Teaching a criminal to be financially literate is as futile as trying to teach Ebenezer Scrooge to establish a charitable foundation. Without a fundamental change in the way the criminal thinks, such an endeavor is doomed.

Related to instruction in financial management is providing criminals with career counseling. Many criminals never had a career. Some had careers but must forsake them because of their criminal record. Contrary to popular belief, a felony conviction often entails much more than losing the right to vote. States often ban felons from working in a host of jobs or professions, limit their access to firearms, force them to forfeit public assistance payments, and restrict their public employment.

Offering guidance and occupational assessments to determine where inmates' abilities and interests lie may be useful. But this does not mean that they will cease thinking like a criminal or be realistic about a career. During conversations with inmates, I have heard criminals assert over and over that they intend to run their own business because they detest the idea of working for someone else. On the face of it, there is nothing wrong with wanting to become an entrepreneur. Ask a criminal what he thinks this will entail, and he is likely to tell you that he envisions himself growing rich while employing people who will do his bidding. He assumes that because he is in charge, success is assured. In his mind, he is already spending the profits—despite knowing nothing about what establishing a business requires: capitalizing the business, screening prospective employees, dealing with personnel problems, obtaining licenses, ordering supplies, marketing the product, and so forth. The criminal is used to living life on his terms. He does not deal constructively with the frustrations, irritants, and disappointments that arise almost daily in any legitimate enterprise. The particular career he chooses is far less important than acquiring the thinking patterns necessary for success in any endeavor.

In correctional facilities, many types of programs teach inmates about relationships: parent-child, husband-wife, employee-supervisor, and so forth. According to a 2010 report, 2.7 million children had a parent who was incarcerated.[7] It is hardly surprising that inmates have a poor track record in being responsible parents. Because many had offspring by different partners, they did not live with their children. And because of their lifestyle, they spent little or no time with their sons and daughters.

Curricula have been developed to help criminals become responsible parents. The Michigan Family Impact Seminar notes, "Because many men in prison may not really know how

to be good parents, most responsible fatherhood programs include parent education as a fundamental component of the
programming."[8] The federal government has provided grants
to teach parenting skills. One federally funded program noted
that because criminals distrust people within the "prison authority structure," instructors were selected from among "incarcerated fathers who had graduated from a prior course and been
trained as peer leaders."[9] This seems akin to asking patients of
dentists to perform dentistry. Unless the incarcerated peer leader
has made enduring major changes in his own flawed thinking
patterns, he is unlikely to be qualified to teach criminals about
relationships. A self-centered, hypersensitive, deceptive, pretentious individual who sees the world in extremes does not make
for a nurturing, dependable father or mother. How is a father or
mother going to become an effective communicator unless he
develops empathy, fulfills obligations, and puts others ahead of
his own self-interest? Teaching parenting skills, worthy as the
idea is, remains a futile endeavor unless the criminal makes far-
reaching alterations to lifelong thought and behavior patterns.
Without doubt, most criminals, if asked, could rattle off a list
of desirable qualities of effective parents. There is a huge chasm
between talking the talk and walking the walk.

Programs in the arts are designed to discover and nurture
the creative potential of inmates. Proponents believe that criminals who participate will experience a lift to their self-esteem as
they cultivate undiscovered or undeveloped talents. Hundreds
of programs, most funded privately, aim to help aspiring art-
ists, musicians, poets, writers, and thespians. The following
programs exemplify the diversity of activities being offered to inmates. There is a women's string orchestra at the Hiland Mountain Correctional Center in Alaska. The orchestra, now more
than ten years old, is said to "showcase the rehabilitative and re-
demptive power of music in the lives of young women struggling
to find their way back into society."[10] For the past eight years,

Washington State's Denney Juvenile Justice Center has held a poetry workshop from which books of residents' poems are published. A group called Rehabilitation Through the Arts (RTA) had its beginning in the famous Sing Sing penitentiary with the writing and production of a play. RTA was a successful enterprise and expanded so that it operates a creative arts program in five New York State correctional facilities. The Anne Frank Center USA provides a copy of *The Diary of a Young Girl* to inmates who agree to write about their own lives and thoughts, then return their journals to the Center for possible publication.

Arts in Prison (AIP) was established in 1995 and continues to operate through volunteers and private donations at Kansas adult and juvenile correctional facilities. AIP states as its mission that it "uses the arts to inspire positive change in the incarcerated, to reduce recidivism, and to reconnect ex-offenders with their communities."[11] Arts programs have even been established in supermax institutions. Prisoners from California's Pelican Bay State Prison and students from the Dell'Arte International School of Physical Theater have collaborated in drama, writing, and musical projects. Programs that constructively occupy inmates invariably contribute to a better institutional climate. But there is no evidence that cultivating creativity translates into eliminating criminality.

Individual psychotherapy is not widely available in correctional facilities or even in forensic psychiatric facilities where offenders are patients. Individual treatment is expensive, but it is available in some juvenile detention centers. Therapy groups in prisons have a variety of formats—from a highly structured agenda for imparting skills, to unstructured and more traditional formats for effecting personality change. Some groups in the form of a "therapeutic community" help inmates address day-to-day problems of living while incarcerated. Not only is group therapy less costly than individual treatment, but many mental health professionals prefer it because peer pressure can be a powerful force for change. Also, presumably it is more difficult to deceive a group than it is to hoodwink an individual therapist.

Some psychologists have asserted that their profession has fallen short in contributing to an area that badly needs experts in behavior change. Psychologist Joel Dvoskin of the University of Arizona School of Medicine stated, "With all the knowledge of psychology . . . our entire criminal justice system does almost everything wrong. Probably the single most important area for behavior change in the U.S. is crime."[12]

Critics of the criminal justice system point out that the United States incarcerates a higher percentage of its population than does any other country. Psychologist Stephen Ragusea observed that this is equivalent to the total number of people residing in Philadelphia, Columbus, and Seattle, or approximately 1 percent of the U.S. population.[13] From almost all points on the political spectrum, a consensus has been forming that it is too expensive and unnecessarily restrictive to incarcerate so many offenders, especially if they are not violent. Efforts to find alternatives to incarceration have spawned numerous ideas for increasing services for offenders living in the community.

Since the late nineteenth century, offenders have often been placed on probation in lieu of incarceration or after they serve a portion of their sentence. In 2012, slightly more than 2 million offenders were on probation in the United States. Probation monitors inmates and imposes certain conditions, which may include holding a job, taking drug tests, receiving counseling, and performing community service. In many communities, probation has no teeth; it barely poses an inconvenience to the offender, much less a sanction. A half-hour appointment every other week (or even less often) barely provides enough time for an overburdened probation officer to complete paperwork, much less hold a meaningful discussion. Some probation officers have such heavy caseloads that they would not recognize many of their clients if they saw them on the street.

More than a dozen states as well as the federal criminal justice system have abolished parole—the release of offenders before they serve their entire sentence. Critics of parole call for "truth in sentencing." They maintain that juries become confused because they do not always know how long a sentence an offender will actually serve. A jury might impose a life sentence, only to learn later that the individual was released after a short period by a parole board. Also, victims remain on tenterhooks, never knowing when a criminal might be released. Critics of parole contend that there is little science and considerable arbitrariness to decisions by parole boards about when to release offenders. Disenchantment with parole is expressed whenever prisoners released early commit new crimes. Efforts many years ago to treat offenders with psychotherapy in hybrid facilities such as Atascadero State Hospital in California and the Patuxent Institution in Patuxent, Maryland, were discontinued after violent crimes were committed by released felons, some of whom were originally sentenced to life in prison.

To help offenders on either probation or parole, centers providing a variety of services are being established in communities. The *San Francisco Chronicle* reported that during 2013, a reentry center opened containing classrooms, vocational training services, GED classes, substance abuse treatment, and information about housing and employment.[14] San Francisco's chief probation officer, Wendy Still, attributed the city's lowest jail population since the 1950s to its investment in the Probation Department. The building cost $2 million with another million required each year to operate the center.

Compensating the victim or engaging in community service—commonly referred to as "restorative justice"—may be court-ordered as a condition of probation and as an alternative to serving a sentence. Restitution programs may have deterrent value for some offenders, who may work for many weeks to compensate their victims. But how does a rapist, or an arsonist who causes a merchant to lose the source of his livelihood, make restitution? And how does a woman who embezzled hundreds of thousands of dollars from her employer ever make restitution, especially while she is serving a penitentiary sentence and then is barred from many types of jobs because she is a convicted felon? For the repeat offender, it is possible that making restitution will have an effect opposite to what was intended. The criminal does not regard the victim as a victim at all. *He* is the victim, for having been caught. Compensating the real victim may bolster a criminal's already elevated view of himself as a decent person and thereby give him even greater license for crime.

Restitution may leave the victim better off, and that is worthwhile in and of itself. The fact that a chronic offender is unlikely to be deterred or "rehabilitated" is not a reason to forgo restitution altogether. However, it argues for selectivity in application. The shortcomings lie not with restitution—or, for that matter, with any other program—but rather with a sponsor's unrealistic expectations of its power to change criminals. Like the institutional programs described above, community correctional programs may help criminals acquire skills or pay a debt to society, but have not demonstrated an overall impact on how they live their lives.

Community corrections organizations face major challenges. They have the technology to keep track of offenders on probation and parole, which helps to achieve the primary goal of holding criminals accountable and keeping the community safe. Rather than continue to offer palliative and superficial measures, however, community corrections must offer well-thought-out, intensive programs that will equip nonviolent criminals with a new set of concepts that correct lifelong patterns of thought and action. In the long run, this may be far less costly than building more prisons.

Unless criminals are serving terms of life without parole, which very few do, they will eventually be free to prey upon us all. There is a job for corrections to do in the institution and in the community—that is to correct. But rehabilitation as it has been practiced cannot possibly be effective. Just as "rehabilitation" is a misconception, so too is the notion of "reintegrating" the criminal into the community. It is absurd to speak of reintegrating a person when he was never integrated in the first place. The criminal has long stood apart from the community, contemptuous of people who live responsibly.

Some people in the criminal justice system and in the community at large overlook a fundamental and seemingly obvious question: If a criminal gives up crime, what will replace it? Change demands more than keeping his hands off others' property or keeping his fly zipped. It requires giving up a whole way of life.

Rehabilitation specialists recognize that the criminal must find alternatives to crime. Some suggest that, as a substitute, he may experience excitement by participating in extreme physical activities such as skiing, skydiving, rock climbing, or mountain climbing. It would be extremely efficient and inexpensive if changing from forbidden excitement to legitimate excitement would do the job. Unfortunately, it falls far short. Becoming skilled at such endeavors does not begin to address the thinking patterns that give rise to criminal activity.

Many rehabilitation programs have the objective of providing "success experiences," thereby enhancing the criminal's self-esteem. Robert W. Reasoner of the International Council for Self-Esteem stated that that "low self-esteem is an underlying reason for such problems as bullying, drug and alcohol abuse, school dropouts, crime, [and] violence."[15] It is understandable that many people think juvenile offenders and criminals have low self-esteem and that people like Reasoner, who is specifically addressing school curricula, advocate programs to raise it. After all, many juvenile and adult offenders appear to have failed in most areas of life—school, work, their families, their communities, and even in crime (since they have been arrested). Their narcissism, Reasoner maintains, is "actually a form of low self-esteem" in that it attempts "to compensate for an underlying fragile sense of self-worth."

The reality is that the predatory criminal does not lack self-esteem or consider himself to be a failure, even when he is apprehended for a crime. If he failed at school, at work, or elsewhere, it is because of choices that he has made. He is not a reticent, neurotic individual who feels out of place and unable to do anything right. Rather, he conceives of himself as an exceptional person who is superior to others. If people want to pat him on the back as he acquires new skills and complies with what is asked of him, then that is fine with him. While receiving praise for success in self-esteem-building programs, he may be planning his next holdup or thinking about where to find the most potent heroin.

Sometimes a criminal convinces himself that the key to becoming a responsible person is to live a drug-free life. He may participate in substance abuse treatment, often because it is court-ordered. Self-help programs, like the twelve-step Alcoholics Anonymous and Narcotics Anonymous, meet daily in all sorts of venues from churches to cruise ships. Long-term residential treatment programs educate participants about substance abuse and provide intensive therapy. Criminals misuse anything, and may have ulterior motives for participating in substance abuse programs. They know that if they become drug-free, they may be more adept in their criminal activities because they will have clearer thinking. If a criminal stays off narcotics, he doesn't have to risk dealing with shady characters, buying contaminated drugs, or worrying about overdosing or undesirable side effects. But abstinence is only a beginning. Alcoholics Anonymous recognizes that change demands more than sobriety. "Stinking thinking" is an A.A. term referring to the fact that, even if an A.A. participant is sober, he may be a "dry drunk." That is to say that, despite giving up alcohol, he remains dishonest, controlling, self-centered, and blameful of others.

Some programs have been designed with the hope of doing something to promote change in offenders quickly and inexpensively. "Scared Straight" was launched in a New Jersey prison during the 1970s. Its purpose was to bring youthful offenders face-to-face with adult inmates who would relate in graphic language what serving hard time was like. In a 2011 report, the U.S. Department of Justice stated, "Decades of research have shown that this approach is not only ineffective, but possibly harmful to youth."[16] Some researchers found that "such programs generally increased crime" and violated a law that prohibits court-involved youths from having contact with adult inmates.

There are different methods for evaluating the success of rehabilitative programs. Assessment of change may be based on observations of the criminal's day-to-day conduct in the institution. Some criminals are chameleons who adapt quickly to their surroundings. Seeking to avoid hassles with staff, they abide by rules and participate in programs voluntarily, sometimes even with enthusiasm. An observer might be so impressed by the inmate's deportment that he would wonder why that individual needed to be confined at all. When a criminal voices intention to change but in fact only temporarily adjusts to confinement, a deterioration in his attitude and behavior will occur once he is released, if not earlier. Successful adaption to a highly regimented environment by no means ensures that a person will cope responsibly with exigencies and challenges of life outside prison.

Bradley had adapted quite well to the county jail. A model inmate, he had never been written up for misconduct during months of confinement. However, churning beneath his placid, accommodating demeanor was a mind that could not fathom living in a similarly conforming manner on the outside. Bradley took me into his confidence when he confessed, "I am not completely at the point where I want to change. I'm afraid that my personal 'rock bottom' would be at a point which was too late. It all comes down to me getting what I want. I've had this mindset my entire life. Eventually, I might begin committing crimes again. Some days, it's all I think about—making a small fortune fast and easy, all the while getting my kicks and showing people how 'bad' I am."

"Recidivism" is the criterion for tracking whether an offender has changed. The Department of Justice defines recidivism in terms of "the criminal acts that resulted in the rearrest, reconviction, or return to prison with or without a new sentence during a three-year period following the prisoner's release."[17] Arrest statistics are not based on subjective assessments and can be readily procured from official sources. However, statistics cannot reflect how a criminal lives from day to day. They reveal nothing of his integrity, dependability, soundness of decision making, or how he treats other people. Recidivism statistics indicate only whether an offender has been careless enough to get caught, which likely represents just a fraction of the crimes he has committed. Psychologist Stephen Brake pointed out that this is especially true of sex offenders, noting, "Somewhere between 64% and 99% of sexual assaults are never reported by victims."[18] He cited a chilling report by psychologist Gene Abel, who found that, when guaranteed anonymity, "adult sex offenders disclosed having committed an average of 533 sex offenses over a 12-year period before being detected." From Dr. Brake's study, the three-year window for measuring recidivism is too short. He cited studies in which investigators reported recidivism increasing over time, to 39 percent for rapists and 52 percent for child molesters after twenty-five years.

The dismal failure of rehabilitation has turned the public cynical about whether it is even possible for criminals to change. Is it reasonable to conclude that criminals are destined to remain the way they are? This, too, would be a misconception. There are times when a criminal is vulnerable, when his life is not working out as he expected, and he casts about for an alternative. Vulnerability is greatest when a criminal is faced with losing something he values, usually his freedom, perhaps a girlfriend or his family. When the doors of the detention facility slam closed behind him, he may be vulnerable in that he sees life passing him by, and he has lots of time to think. During such periods, straightening out may have its strongest appeal. Even when he is not behind bars, he may become fed up with himself, sick of running, looking over his shoulder, and harming those who care about him.

The work of habilitation can begin in prison or in the community. The critical factor is not where it takes place, but the state of mind of the criminal. Reflecting on his wasted life, a middle-aged inmate of a state penitentiary posed to me what remains a challenge to society. First, he said that people like himself were rarely reached by current methods. Then he despaired that it might not be possible to change at all. "In my opinion," he said, "the human mind is ever reduplicating itself, acquiring more finesse, sophistication, technique, subtlety, and science. I am sure that a controlled setting that is humane in its approach, that is moral, principled, and courageous, can inspire the most lowly to become a working and functional part of this country." Said another criminal, "I know it is not easy to change someone's whole concept and evil ways, but I am aware of this. For me to become a law-abiding citizen would be my greatest triumph."

Little has changed since I wrote in 1984 about what passes for "rehabilitation." There is not only public disillusionment about the effectiveness of rehabilitation, but also outrage about how much incarceration is costing the public in dollars. A 2014 headline on FoxNews.com called attention to an issue that continues to fuel criticism of the criminal justice system: "States Spend Almost Four Times More Per Cap Incarcerating Prisoners Than Educating Students."[19] The article that followed pointed out that California spends about $47,000 per inmate while only $9,000 is spent per student. Many years ago, George Beto, a professor of criminal justice and a former chairman of the Texas Department of Corrections, stated, "The history of corrections is 150 years of undocumented fads." Token measures continue to be instituted in sometimes frantic, usually fruitless attempts to do something rather than nothing with respect to rehabilitation, and to do it as quickly and cheaply as possible. I ask the same question I asked thirty years ago: Will society effectively use its resources to help criminals become responsible, or will it continue to throw billions of dollars into human warehouses and down the drain into well-intentioned, but misguided, partial solutions that turn out not to be solutions at all?

All of the above-mentioned efforts directed toward helping juvenile and adult offenders have positive features and have the potential to facilitate change. But it is fruitless to construct a fine house on a rotten foundation. Behavior is a product of thinking. The key to habilitation is to help an offender change his thinking. That remains the focus of the next two chapters.

15

To Change a Criminal

With the exception of a followup note at the end, this chapter appears as it was written for the 1984 edition. The rationale for leaving the content unaltered is that it presents the essence of an effective approach to helping criminals change. Many readers of the earlier edition told me that they found the story of Leroy both instructive and inspirational.

A tall, gaunt, white-haired elderly psychiatrist was doing most of the talking as he leaned back in the chair across from Leroy, a bearded black housebreaker and armed robber, who appeared cowed into silence. In a direct yet polite manner, Dr. Samuel Yochelson was telling Leroy that he was a menace to society.

Yochelson had dealt with criminals this way many times before, but he was a different man in his approach to them than he had been ten years earlier in 1961, when he arrived at St. Elizabeths Hospital in Washington, D.C., to begin a second career. One of Buffalo's most eminent psychiatrists, he was known not only as a successful practitioner but also for his contribution to the public's knowledge of psychiatry through his regular appearances on a local television series. As he approached his mid-fifties, the time had come when he aspired to make a contribution to this field that would be both scholarly and practical. Having been a public figure in Buffalo, he chose the obscurity of a new environment, where he would not be heard from for fifteen years. Yochelson undertook the research-treatment program in criminal behavior at a hospital rather than a prison because he thought that a treatment environment would be more conducive to a clinical study, and in addition he could draw upon the expertise of the huge hospital's medical and social work departments.

When he began the research, Yochelson didn't consider his patients "criminals." Rather, he regarded them as disturbed people who were products of adverse family situations and oppressive social conditions. He spent hundreds of hours taking detailed histories, and hundreds more treating them in individual and group psychotherapy using traditional techniques with which he had been successful in Buffalo. Yochelson believed that if he could help the St. Elizabeths patients gain insight into their past behavior, they could resolve their conflicts and would no longer commit crimes. After several years of probing into their early experiences and psychosocial development, he observed something quite sobering. Despite all their insight, these men were still committing crimes right on the hospital grounds and, when caught, used their newfound understanding as justification.

Undaunted, Yochelson realized that he would have to take a new tack. Having discovered that the search for causes was futile and contributed only to rationalization, he stopped swallowing his patients' self-serving stories and concentrated on their current thinking. As he did this, he saw that they were rational, not crazy at all. He concluded that the insanity defense through which they had escaped imprisonment was a farce. In fact, they were no different from criminals whom he studied who never were hospitalized for a psychiatric condition.

Increasingly, Yochelson became a hard-liner, not in the

sense of wanting to punish criminals but in insisting that they be treated as responsible for their behavior and held accountable. Only by seeing them as the victimizers they were, not as the victims they claimed to be, could he surmount the barriers that they set up to confuse and distract not only him but everyone else they encountered.

The work with these men whom he now called "criminals" was arduous and unrewarding for a long time. But Yochelson persisted, meticulously recording on thousands of pages all of his observations, even those he couldn't immediately make sense of. Eventually he realized that significant and lasting change in the behavior of criminals could occur only with a 180-degree alteration in their thinking. He developed a technique to teach criminals to report their thinking so that it could be monitored, and errors pointed out and corrected.

In its format, Yochelson's new program resembled a classroom more than a therapy group. The procedures that he developed are time-consuming to apply, but they offer promise of revolutionizing practices in many parts of the criminal justice system and in the mental health field.

LEROY DID NOT walk into the doctor's office from the streets begging for help. Yochelson had encountered a few criminals who did this. Some wanted to kick a drug habit or lay off booze. Others were momentarily depressed or anxious and wanted him to get a wife or parent off their backs. But they were not interested in making profound changes in themselves. Leroy declared that he had nothing to show for his thirty years. He had abandoned his wife and children for sex, heroin, alcohol, guns, and other excitement in the streets of Washington, D.C. After beating a charge for bank robbery by faking insanity, Leroy was committed to St. Elizabeths Hospital, where he met Yochelson. Now he wanted two things—to get out of the hospital and to make changes in his life. What changes he wasn't sure, but he was certain that he wanted things to be different.

Yochelson began by stating that he knew Leroy sized up everyone he met. Since the purpose of the first meeting was primarily to let Leroy know whom he was dealing with, the psychiatrist did not worry about establishing rapport. Instead he assumed control of the interview by presenting his own view of what Leroy was like. Yochelson was not searching for explanations, which Leroy would readily feed him in the form of self-serving stories and excuses. He declared that he would not fall prey to Leroy's diversions, excuses, and other attempts to mislead and confuse him. Leroy would be offered no chance to ramble on about his mother, his father, his "bad breaks" in life, or even his crimes. Yochelson knew practically nothing about Leroy's background, nor was he interested. He didn't even know the charge on which Leroy had been declared not guilty by reason of insanity. But having studied many criminals in depth, and having found identical elements in many of their thought patterns, the doctor knew a great deal about the workings of Leroy's mind.

Yochelson asked Leroy to listen to his statements and then tell him whether he agreed. He asserted that very early in life Leroy had carved out a path different from most of those around him, that he had lived a secret life and gloried in being slick enough to fool others. Yochelson pointed out that Leroy's early and frequent violations grew out of a demand that the world suit Leroy rather than that Leroy suit the world. He cited Leroy's insistence that others respect him while he respected no one. Whereas Leroy paid lip service to responsibility, he had actually scorned all but extremely successful people, whom he thought he could surpass in brilliance and accomplishment. Yochelson stated that Leroy had a "glass jaw"; he could dish out abuse but couldn't take even the slightest criticism. He told Leroy that although he might brag about his friends, he didn't know what friendship was. He contended that by a twist of mind, Leroy considered himself decent despite having committed crime after crime and having neglected and then abandoned his wife and children, whom he still professed to love. After each statement, Yochelson would pause, gaze intently at Leroy, and ask him, "Am I right?" Sometimes Leroy nodded solemnly. At other times he would shrug his shoulders and remark, "You could say that." Yochelson would pounce on that statement and point out that it showed Leroy to be a coward who presented a tough exterior to the world, but who didn't have the guts to face up to who he was. When Leroy replied, "I don't know," Yochelson said that "I don't know" is typical of a criminal who fears tarnishing his image by being truthful. Yochelson demonstrated how everything that Leroy said was revealing of his personality.

Like a bloodhound, Yochelson pressed on for close to three hours, unmasking Leroy. Leroy didn't like what he was hearing, but he found it hard to deny. He quibbled with a word or phrase here or there, but found his resistance crumbling. Later Leroy admitted that early in the interview he had sensed that this wasn't another "shrink" whom he could lead by the nose; that it was going to be a lot tougher than he had expected to take on Yochelson. Leroy began to wonder if the doctor was reading his thoughts. Fleetingly he thought that because Yochelson knew so much about criminals, he might be one himself. What amazed him most was that he was sitting there and taking it while this elderly man painted a dismal picture of him as a human being. Although he was being exposed, he did not feel attacked. Yochelson had remained calm and polite, even when he expressed his total opposition to Leroy's way of life. He did not ridicule Leroy, browbeat him, berate him, or treat him with anything less than respect. So Leroy continued to sit there and take it, almost mesmerized while Yochelson picked him apart and presented him with a mirror image of himself.

This was only the beginning. The doctor invited him to

return for more of the same. Leroy had heard about Yochelson's program, but in the interview not a word about it had been mentioned. The doctor stated that until he completed laying out Leroy's personality, there would be no discussion of a program.

Leroy did return for further interviews. No aspect of his life was sacred, not even Leroy's new girlfriend, whom he regarded as responsible because she had gone to college. Yochelson's probing questions revealed that she was not the Madonna-like figure he portrayed. She smoked marijuana, was an "easy lay," and offered to be an accessory to his crimes by concealing his guns in her home. After several meetings it became apparent that Yochelson did not detect any redeeming feature in Leroy. Even his musical talents had been misused, as he played in dives where criminals hung out. Bluntly, Yochelson told him that he was a thoroughbred criminal and that three options were possible: Leroy could continue in crime and experience the consequences; he could commit suicide, in which case society would be better off; or he could learn to live like a civilized human being and become a responsible person. Leroy had ruled out the first two. That left only change, which he thought would be a snap.

Behavior follows in the wake of thought. To eliminate criminal behavior, it is essential first to change the way a man like Leroy thinks. This is by no means a fast or easy process. The task requires demolishing old thinking patterns, laying a new foundation by teaching new concepts, and building a new structure wherein the criminal puts into action what he is taught. All his life, Leroy had heard the word "responsibility" bandied about, a word used so promiscuously that it means everything and nothing. Leroy was used to parroting the word, even though he knew nothing about being responsible. To him, to be responsible meant to erect a facade and appear respectable. He commented, "Once a person is responsible, he can get away with a hell of a lot." Responsibility also meant to be a big wheel, to acquire fame and fortune overnight by any means that he could think of. But in the program that Leroy was about to enter, "responsibility" embraced all it takes to be an effective, constructive person with total integrity. It meant learning and putting into practice specific patterns of thinking that are second nature to most people but brand-new to the criminal.

Leroy was told that none of his hard-luck stories was relevant. The circumstances of his life were of no concern. He was not a victim. At the heart of the program was the premise that man can choose between good and evil. Rather than relieve Leroy's fears and guilt, Yochelson would try to intensify them. Having had some psychotherapy, Leroy was used to expressing feelings, ventilating anger. He was surprised that Yochelson, a psychiatrist, had no interest in his feelings. There would be nothing in this program to make Leroy "feel better" about himself or accept himself. Rather, in order to change he would have to grow intensely fed up with himself. Leroy was intrigued, but, more important, he saw no choice but to trust this man and see what the program was all about. He told Yochelson he would make an "honest effort." Refusing to let that phrase slip by, Yochelson pointed out that there could be no effort that wasn't honest. He asserted that Leroy seemed to be placing the program on trial. If things did not go the way he wanted, Leroy would then do what he pleased, secure in the belief that he had tried. Yochelson continued to unmask Leroy by dissecting his every statement or question.

Leroy was then permitted to join a group of five men who already were at different points in the change process. Groups were organized in this manner so that a new man could see how others were functioning and the current members could see themselves all over again as they heard the questions, arguments, and excuses of a totally unchanged criminal. Leroy had been accustomed to therapy groups where patients decided what to discuss and where the doctor said little. Yochelson's group did not begin to resemble those freewheeling discussions. In this situation the doctor, not the criminals, was running the meeting. From a sheaf of notes made during the past twenty-four hours, each criminal reported what he had been thinking—thoughts about other patients on the ward, thoughts about the nursing staff, thoughts about family, thoughts about a violent movie on television, thoughts about the group, thoughts about Yochelson, thoughts during masturbation. The others listened in silence until Yochelson broke in to comment on a particular thought or sequence of thoughts. That became the focus of discussion, with Yochelson applying corrective concepts to everyone in the group, not just to the man who was giving the report.

When Leroy entered the program, he had been given a preview of the life he would lead. Yochelson warned that it would seem like the cloistered existence of a monk. He would have to sever ties with other criminals. There would be no drugs, not even a beer; no sex until he learned how to have a responsible sexual relationship. Every day he would have to attend group meetings. Even after he left the hospital, participation would still be required. His existence would seem regimented and frustrating as Leroy encountered problems that he never knew existed. Leroy heard these words and pondered them. The program sounded extreme to him, but what other choice did he have? His disgust for the past and his fear about the future were strong enough for him to make a new beginning.

Neither Leroy nor any other criminal can be passionately committed to change from the outset. It is impossible for a person to embrace immediately a way of life that he has previously scorned and about which he knows nothing. Commitment grows with experience. It's like learning to play tennis. This analogy made sense to Leroy, who had learned tennis while in the hospital. At first the sport seemed glamorous, and he was eager to try it. After chasing the ball around and fighting off the gnats on one of Washington's miserably humid August days, Leroy was anything but committed to tennis. However, with lessons and practice, he improved. The harder he tried, the more skillful he became and the greater his eagerness to play and improve. Unfortunately, he had not made the generalization from tennis to life. Yochelson did, however, and told Leroy that with more experience and knowledge, commitment to change would develop just as had commitment to tennis.

Yochelson had no way of knowing why Leroy had agreed to be in the program. Was it to impress the hospital authorities so they'd let him out earlier? In his years of experience with criminals, Yochelson had learned to be neither gullible nor cynical. He knew if he believed everything that Leroy said, Leroy would manipulate him and lose respect for him. But Yochelson also knew that if he constantly disbelieved Leroy, there could be no dialogue between them. He made no immediate judgments, preferring to take the position that "time will tell." As he saw it, Leroy's life was at stake. The burden was on Leroy to be truthful and then to put what he was learning into practice. Otherwise the failure would be Leroy's, not Yochelson's.

Having heard that Yochelson's group met all morning every day, Leroy wondered what in the world consumed so much time. He quickly found out. Discussion was not limited to events or problems. Events may be few and unremarkable, especially during a routine prison or hospital day. A criminal considers himself having a "problem" only when he gets into a jam by doing what he isn't supposed to. So there was little point in limiting discussion to that. The heart of the meeting was the daily report of thinking. Then even the person who languished in bed all day with the flu would have plenty to report. First, Leroy had to be taught to stop and recollect what he had thought, then to make notes on paper. He was instructed to think of this exercise as though a tape recording of his thinking were being played back. The reason for the emphasis on thinking was that today's thoughts contain the seed of tomorrow's crime. Leroy began to understand this very quickly.

One morning he reported being furious when he was called into an office and accused by a nursing assistant of being high on marijuana. He was especially outraged because he had used no drugs for a week, now that he was in the program. The thought flashed through his mind, "I'll bust the SOB's head wide open." In the group meeting, Leroy's thought of assaulting the attendant was treated as seriously as if he had actually done it. Yochelson knew that unless such thinking was controlled, it would be only a matter of time before Leroy became violent. But it was not only thoughts about committing crimes that were considered important. No element of Leroy's thinking was to remain obscured. As an unchanged criminal, he was in no position to determine what was important. What seemed trivial to him could provide the substance for a morning-long discussion. As reports were made, Yochelson listened carefully and, from the hodgepodge of thoughts, selected a focus. One criminal living in the community happened to mention that en route to the meeting, he had thought of cutting off a driver who abruptly pulled out in front of him. This thinking flashed by, consuming seconds out of a twenty-four-hour day. Though most people would forget it instantly, this man had been trained to turn a magnifying glass on his thinking. Reporting this seemingly insignificant incident provided substance for a discussion that touched on several themes—the criminal's expectations of other people, his attempt to control others, his fears, and his anger.

Leroy found that the morning meetings were like a classroom in that they were structured and orderly. But they were not in any sense dry or academic, because the teaching was directly related to group members' immediate experiences. Leroy initially wanted to impress others by showing how perceptive he was. During the first meeting, one criminal was arguing heatedly with Yochelson. In a self-righteous tone, Leroy lambasted the other man for arguing at the expense of learning something. He advised the criminal, "Doc knows what he's talking about.

You better listen!" Leroy expected praise, but was taken aback by Yochelson's informing him that the purpose of the meeting was not to criticize one another but to learn from others' mistakes and experiences. Yochelson observed that all his life Leroy was quick to pick others apart, but rarely applied his criticisms to himself. The doctor's most frequent question to each criminal in the group was "What did you learn?" Early in the program, Leroy persisted in pointing out flaws in the group members or in Yochelson, but shrank from looking at himself. He had never believed that he was a criminal, and fought that notion with all his being.

One afternoon an attendant offered him a ride from the tennis court to his living quarters. Leroy accepted, only to find that the attendant went by way of the grocery store and purchased beer. Leroy took a few gulps and returned to the ward. No one had missed him, and no one knew about the beer except for the attendant, who wouldn't tell. When Leroy reported the incident to the group meeting, Yochelson reacted to it as though he had murdered someone. Leroy saw no big deal because "everyone" wandered off the grounds. For an experienced criminal, it was easy to get past the guards. Beer didn't hurt anyone. No one was the wiser. Wasn't he entitled to a slip? He wasn't perfect. In this single incident lay many errors in thinking. First, he had committed two violations of hospital regulations, as well as a violation of the program, by leaving the grounds without permission and drinking. Then there was Leroy's insistence that he could make exceptions for himself. It was the old story of making what was wrong right because he considered it right for him at the time. It wasn't the danger of a few gulps of beer that was at issue, but Leroy's lifelong practice of making exceptions, with one offense leading to another. Furthermore, Leroy rarely stopped at one beer. Rather, beer was the first link in a chain of Scotch, heroin, women, crime. His claim that he had slipped and wasn't perfect only meant that he had not exercised the necessary restraint to eliminate old patterns. Whether everyone went off the grounds and drank was irrelevant, a lame excuse. Everyone was not in the program. Leroy was. The main question was whether a beer was worth the sacrifice of his opportunity to become a responsible member of society.

One of the obstacles that criminals pose to nearly every interviewer or change agent is the argument that "everyone does it," or "people are like that." Criminals point an accusing finger at society for being corrupt, and claim that the only difference between them and others is that they have been caught. They'll point out how people in business and government get away with things, citing specific scandals. Leroy did his share of this. While acknowledging that many offenders avoid getting caught, or if caught don't get punished, Yochelson refused to be diverted from the task at hand—dealing with Leroy's irresponsibility.

The standards in Yochelson's program were stricter than almost any Leroy would find in the straight world itself. Leroy found it difficult to accept the fact that to change he had to go from one extreme to another. He didn't view himself as an evil person to begin with. Coming to terms with the truth about himself was excruciatingly painful, the most difficult undertaking he had ever experienced. The criminal's reluctance to face the truth was verbalized by one group member who confessed, "The reason I don't examine this stuff is that when I really look at it, it's like touching a live wire." The most basic requirement of the program is that the criminal report his thinking without embellishing, editing, or omitting. Leroy deliberately concocted some lies because he didn't want to touch the "live wire." At other times, lies spilled out of his mouth automatically. He would deny something, admit to only a part of the truth, or shade his answer to make himself look good. As he pointed out, he had lied since he could talk, so lying was second nature to him.

Because of the criminal's habitual lying, it is important that in a program like this the agent of change maintain contact with a responsible person who knows the criminal well, such as a parent, wife, or employer. This must be done regularly with the criminal's knowledge and consent, especially once he is released. Yochelson was able to talk to the institutional staff who lived around the clock with Leroy and later to family members, once Leroy was in the community. Access to an outside source is essential to evaluating the criminal's progress, and also because another person may see a problem brewing that the criminal fails to recognize because of a lack of experience in the responsible world.

Leroy found the first month of the program new and exciting. He was sure that he could change faster and more completely than anyone else. He got a high out of small accomplishments. On a pass, he went to the cleaner's and asked to purchase some storage bags. The owner graciously gave them to him. He stopped by the grocery store to ask for cartons, and was loaded up with more than he could carry. His asking was a real change. In the past, he'd just take whatever he wanted. Leroy proclaimed that he was getting high on responsibility. The trouble was that he still was in search of highs. It wasn't long before the novelty of the program wore off and Leroy grew bored. Whereas he had had tremendous stamina in his criminal life, he had little endurance for this. In the past, he always did things his way and found shortcuts, but in this program there were no shortcuts, only endless drudgery. Every time he opened his mouth, the doctor discovered something to criticize. There were no rewards for doing the expected. Yochelson would ask, "Do you want orchids for living like a civilized human being?" Observing that there seemed to be so much to learn at once, Leroy commented, "The more I do, the more there is to do." He found the whole program literally a pain in the neck and complained frequently of tension in his neck and a blistering headache. Although Leroy had been off drugs for months, he suffered other symptoms identical to those he had experienced during withdrawal from heroin. He knew that stomachaches, sweating, and other miseries would disappear if he cheated on the program. "Violation is the only comfort," he thought.

This man, who had always considered himself at the top of the heap, in control of all around him, suddenly seemed a helpless victim, if not of others, then of his own makeup. He acted as though his emotions arose from outside himself and he had nothing to do with them. Leroy claimed that because he couldn't control his anger, he slapped his girlfriend during an argument when she came to visit. He said he resorted to smoking reefer because he was so bored and depressed. He skipped a ward meeting because he was so anxious he couldn't sit still. It was up to Yochelson to alter his feelings and interest him in change.

Leroy's feelings had governed his interests, and so he'd repeatedly balk at others' requests, saying, "I don't feel like it," or "I'm not interested." In fact, Leroy thought it was the duty of others to give him reasons why he should fulfill an obligation that he didn't recognize as an obligation at all. The hospital eventually permitted Leroy to work in the community, returning to the institution just for sleeping. He was also allowed passes on weekends. Yochelson had stressed repeatedly the importance of structuring time, especially on weekends. On one of his first Saturdays out, feelings prevailed. Leroy didn't feel like doing much at all and made no plans. After visiting his mother, he went to the heart of the drug and crime area. Despite ideal spring weather, he didn't give tennis a thought. He had no interest in visiting friends of the family. He wandered by the bars and roamed through pool halls, feeling as if he wanted to get drunk more than anything else. He paused in front of one of his old haunts, told himself no, and returned to his mother's. On Sunday he had a couple of beers, returned to the hospital grounds, and began flirting with a female patient. As the sexual repartee grew increasingly animated, Leroy grinned and patted her buttocks. The woman was ready for anything, but Leroy stopped, asked himself what he was doing, and returned to his ward. Monday morning, he complained that he just couldn't get interested in the program. He was angry at Yochelson for trying to make him a lackey and rob him of his manhood. He exclaimed that he wasn't going to be like "no white man." Throughout the program, every time Leroy injected the racial issue he was angry and seeking an excuse for irresponsibility. Then Yochelson was a "no-good honky."

LEROY DISCOVERED THAT Yochelson was on a crusade against anger—quite the opposite of Leroy's earlier psychiatric treatment, in which doctors encouraged him to express his anger. Yochelson asserted that the angry criminal does far too much damage "ventilating" his fury. Whenever the world does not suit him, whenever he fails to control a situation, the criminal flies off the handle. Anger is his habitual response whenever he thinks he's being threatened, and this happens many times every day of his life. When a responsible person is angry, he may offend others, think less clearly, and be less efficient at whatever he is doing at the time. But the anger usually stops there. For the criminal, anger is a malignancy that must be removed before it spreads and results in a crime. Leroy was shocked when Yochelson told him to swallow his anger rather than unleash it. Yochelson advised Leroy that for the present it was better to risk an ulcer than for someone to suffer a cracked skull.

But neither ventilation nor suppression is an adequate solution. What must be done with a criminal like Leroy is to help him gain a realistic view of himself and of the world, so that fewer things bother him and he reacts constructively when things go wrong. The thin-skinned criminal has to learn to benefit from criticism, cope with rejection, and roll with life's punches. Columnist Ben Stein put it succinctly when he wrote that life requires "taking the lumps and calling them sugar."[1]

But the criminal must do even more than that. He must learn to anticipate situations in which he might be angry, and think them through in advance. For example, if he leaves his car at a repair shop, he already knows from experience that mishaps are likely. The car won't be ready on time, the car will not be fixed, the bill will be higher than expected, the wrong thing will be fixed, or, worst of all, the service manager won't be able to find the car anywhere on the lot. A customer can be realistic in his expectations and thereby avoid anger. He can phone before leaving to check if the car is ready. He can request an estimate before a repair is made. He can instruct the shop to notify him before making any additional repairs. En route to pick up his car, he can remind himself that even though he has taken precautions, something still may go wrong. This does not mean that he will be a doormat for others to step on. But by anticipating problems, he can preempt anger. If the need arises, he can be firm without being angry. Psychologist Paul Hauck makes the point that it is possible to live without anger: "It is perfectly possible to raise children who will not get angry over most normally provoking situations." He asserts, "One can be as solid as the Rock of Gibraltar and as peaceful as a sunny day, both at the same time."[2]

The responsible person may not take such steps to avoid anger. But the consequences of his anger are usually far less devastating than what ensues when the criminal becomes enraged. Criminals like Leroy establish their place in the world through anger, often at enormous cost to others. Who is Leroy if he can't control people? What is life if others don't jump to his command and anticipate his every wish? From a report of a single episode of anger, the role of anger in his life is examined.

One Saturday, Leroy dropped by his girlfriend Jackie's apartment. When her phone rang, he grabbed it and heard a man ask to speak to Jackie. He handed the receiver to her and stood next to her, straining to hear both ends of the conversation. She tried to get rid of the caller by pretending that he had reached the wrong party. Leroy accused her of lying about not knowing the caller, since he had asked for her by name. Jackie denied it, and Leroy had sense enough to drop it. That evening they went to a nightclub. While Jackie was in the ladies' room, a buxom, stylishly dressed girl asked Leroy to dance. Jackie returned and, seeing the couple cheek to cheek on the dance floor, created a commotion that wound up with Leroy's proclaiming that no "bitch" was going to tell him what to do, particularly after being called by every guy in the city. As Jackie rose from her chair to leave, he wheeled around and slapped her across the face. This was how Leroy handled life.

Leroy had not yet relinquished his view of himself as divine monarch, nor was he putting himself in the place of other people. He expected to be Jackie's "man," her one and only, no matter how many women he had or how he mistreated her. When others did not fulfill Leroy's expectations, he was outraged. And so he lived in a perpetual state of anger. To help him become more realistic, Yochelson introduced Leroy to "Murphy's Law" (If anything can go wrong, it will). Leroy heard a group member quip that he had discovered a corollary to Murphy's Law: Things that he was absolutely positive couldn't go wrong also went wrong. For the rest of his life, Leroy could expect to be plagued by Murphy. Murphy's Law was only one tool. Basic questions to be addressed throughout the program were: Who are you, Leroy? How do you affect people? What do you want to become? What do you expect of others?

Despite doubts about the program and whether the whole thing was worth it, Leroy saw little choice other than to stick with it. Leroy's state of mind was captured by thoughts he jotted down late one Friday afternoon.

"Near the first gate where I spend some afternoons, I saw a guy who I talk with often," Leroy reported. "I don't know his name and doubt seriously if he knows mine. We talked, and it was very obvious he had been drinking and was feeling no pain. I thought to myself that everybody I came in contact with was high on something and enjoying themselves. Then I wondered is the square life worth it, with all its loneliness and no fun. As the pretty cars left the grounds through the gates, I thought the cars were only just a small portion of what square people have along with homes, children, sweet, beautiful wives who love them, relatives and friends who respect them, and many other small but wonderful things. Then I felt my struggle and fight would bring to me those wonderful things, or I could get hip again and go no place, but the hell with it all, it's agony." His report ended with his writing, "I don't know why, but right now I feel like crying. So I'll stop and continue tomorrow. I hate this feeling, so help me God."

The worst problem Leroy faced in the early period was that as an unchanged criminal, criminal thoughts flooded his mind every day. The only barrier between himself and his life on the streets was a fear of getting caught and a threadbare conscience. These had not been very potent before, and he knew he could not rely on them in the future. Yochelson began to teach him ways to deter criminal thinking. The first method was to consider the many consequences of acting on a thought. At his job as a clerk, Leroy was positive that the boss was prejudiced against blacks and was afraid that he would be passed over for promotions. Each day he took a dimmer view of his boss, who appeared indifferent, if not antagonistic, to him while being cordial to the other personnel, all of whom were white. One day Leroy was reprimanded for coming in late. He had never seen anyone else spoken to so sharply. He held himself in check, but stalked into the group meeting vowing that he wasn't going to take "shit from that motherfucker" any longer. The next time he was going to let him have it. Patiently, Yochelson pointed out that this declaration told the story of Leroy's life. If something didn't go as he wanted, he'd teach the other person a lesson. If a situation was bad, he'd make it worse. He had always demanded fair play but had treated others shabbily.

Yochelson pointed out that, in typical fashion, Leroy was jumping to conclusions after only a few months on the job. He warned Leroy that he would encounter situations far more trying than this. In fact, Yochelson advised criminals to be grateful for things going wrong, because it could help them learn to cope with adversity and be better equipped for it in the future. If Leroy told off the boss, he'd not only enrage him, but if the boss was racially prejudiced, Leroy's behavior would reinforce that prejudice as well. Furthermore, Leroy would make other enemies in the office and find it more difficult to get work done. He might be fired and lose a job reference. Most important, his anger would unleash a chain of events that would be apt to culminate in his committing a crime, for this had been his pattern. Thinking of the consequences in advance was one form of deterrence. Later, Leroy would learn new concepts that would offer greater insurance against repeating old response patterns. He would understand the need for long-range thinking, the necessity of teamwork, and the importance of putting himself in the place of others. But until then, it was critical to equip him with deterrents for immediate use. Just as the criminal learns to abort anger, he also learns to nip criminal thinking in the bud before it flowers into criminal activity. He does this by preparing himself for any adversity.

Mark, one of the men most advanced in change in the group, reported that he and his wife, Liz, were driving to the mountains for a holiday weekend. In the past, the two of them had had arguments, long, cold silences, tears, and bitter recriminations whenever they were together, but especially on vacation. Weekends and trips had totally fallen apart over the most inconsequential incidents because Mark had always insisted on having his way. He tried to control Liz, even to the point of deciding what she should order from the menu for dinner. This time,

Mark was trying to anticipate everything that could possibly go wrong—getting lost, car trouble, illness, dirty accommodations, cold weather, rain, weak coffee, inconsiderate people, crowds at recreational facilities, a wife wanting to do something he didn't have any interest in, her moving at a slower pace, her having her period and refusing sex.

This was all new to Leroy, who had planned little in his life other than a bank robbery. In this program he was taught to think not only about future events, but also about what his future thinking might be. Yochelson stressed the importance of thinking about thinking.

Summer was approaching, and the days were hot and sultry. Pete, another member of the group, reported being "dizzy with desire" as he gazed at young women in shorts, halters, and bikinis. He contrasted the "lush female animal" on the third-floor balcony across the way with his "old hag" wife, who actually was neither old nor a hag. He caught himself thinking this way and reported to Yochelson that he had put a stop to it. If he had allowed it to proceed, he would have mentally stripped his neighbor nude and imagined "balling her like she had never been balled before." From past experience, he knew that then he would go beyond fantasy, prowling the corridor, seeking an opportunity to accost her and drag her into an area where he would tear her clothes off and gratify his desires.

Leroy was impressed with how quickly Pete had put the brakes on thinking. But Leroy pointed out that there were occasions when he didn't have time to ponder the consequences. Furthermore, he couldn't anticipate everything he'd think about, much less do. There had to be a more efficient way to deal with his immediate desires. How could he quickly squelch thinking about the pleasures of snorting coke when the thoughts seemed to hit him out of the blue? Yochelson suggested that perhaps the best way to deal with thoughts about drugs or other violations was simply to ask himself if they were worth throwing away his life and returning to the gutter. If Leroy answered no, he could direct his thinking elsewhere. This Leroy tried.

At the office, Leroy saw a young woman removing a splinter from her foot with a needle from a syringe. Immediately he thought about drugs. He dealt with this thinking by reminding himself that "drugs are death," then thinking about something else.

Pete reported spotting a pair of rubber gloves lying on a shelf in a physician's examining room. He thought about putting them on, grabbing the nurse, and raping her. Immediately, Pete stopped this stream of thought and began to think about problems at work. Another man reported going out to buy a quart of milk and passing a liquor store. He instructed himself, "Keep your mind on the milk." A thought that a responsible person can allow himself to have and perhaps savor may be dynamite to the criminal, who will elaborate on it and translate it into action.

Finally, Yochelson was teaching each of the men to take stock of himself, a deterrent process that he emphasized repeatedly. Yochelson had been holding a mirror up to Leroy, rubbing his nose in the slime of the past. Now it was time that Leroy held it up to himself. Alcoholics Anonymous requires its members to conduct a "searching moral inventory." In the same way, if a criminal does not make a habit of reflecting on his life, he will not progress because there is little incentive to change.

Inculcating fear and guilt are essential to change inasmuch as they prompt consideration of other people and the making of responsible decisions. Leroy knew well the spine-tingling fear and knot in his stomach that came whenever he was approaching the scene of a crime and leaving it to make his getaway. The only conscience he knew was that of momentary remorse when he realized he had hurt or disappointed someone. Leroy could shut anything out of his mind long enough to do whatever he wanted. The criminal must learn that fear is built into life. Some people diet out of fear. They exercise because of fear, and drive safely because they are afraid. Fear is an incentive to do better. Out of fear of hurting others, people take precautions before they act. Fearing for the future, a person does what he must for his family and himself. He purchases life insurance, saves money, schedules health checkups, services the car. Leroy was told that if he hurt someone or acted thoughtlessly, he should experience pangs of guilt. Without fear and guilt, he could never live responsibly. Leroy's fear and guilt would grow only by subjecting his irresponsible thinking to scrutiny, then by struggling to grasp corrective concepts, and finally by putting them into practice.

Leroy believed that once he learned to be responsible, he would have no worries, but Yochelson warned him that he'd be tension-free only when he was dead. Through new experiences, Leroy was learning what the doctor meant. He began to worry about work because he had processed fewer requisitions in November than in October. It wasn't just that, or the boss hassling him. There were constant interruptions, incompetent coworkers asking asinine questions, unreasonable deadlines, being placed interminably on hold while people in other agencies looked up information that turned out to be inaccurate so that eventually he had to redo work. Leroy complained that all this was meaningless. There'd be a ray of sunshine as one problem was solved, and then clouds seemed to descend—another day, another set of problems. Leroy wanted to say the hell with it. Why should he bother? Why should he worry? If this was life, it was not what he bargained for. Patiently, Yochelson did what he had done so many times before. He asked Leroy what alternative he had. Every job had its difficulties. Yochelson was having his own with St. Elizabeths. Life was full of problems. It was only reasonable to expect that before one was solved, another would crop up. Did Leroy want to return to hustling, holdups, and heroin? Did he want to kill himself? If not, the only other course was to press on and do what had to be done.

The program required massive amounts of endurance,

because life itself demands that. This is a quality that Leroy was short on. He was forever expecting to reach the summit of achievement without taking the beginning steps, and was angry when it didn't happen. His had been a life of emergencies, all of his own making. There were no goals, only an interminable series of conquests to shore up an inflated but precarious self-image. Leroy could not see any light at the end of the tunnel. He couldn't understand why anyone would work and work and work without a guarantee that it would all pay off. He demanded insurance against failure, and by failure he meant being anything less than tops at whatever he did. He said, "For some reason or other, I'm unable to go into a situation where there's a chance of failure." Since a guarantee of success was not forthcoming, Leroy began to doubt everything. "What's the purpose of it all?" he asked. "Every day is like you have to put on your armor to fight a battle. It's too much."

While Leroy was entertaining doubts, the hospital thought he was doing superbly and discharged him on a conditional release. By this time he was immersed enough in Yochelson's program to keep attending the group meetings each day. Although there was a momentary flurry of elation at being released, Leroy still found himself in a prison—the prison of a program that demanded making what he considered extreme sacrifices. All he could see was deprivation, not opportunity to start life anew. He had rejoined the wife and children whom he had abandoned years before. But still, what was life? Day after day, it was work, home, and the program.

Leroy lamented that all he had gotten out of the program was an aching head, upset stomach, and constant fatigue. He had reached the point of saying what he had said all his life when he tired of something: "Fuck it." At this point he had ruled out crime, but not other things. After working overtime one Saturday, Leroy came home late in the afternoon and found that his wife, Mary, was not yet back from shopping. He strolled down to the corner and started chatting with some of the winos hanging around. As they were talking, friends of Mary's called to him and offered him a ride home, chiding him about his poor choice of companions. Leroy replied that he was lonely. Seeing that Mary was still not home, he knocked on the landlady's door, and she invited him in to a party. Leroy had a drink or two and eyed a young lady who seemed to be about twenty. She was aware that he was watching her, and soon came over to him. They bantered flirtatiously. He nuzzled her cheek, then planted a kiss on her lips, and finally drew her into the bedroom, shutting the door behind them. After embracing and kissing, they undressed, and the girl began lionizing Leroy, telling him what a great build he had and admiring and fondling his penis. In a frenzied manner, they had intercourse and dressed. In the nick of time, Leroy returned to the party to find his wife just bursting in the door, looking for him. Mary accused him of nothing, but he was angry because "she shouldn't have been checking up on me." Leroy saw no harm whatsoever in this rendezvous. He claimed he was entitled to a "release." Yochelson viewed it differently, asking Leroy if a quick tumble with a tramp was worth risking the loss of his wife and children and the stability of the life that he was trying to build. He was not sexually deprived. He had sex with his wife almost every night. Finally, Yochelson reminded Leroy that once he made an exception for himself, it would be only the beginning. Whenever he said "fuck it" because of a momentary dissatisfaction, he came perilously close to abandoning the entire effort to become responsible. It was a question of his choice and will. Leroy became contrite, admitted he had erred, and moaned that he was a hopeless case. Yochelson was unrelenting. He reminded Leroy that he said "I can't" only when he didn't want to do something. "Are you a man or a mouse?" queried the doctor. Then he asked Leroy if he'd take criticism like a man and improve, or give up and blame others.

In Yochelson's program, the theme of the criminal's injury

to others always hung heavily in the air. Leroy knew what injury was when his own home was burglarized. He knew what injury was when his son was threatened by a boy with a knife. But he never thought of himself as injuring others. He equated injury with drawing blood, something he rarely did. But he was completely oblivious to others' rights and feelings. A fellow in the group reflected, "I do have feelings for other people. If I saw people trapped in a burning house, I'd experience a certain horror." The man continued, "And yet I really don't have any feeling for those I hurt. Were I to rape a woman, I wouldn't feel one second of her pain or anguish. I can't explain the contradiction between my pain for those in the burning building and my complete lack of feelings for my victims. I think it's because, where my own interests and pleasures are concerned, my feelings for others are automatically so totally suppressed and discarded as to be totally absent. I don't know. I only know that if I could appreciate the sufferings of my victims, they wouldn't be my victims."

Learning what constitutes injury is critical to learning about oneself. Throughout the program, Leroy experienced new waves of awareness and then disgust as to the scope of the damage that he had inflicted in almost three decades as a criminal. Beyond physical suffering and financial loss, injury extends to the emotional damage, to the climate of fear engendered in the aftermath of a crime, and to the disruption of lives. A small violation has a far-reaching effect. If a man pays for a meal with a bad check, the business suffers a direct loss. But the customers are hurt too, because if enough of these losses occur, management will refuse to take checks and customers will have to pay by cash or credit card. Furthermore, because the cost of losses is passed on to customers, the offender's own mother will have to pay more in that very restaurant. One of the men in Yochelson's group had committed burglaries and been in a few fights. But he hadn't fought or broken into anyplace lately. He asserted that he wasn't much of a criminal because he "only dealt drugs."

Yochelson pointed out that there was no telling how much injury this man contributed to through his drug sales. The criminal did remember that one of his buyers, after purchasing some heroin, had held up a store, terrorized the customers, and shot the lady behind the cash register. But never before had he thought about these or other injuries resulting from his drug trafficking.

The criminal's habit of blaming others is a persistent obstacle to the process of change. Yochelson told Leroy that what others did made no difference in this program. Only what he did mattered. Does he create a bad situation? Does he make an already bad situation worse by anger or poor judgment? He must evaluate himself before criticizing others. If his wife is unreasonable, the important issue is how he reacts. If he fails to meet a deadline at work because of someone else's incompetence, what matters is not the shortcomings of the other person, but how he deals with the situation. Even were he to be attacked totally without provocation, the focus in the group meeting would be on his thinking about his assailant. Leroy and the others were totally accountable for changing their own lives. Blaming circumstances was futile and only gave vent to anger. One of the fellows reflected, "When you look over your whole life and you see the total harm, it is up to you to create a new life for yourself. Nobody else does it for you."

As Leroy learned new ways to think and behave, he gradually emerged from his own private universe into a world of sharing, teamwork, loyalty, and trust. His attitude shifted from "screw everybody else but me" to "I have to learn how to share. I don't even know what it means." He slowly relinquished his perch of solitary grandeur to discover the give-and-take of relationships. In the group meeting, he found out what a discussion is, witnessing that it is possible to disagree with a person without insulting him. He learned to listen. In the past, Leroy didn't think anyone could teach him anything, because he knew it all to begin with. First in the group and then at work and with his family, he began to learn and practice the rudiments of civilized behavior. He became a team member instead of demanding to be the captain.

As Leroy traveled along this new road in life, unremarkable everyday events called up memories of his sordid past. Leroy and Mary were discussing their priorities in fixing up the apartment. Because both were working, they had been able to set aside more than $500 for the project. But they needed so many things, it was hard to decide whether to purchase a couch, chairs and a lamp, or some drapes and a coffee table. They listed each item they hoped to buy, and what it was likely to cost. The next morning, as he rode the bus to work, Leroy was absorbed in thinking about their discussion. He winced to himself as he thought about the way he used to "borrow" Mary's hard-earned wages on false pretenses and spend it on drugs and other women. He gasped as he realized what they could have owned by now had he been a responsible person.

Two other fellows who had been in the program longer also reported sobering reflections arising from their current progress. Pete had done well in sales and had received a promotion. Now he was authorized by management to attend an out-of-town convention. Pete picked up the phone book to look up the airline's number to make reservations. As he ran his finger down the page, he thought of the obscene phone calls he had made to clerks at nearly all the airlines as he tried to find a female agent who would engage in sexual repartee while he clung to the other end of the line, masturbating and fantasizing. As these recollections flashed through Pete's mind, he was revolted to the point of feeling physically nauseated.

Tony talked about his experience reading a psychology book in the library now that he was out of prison and in school part-time. He reported with satisfaction that by concentrating for two full hours, he had absorbed a tremendous amount. His head was swimming with ideas, and he was bubbling over with enthusiasm. However, he remembered that before prison, his library habits were very different. He rarely could sit still for two hours, and when he did, only fifteen minutes were spent in study. The rest of the time his mind was in the streets or he was staring at girls' legs or breasts. He also reflected how during that period of his life he'd wasted thousands of the dollars that his parents had saved over the years for his college education.

Several years before meeting Yochelson, Leroy had been in psychotherapy, during which the therapist probed his unconscious mind and searched for hidden complexes. He had also participated in programs where he was rewarded or punished for his behavior. Yochelson's program was neither as complicated as the psychodynamic approach nor as simplistic as behavior modification. He found its concepts made sense, and he could glimpse progress when he allowed himself to be guided by them. The more he learned, the more starkly the present contrasted with the past, and the more he saw there was to learn. Leroy was surprised to discover that he knew virtually nothing about making decisions responsibly. He had been one of those people who didn't like to ask a question because to do so was a humiliating admission of ignorance. He had no need to plan ahead except in scheming a crime. He recalled, "I thought about tomorrow, tomorrow." Now he was beginning to realize that to admit ignorance was wiser than pretending to know it all. Leroy began to weigh alternative courses of action and consider both short- and long-range consequences.

There are other programs that teach criminals how to make decisions as well as acquire many other skills. However, they focus upon situational problem solving and feelings, not upon thinking patterns that are all-pervasive. Yochelson's program aimed to help a criminal change 180 degrees by learning an entirely new way of thinking and acting that would permeate his entire life. Leroy continued to be amazed at the tremendous attention to tiny details. For example, he reported that from time to time he put a quarter in a pay phone rather than twenty cents, because he didn't want to take the time to get the proper change. Yochelson developed this pattern into a major theme for discussion—the criminal's view of money. Leroy had never valued money. A nickel, a quarter, even a thousand dollars meant little. More money had passed through his hands in a few weeks than most people earn in years. To manage money, Leroy first would have to keep track of it. Again, it was a matter of going from one extreme to the other, from squandering thousands of dollars to counting every penny. Establishing the discipline of saving was what mattered, not whether the phone company gained five extra cents on the pay phone. In this program, the smallest breach of integrity became a major issue, even when no one was hurt by it. One of the men in the group ate ham at Thanksgiving rather than turkey. When asked by a friend whether he'd enjoyed his turkey, he responded that he had. This was a lie, a trivial one to be sure, but one that a criminal could ill afford. Leroy and the others in the group had lied all their lives, even when there seemed to be no advantage to it. One lie had led to another. To destroy this pattern, a criminal must maintain total integrity. Leroy's fellow group member could have replied, "This year it was ham." The discipline in being totally truthful is important in the same way as the discipline in accounting for every cent.

LEROY HAD UPS and downs in change, as did all the men. As he achieved more and more in the responsible world, it became increasingly hard to think of turning back. He viewed the old life as a living death. It was true that meeting deadlines at work, worrying about bills, balancing his checkbook, enduring the stresses of raising children, and working out differences with his wife were not the highs he was accustomed to. There were periods of self-pity and departures from the program—a nip of sherry, followed by a tumbler of Scotch, staying home from work on a day when he just didn't feel like going, slapping Mary in a fit of pique because now she was spending too much money. But from each such departure, Leroy learned. The most important reinforcer of change was that by adhering to the program, he was accomplishing new goals he had set. Leroy and Mary bought a small house in which Leroy took great pride. After coping with delays in securing financing, and then the drudgery of moving, he plunged into fixing up the place, spending practically every spare moment plastering, painting, cleaning, and working on the yard. Tending a vegetable garden became almost an obsession. After months of physical labor he was finally able to say, "As soon as you hit the corner, my house stands out." But many more projects remained—repairing the fence, enlarging the garden, sodding the front lawn, and painting the bedrooms.

Leroy's family life meant more and more. His boys, approaching adolescence, looked to him for approval and guidance. He fought back tears of joy as Tommy powered his school football team to victory with the encouraging cheers of the fans. Leroy had always believed he had to have more than one woman or else he was not a man. But he was starting to change his mind about this.

One day in the group, Leroy reported that a "sexy-looking thing" was waiting at the bus stop. Catching himself thinking, "She'd be a nice piece to have," he shifted his gaze, then boarded the bus and buried himself in the newspaper. She made her way down the aisle, plopped down beside him, and brushed her thigh against his. Leroy shifted his leg and responded politely to the conversation. Deciding to keep things light, he discussed the weather and bus breakdowns. When he got off, he thought he was a "damn idiot" for not taking her phone number. But as he walked to his office building, he had an image of Mary, who had suffered so much in the past because of him. Now she was beginning to trust him, to plan a life with him as her husband

and the father of their two boys. He felt ashamed of his thoughts about the girl on the bus and dug into the work piled up on his desk.

As things continued to go relatively smoothly at home, Leroy found he was thinking less about other women and looking less, too. "I look once and don't allow myself to look again," he reported. "I am never going to let myself go. It makes me feel good to be in control of myself."

Leroy believed that he had gone through too much in the past, and was working too hard now, to soil a clean record. Hard work was yielding results—a promotion at work, an attractively decorated and immaculately clean home, two sons who loved him, a wife who depended on him, neighbors who respected him. Leroy had altered his spending habits. He and his wife had a savings certificate in a bank and had far fewer debts. Leroy said, "I value money. Excitement is when I have it stashed away." Leroy saw similar changes occurring in some of the other men in the group. One who had been insensitive and angry was referred to at his job as "the Easter Bunny" because he was so affable. Another rose from busboy to manager of a large restaurant. Perhaps what Leroy and the others prized most was not so much the tangible accomplishments as the feeling of being clean. One man asserted, "I so prize the cleanliness that everything could go, including my health, but I'd still prize the cleanliness." What had been tempting was no longer tempting. Leroy severed his connections with other criminals, prostitutes, the drug world. No more looking over his shoulder for the police. He said with pride and some amazement, "That world is like a dream."

Leroy did not become complacent. The criminal life may have seemed like a dream, but Leroy knew it could quickly become real if he failed to be self-critical or ceased to struggle to improve himself. Although he was no longer legally accountable to the hospital, he put himself on parole, so to speak. Voluntarily, he continued to seek Yochelson's counsel long after the intensive phase of daily sessions was over. Meeting with Yochelson once a week, he spontaneously described his thinking. Rather than fearing the doctor's picking him apart as he used to, Leroy welcomed it. He was afraid of getting too cocky from compliments that were being showered upon him at work, at home, and by his friends. Leroy agreed with Pete, who drew an analogy between his current status and rowing a boat away from the brink of Niagara Falls. Pete contended that unless he kept straining at the oars, he'd drop over the edge of the falls. Another man put it this way: "My wife, our little apartment, the car, the stereo. It's like it's all sitting on sand that could be blown away with one little slip."

In November 1976, tragedy struck Leroy, something he'd never envisioned, although Yochelson had warned him it might occur. On Yochelson's first trip away from Washington to speak about his work, the seventy-year-old psychiatrist collapsed in the St. Louis airport and died a few days later. Leroy was stunned, but he knew what he had to do: "Damn what I feel, do I must. I have got to be stronger than ever." More than a year later, he was still watchful of his own thoughts, had received another promotion at work, and, above all, had continued to make the program his life.

As Yochelson had instructed him, Leroy continued engaging in a daily moral inventory. He knew that he would never reach a point at which he would "have it made." Rather, he was positive that the effort had to be constant and that he had to bear in mind what his life had been. This program seemed less and less burdensome because Leroy no longer harbored his former grandiose view of himself. The more he reaped the rewards of this new life, the more crime repulsed him. He lived a quiet life, one that he could never have imagined before, dividing his time among family, work, and a few friends. Leroy budgeted his money and his time, the latter being too short for all that he wanted to accomplish. He knew what had to be done to progress. He had the tools—the new patterns of thought that Yochelson had taught him. Leroy reflected, "It's easy to figure out things when my mind isn't bollixed up." Going back to crime was unthinkable. Declared Leroy, "There are too many things I want. I don't want anything interfering with my goals."

TWENTY YEARS AFTER this was written, Leroy had maintained steady employment. He still lived with his wife, Mary. His children were grown. Leroy had a clean record—no arrests. He reported that he tried to take care of himself by exercising and remaining in good physical condition. He continued to abstain from the use of illegal drugs. The only major correction he reported making was voluntarily to attend meetings of Alcoholics Anonymous at a time when he realized his consumption of alcoholic beverages threatened to destabilize what had become a responsible and productive life.

ANOTHER FOLLOW-UP, TEN years later, found Leroy fighting for his life in a hospital. While recovering from cancer surgery, he suffered cardiac arrest. According to a close family member, Leroy had retired from his long-time municipal job, worked part-time at a store, and remained devoted to his wife and adult children. He was still arrest-free and, according to his relative, "living a normal life."

16

"Habilitation" or More Crime?

Forty-four years ago, I knew nothing about "the criminal mind." I thought that people who committed crimes were like anyone else, but that their criminality was a response to environmental adversities, poor parenting, or mental illness. It was eye-opening as I watched Dr. Yochelson interview men who had made crime a way of life. I saw that their way of looking at life had little in common with people whom I personally knew, and was very different from individuals whom I had treated professionally. On the face of it, they seemed to want what most people want—friendship, security, love, and a legitimate way to support themselves. What I came to realize is that even if criminals say they want these things, they have a radically different way of pursuing them from people who are basically responsible. Their self-image is based on overcoming and controlling others through deception, intimidation, or force. They seethe with anger at a world that doesn't accord them what they think they are owed. And, in a most chilling manner, they shut off fears of consequences and conscience long enough to do whatever they want.

Since the publication of the first edition of *Inside the Criminal Mind,* I have received hundreds of letters, e-mails, and phone calls from people in all walks of life who reported that the book helped them make sense of what had baffled and grieved them for years. Parents, exhausted by lengthy and expensive consultation with mental health professionals who blamed them for their offspring's criminality, expressed relief upon learning that they were not the cause.

Men and women who encountered criminals daily in their professional roles found the concept of a "criminal mind" invaluable, especially as they became acquainted with the "errors in thinking" that give rise to criminal behavior. This frame of reference improved their understanding of what they were observing from day to day. It helped them perform better at their jobs.

Professionals working in institutions and in the community with adult and juvenile offenders wanted to learn more about how to help criminals identify errors in thinking, and they sought guidance as to how to teach corrective patterns to this very difficult population. Nearly 7,000 sets of DVDs and workbooks elaborating on some of the concepts from *Inside the Criminal Mind* were ordered by state and federal institutions to help in this endeavor.[1]

After reading earlier editions of this book, people in relationships with individuals whom they did not conceive of as "criminals" came to realize that the person they thought they knew intimately was in many ways a stranger. The new perspective helped these individuals liberate themselves from entanglements that left them feeling confused, victimized, and guilty.

And criminals themselves who either read *Inside the Criminal Mind* or were exposed to my DVD curriculum reported that, finally, they started to understand their own thinking, and this helped them change their lives for the better.

THIS WORK, WHICH I have been engaged in since 1970, began in 1961. Dr. Yochelson developed an approach of "habilitation" that was based on an in-depth understanding of the criminal mind. His findings and approach to change have been adapted and implemented in a variety of settings, including some that he may not have anticipated, such as faith-based programs, and juvenile facilities. Dr. Yochelson pioneered a cognitive approach, now considered to be mainstream. But, unlike mainstream cognitive psychology, his method was based on an understanding of the day-to-day thought processes of criminals. This required a "phenomenological" approach—understanding the world from the criminal's point of view, rather than dwelling on causative factors that still remain matters of theory and conjecture. Once Dr. Yochelson and I understood how criminals think, we were in a position to develop a program to help them change that thinking.

IN DESCRIBING THE change process, I have referred to "the criminal" over and over, with few distinctions as to the severity of their crimes. Obviously, not every person who commits a crime is a hard-core criminal. But still, crimes of all types result from the way a person thinks. The program described in the previous chapter has been modified to help youths and adults who have not yet developed into career criminals become more responsible. However, nothing short of an intensive process will suffice for career criminals.

As he begins a "habilitative" program, no criminal can be aware of all that will be required to change. Some criminals will reject any opportunity to reform. Some will make a stab at changing on their own, but eventually abandon it. Criminals who refuse to change remain a danger to society as well as to themselves. In such cases, only two alternatives exist: lengthy confinement in humane institutions or release under a kind of close supervision that does not now exist. Supervision would first require that the offender meet weekly with an officer of the court. Second, that officer must make home visits and maintain close contact with a reliable person who knows the criminal well. This reliable individual could be a spouse, parent, other relative, or employer. Criminals who are amenable should be offered the opportunity to participate in an intensive program designed to help them make fundamental changes in their thinking and behavior.

Change demands not only that an offender remain arrest-free, but also that he experience a reduction in his desire to commit crimes. Offenders like Leroy must account for how they spend money and time. Not only must they hold jobs, but they also must establish stable work patterns. Those who have families must function in an accommodating and interdependent manner, and this needs to be verified by family members.

THE MOST IMPORTANT part of the change process transpires in the community. It is a pipe dream to release a criminal from an institution and expect him, without guidance, to function responsibly in a world for which he is not equipped. It would be like asking a second-grader to solve algebraic equations. Once a criminal is released, the effort to help him change must continue in the community on an intensive basis. For those who are not confined at all, a period of "trial probation" is necessary. That is, the criminal could be placed on probation with the understanding that he must participate in an intensive program for change. If he decides to leave the program, a court would determine whether probation should be continued under different conditions or revoked altogether.

Because technology exists to monitor offenders in the community more effectively than ever before, such a habilitative effort is somewhat less risky than it might have been earlier.

Society need not rely solely on a criminal's good faith or on hit-or-miss supervisory efforts. Through GPS technology, it is possible to know, with considerable accuracy, where a criminal is at any given time.

The program does not require new types of facilities or tremendous manpower. Personnel must be trained in order to become thoroughly familiar with the thinking and behavior patterns of criminals. A cadre of psychologists or psychiatrists is not required to help criminals change. The concepts and methods are straightforward and can be transmitted to people who do not hold advanced professional degrees, but who do have the dedication and stamina for this arduous work. It is essential that the men and women who staff such programs be responsible themselves. Nothing is more futile than having one irresponsible person try to teach another irresponsible person how to become responsible. In other words, the personal qualities of those who are to help criminals change is important. To undertake the task, a person must be firm, compassionate, and patient. Quick results are unlikely.

Whether working in the institution or the community, the person guiding the criminal in this enterprise will show compassion not by shedding tears for his plight, but rather by devoting considerable time and effort to a monumental undertaking that has life-and-death importance to both society and the criminal.

The greatest occupational hazard of working with criminals may be the risk of physical assault. Also extremely inimical to a gratifying career is the prospect of a rapid burnout of enthusiasm, commitment, and interest. Mention the word "burnout" to seasoned people in corrections, and they know what you mean. Increasing numbers of idealistic, conscientious young adults are entering corrections, eager to do a good job. Almost immediately, they confront a formidable array of obstacles for which they are ill prepared. Despite the fact that their clients are among the most difficult anywhere, these novice counselors think that they are expected to accomplish what parents, teachers, employers, clergy, and others have failed at for years. One senior corrections official described the progression from enthusiasm to burnout. "The first year," he said, "the new person can't do enough *for* the criminal. The second year, he can't do enough *to* the criminal. The third year, he doesn't give a damn." The human element vanishes when workers become cynical or indifferent. Some quit their jobs. Some persist and endure, grateful simply to survive each day and receive a paycheck. A minority plug along, still hoping to accomplish something worthwhile.

Criminals cannot be forced to change; they must reach a point in life when they are becoming fed up with themselves and, consequently, desire to change. There are just three paths—crime, suicide, or change. Many offenders cling to a belief that there is a fourth option—to appear responsible while committing crimes on the side. Partial participation in this program is analogous to being a little bit pregnant. It is not a viable option. A person either shuts the door completely on crime or he does not. No middle ground exists. There is a parallel between criminal habilitation and Alcoholics Anonymous. A.A. calls for total abstinence. A sip of alcohol becomes a glass, then a bottle, and in time the alcoholic reverts to where he was. And so it is with the criminal. If he permits himself to lie, lying eventually becomes pervasive. If he steals a few tools from work, it is not long until he is cheating or stealing from his employer in other ways. Minor offenses are like a snowball rolling downhill; they just increase in size.

An effective program for change places total responsibility upon the criminal, who has the opportunity and capability of making new choices. The approach emphasizes not what happens to the criminal, but on what he does to others. For example, if his employer was harshly critical, what had he done to provoke it? If truly nothing, then did his response improve the situation or make it worse?

Decisions are not made for the criminal. The *process* of decision making is the focus, but each specific decision is made by the individual. Eventually a criminal, like law-abiding citizens, chooses his life's work and advances as far as his talents and efforts allow. Many and varied opportunities will always reside within the limits of responsible choices. The change process calls for criminals to acquire moral values that have enabled civilizations to survive. The objective is to teach offenders to live without injuring others.

THE ISSUES I'VE addressed here are not new: the power to choose, free will, good versus evil, one's response to temptation, and whether one demonstrates courage or cowardice in the face of adversity. The sacred books of most religions are filled with admonitions against deceit, anger, and pride. In addition, the Old Testament says, "As a man thinketh in his heart, so is he" (Proverbs 23:7). We are as we think. It is impossible to help a person give up crime and live responsibly without helping him to change what is most basic—his thinking.

1. The Failure to Identify Causes of Crime

1. O. Hobart Mowrer, "Does Psychoanalysis Encourage Sociopathy and Paranoia?" In O. Hobart Mowrer, *The New Group Therapy* (New York: Van Nostrand, 1964), 181–214.

2. "On Edge of Society, Disaffected Youth Identify with the Infamous," *Rocky Mountain News,* December 15, 2007, 27.

3. "Slave Syndrome Argued in Boy's Death," Associated Press report, June 1, 2004.

4. "Violent Games 'Cause Violence,'" *New Zealand Herald,* October 19, 2005, B3.

5. "Angry Outbursts Linked to Inflammation in the Body," nydaily news.com, December 13, 2013.

6. M. Pakyurek and Z. Gutkovich, "Adenotonsillectomy Reduced Aggression," *C&A Psychiatry Alerts,* extract in *Journal of the American Academy of Child and Adolescent Psychiatry,* September 2002, 1025.

7. "Soda Linked to Behavioral Problems in Young Children, Study Says," *Los Angeles Times,* August 16, 2013.

8. "Japan's Graying Criminals," *AARP Bulletin,* January–February, 2009, 6.

9. "Bittersweet: Candy Causes Adult Violence," *Metronews*, October 2, 2009.

10. "Violent Crime and Cholesterol," *Washington Post,* February 11, 2001.

11. "Crime of the Century," *St. Louis Post–Dispatch,* June 10, 2008.

12. "Top 10 'Bad Boy' Baby Names," *USA Today,* July 17, 2009.

13. "Warmer Climate Could Lead to Increased Conflict, Violence," *Science News,* August 2, 2013, 444–45.

14. Frederic Wertham, *Seduction of the Innocent* (Port Washington, N.Y.: Kennikat Press, 1972).

15. "Violent Video Games and Young People," *Harvard Mental Health Letter,* October 2010, 2.

16. Christopher J. Ferguson, "Violent Video Games and the Supreme Court," *American Psychologist,* 68(2), 57.

17. "Echo of Columbine," *Baltimore Sun,* March 13, 2014. 1.

18. Kevin W. Dowling, "The Effects of Lunar Phases on Domestic Violence Incidence Rates," *Forensic Examiner,* Winter 2005, 13–18.

19. Robert M. MacIver, *The Prevention and Control of Delinquency* (New York: Atheron Press, 1966), 41.

20. U.S. Department of Justice, "Remarks by Attorney General Ramsey Clark to the National Commission on Causes and Prevention of Violence," Washington, D.C., September 18, 1968, 5.

21. U.S. Department of Justice, Bureau of Justice Statistics, *National Crime Victimization Survey,* 2010.

22. United Nations General Assembly, 60th General Assembly, Third Committee, "Crime is Both Cause, Consequence of Poverty," 2005.

23. "Rural Crime, Poverty, and Community," in Joseph F. Donermeyer et al., *Advancing Critical Criminology Theory and Application* (Lanham, MD: Lexington Books, 2006), 199–216.

24. "There's No Defense for Affluenza," *Slate Magazine,* December 17, 2013.

25. Michael Shader, *Risk Factors for Delinquency: An Overview* (Washington, D.C.: U.S. Department of Justice), 1.

26. Centers for Disease Control and Prevention, "Youth Violence: Risk and Protective Factors," August 30, 2011.

27. Richard Cohen, "Bad People, Not Bad Times," *Washington Post,* May 31, 2011, A13.

28. "Cold Weather Creates Climate for Car Thefts," *Washington Post,* March 28, 2013, B3.

29. George N. Thompson, "Psychopath," *Archives of Criminal Psychodynamics* 4, 1961, 4, 736–48.

30. C. R. Jeffrey, "Environmental Design and the Prevention of Behavioral Disorders and Criminality," in *Proceedings: Crime Prevention Through Environmental Design Workshop* at Ohio State University, July 19–23, 1972.

31. Adrian Raine, *The Anatomy of Violence* (New York: Pantheon Books, 2013).

32. Sally Satel and Scott O. Lilienfeld, *Brainwashed: The Seductive Appeal of Mindless Neuroscience* (New York: Basic Books, 2013), 71.

33. David Deitch, "Presentation at the 132nd Congress of Corrections of the American Correctional Association" (Anaheim, CA: 2002, unpublished).

34. Adam Gopnik, "Mindless: The New Neuro-skeptics," *The New Yorker,* September 9, 2013.

35. Sarnoff A. Mednick et al., "Genetic Influences in Criminal Convictions: Evidence from Adoption Cohort," *Science* 224, 891–94.

2. Parents Don't Turn Children into Criminals

1. David Cohen, *Stranger in the Nest* (New York: John Wiley & Sons, 1999), 4, 7.

2. Richard Trembley, "Terrible Twos Who Stay Terrible," nytimes.com, December 16, 2013.

3. William B. Carey, *Understanding Your Child's Temperament* (New York: Macmillan, 1997), xxi.

4. Elaine Gunnison, "Psychological Theories and Research on Female Criminal Behavior," in Jacqueline B. Helfgott, ed., *Criminal Psychology: Volume 1: Theory and Research* (Santa Barbara: ABC-CLIO, 2013), 281.

5. Neil I. Bernstein, *How to Keep Your Teenager Out of Trouble and What to Do If You Can't* (New York: Workman, 2001), 102.

6. Ruth Marcus, "A Mother Tragic—and Infuriating," *Washington Post,* November 27, 2013.

3. Peer Pressure: No Excuse for Crime

1. "Signs of Danger Were Missed in a Troubled Teenager's Life," *New York Times,* March 24, 2005, A1.

2. "The Columbine Tapes," *Time,* December 20, 1999, 40–41.

3. "Before Gunfire, Hints of 'Bad News,'" nytimes.com, August 26, 2012.

4. "The Roots of Evil," *Vanity Fair,* May 1989, 142–49, 188–98.

5. Elizabeth Englander, "Addressing Bullying and Cyberbullying," *National Psychologist,* March/April 2012, 11.

6. Michael Nuccitelli, "Cyberbullying Tactics: An Introduction," *Forensic Examiner,* Summer 2012, 20–21.

7. American Psychological Association, "Bullied Children May Be More Likely to Develop Anxiety Disorders and Depression and Have Suicidal Thoughts as Adults," *Monitor on Psychology,* May 2013, 18.

8. Nicholas Pileggi, *Wiseguy: Life in a Mafia Family* (New York: Simon & Schuster, 1985), 19.

4. "To Hell with School"

1. American Psychological Association, "Are Zero Tolerance Practices Effective in Schools?" *American Psychologist,* December 2008, 859.

2. "D.C. Police Adjust Coverage at Schools," *Washington Post,* September 16, 2013, B1.

3. American Psychological Association, "Violence Against Teachers Spurs Urgent Call to Action," *Monitor on Psychology,* March, 2013, 11.

4. "The Classroom as a Battleground," *Baltimore Sun,* February 16, 2014, p. 1.

5. American Psychological Association, "Preventing Violence Against Teachers," *Monitor on Psychology,* November 2013, 61–64.

6. "Are Zero Tolerance Policies Effective in the Schools?" *American Psychologist,* December 2008, 852–62.

7. "Discipline in Schools Revisited," *Washington Post,* January 9, 2014, A13.

8. American Psychological Association, "By the Numbers," *Monitor on Psychology,* March 2013, 13.

9. U.S. Department of Education, Family Educational Rights and Privacy Act (FERPA), 1974.

10. "Letting It Slide: Crimes Often Go Unreported," *Daily Pennsylvanian,* April 4, 2007.

5. Work and the Criminal

1. Ponemon Institute, "2013 Cost of Cyber Crime Study: United States," October 2013, 1.

2. "Trade Secret Theft: Businesses Need to Beware and Prepare," Forbes.com, May 24, 2012.

3. Joseph Epstein, "'Uncle Bernie' And the Jews," thedailybeast.com (excerpted from *Newsweek,* January 9, 2009).

4. "The Talented Mr. Madoff," nytimes.com, January 24, 2009.

5. Gil Weinreich, "Leeson's Lessons," *Research,* January 2005, 34–40.

6. Terry Leap, "When Bad People Rise to the Top," *MIT Sloan Management Review,* Winter 2008, 23–27.

7. "Ex-EPA Official Who Stole $900,000 Gets 32 Months in Prison," *Washington Post,* December 19, 2013, A4.

8. "Former Atlanta Schools Superintendent Reports to Jail in Cheating Scandal," *CNN Justice,* April 3, 2013.

9. "Ex-Cop Drew Peterson Gets 38 Years for Killing Ex-Wife," usatoday.com, February 21, 2013.

10. "Drew Peterson, Accused of Killing Wife, Takes Active Role in Jury Selection Process," *Chicago Tribune* (MCT), July 25, 2012.

6. "Life Is a One-Way Street—My Way"

1. Erik Larson, *The Devil in the White City* (New York, Vintage, 2003), 355.

7. Sex for Conquest and a Buildup of the Self

1. Fara McCrady et al., "It's All About Me: A Brief Report of Incarcerated Adolescent Sex Offenders' Generic and Sex-Specific Cognitive Distortions," *Sexual Abuse: A Journal of Research and Treatment,* vol. XX, 2008, 1–11.

2. John Douglas and Mark Olshaker, *The Anatomy of Motive* (New York: Scribner, 1999), 40.

3. Brett Kahr, *Ideas in Psychoanalysis: Exhibitionism* (Cambridge, Icon Books, 2001), 54.

4. Carolyn M. Bates and Annette M. Brodsky, *Sex in the Therapy Hour* (New York: Guilford Press, 1989), 136.

5. William Nack and Don Yaeger, "Every Parent's Nightmare," *Sports Illustrated,* September 13, 1999, 40–53.

6. U.S. Department of Justice, "Citizens Guide to U.S. Federal Law on Child Pornography," justice.gov/criminal/ceos/citizensguide_porn.

7. Fred S. Berlin and Denise Sawyer, "Potential Consequences of Accessing Child Pornography Over the Internet and Who Is Accessing It," *Sexual Addiction and Compulsivity,* January–June 2012, 39.

8. Simmering Anger Flaring into Rage

1. Michele C. Black et al., *The National Intimate Partner and Sexual Violence Survey, 2010 Summary Report,* National Center for Injury Prevention and Control, Centers for Disease Control and Prevention, Atlanta, Georgia, November 2011.

9. Criminality Is Primary, Drugs Secondary

1. President's Advisory Commission on Narcotic and Drug Abuse, *Final Report* (Washington, D.C.: U.S. Government Printing Office, November 1963), 1.

2. "The Big Story: Ohio Executes Man Who Fatally Shot Security Guard," Associated Press online report, March 6, 2013.

3. Neil Bernstein, *How to Keep Your Teenager Out of Trouble and What to Do If You Can't* (New York: Workman Publishing, 2001), 342.

4. "Teens and Drugs: Rite of Passage or Recipe for Addiction?" time .com, June 29, 2011.

5. Edward J. Khantzian, *Treating Addiction as a Human Process* (Lanham, MD: Jason Aronson, 2007), 572.

6. Substance Abuse and Mental Health Services Administration, "'Bath Salts' Were Involved in Over 20,000 Drug-Related Emergency Room Visits in 2011," *The Dawn Report,* September 17, 2013.

7. National Institute on Drug Abuse, "Drug Facts: Synthetic Cathinones ('Bath Salts')," drugabuse.gov/publications/drugfacts/synthetic -cathinones, November 2012.

8. "Interview with Glen Hanson," *Forensic Examiner,* Winter 2012/ Spring 2013, 84.

9. "Marijuana: Will It Ever Be Legal," *Washington Lawyer,* June 2013, 31.

10. National Institute on Drug Abuse, "Drug Facts: Marijuana," drug abuse.gov/publications/publications/drug facts/marijuana, December 2012.

11. "More Drivers Are Testing Positive for Pot in Washington State," *Washington Post,* November 24, 2013, A2.

12. National Institute on Drug Abuse, "Marijuana Abuse," drugabuse .gov/publications/marijuana-abuse, July 2012.

13. Otto Fenichel, *Psychoanalytic Theory of Neurosis* (New York: W. W. Norton & Co., 1945), 377.

14. Melissa Stone, "Why Can't They Just Stop?" *Mental Health Matters,* December 2010, 3.

15. "89-Year-Old Drug Courier Pleads Guilty in Detroit," Associated Press report, October 8, 2013.

16. American Psychological Association, "In Brief," *Monitor on Psychology,* February 2013, 16.

17. "Gateway to Percocet?" *Yale Alumni Magazine*, November/December 2012, 29.

18. United States District Court for the Eastern District of Virginia, Sentencing Memorandum of U.S. Attorney's Office in *United States of America v. William Eliot Hurwitz*, March 2005.

19. American Psychological Association, "Will Behave for Money," *Monitor on Psychology*, November 2011, 38–41.

20. "Award Nominee Has Drive to Find Cure for Addiction," *Washington Post*, August 8, 2013, B1.

10. The Criminal as Terrorist

1. Federal Bureau of Investigation, Definitions of Terrorism in the U.S. Code, ibi/gov/about-us/investigate/terrorism/terrorism-definition.

2. Robert G. L. Waite, *The Psychopathic God: Adolf Hitler* (New York: Signet, 1977), 47, 188.

3. Mary Anne Weaver, "The Short, Violent Life of Abu Musab al-Zarqawi," *The Atlantic*, July 1, 2006, theatlantic.com/magazine/archive/2006/07/.

4. "The Apostle of Hate," *Time*, June 19, 2006, 37.

5. Stanley Bedlington, "Not Who You Think," *Washington Post*, October 28, 2001.

6. Kenneth L. Woodward, "In the Beginning There Were Holy Books," *Time*, February 11, 2002, 57.

7. Aubrey Immelman, "The Personality Profile of al-Qaida Leader Osama bin Laden," paper presented at the annual scientific meeting of the International Society of Political Psychology, Berlin, Germany, July 16–19, 2002.

8. Philippe Bolopion, "Averting a New Genocide in Africa," *Washington Post*, November 29, 2013.

9. "Hospital Attacked in Central African Republic," aljazeera.com/news/Africa/2013/hospital-attacked, December 8, 2013.

10. "Turning from 'Weapon of the Spirit' to the Shotgun," *Washington Post*, August 7, 1994, A01.

11. "Hill Lives in World of Black and White," *Pensacola News Journal,* August 24, 2003.

12. "Internet Provides Venue for Training Future Jihadists," *Washington Jewish Week,* May 16, 2003, 3.

13. Ibid.

14. Marie Wright, "Domestic Terrorism, Cyber-Radicalization & U.S. College Students," *Forensic Examiner,* Winter 2011, 10–18.

15. Report of the Central Intelligence Agency, "Terrorists: Recruiting and Operating Behind Bars," August 20, 2002.

16. "Homegrown Terrorist: How Al-Shabaab Is Recruiting the Male Teen Next Door," wusa9.com, 2013.

17. "Huge Breach of Data Security at Target," *Washington Post,* December 20, 2013, A21.

18. General Michael V. Hayden, "It's Going to Get Worse," *Washington Post,* October 10, 2013, AA5.

19. "An Ordinary Boy's Extraordinary Rage," *Washington Post,* July 2, 2995, A01.

20. "A Battered Dream, Then a Violent Path," *New York Times,* April 27, 2013, nytimes.com/2013/04/28/us/shot-at-boxing-title.

21. "Ex: Boston Bomber Tried to 'Brainwash' Me to Hate America," *New York Post,* April 20, 2013, nypost.com/2013/04/30/ex-boston-bomber.

22. "The Dark Side, Carefully Masked," *New York Times,* May 4, 2014.

11. "Decent People"

1. Katherine Ramsland, "The Man Who Enters the Mind of the Serial Killer," *The Forensic Examiner,* Fall 2013, 64–68.

2. Sid Kirchheimer, "Scare Tactics," *AARP Bulletin,* September 2013, 24.

12. Mental Illness, or a Criminal Personality?

1. "In Lanza's Chilling Book A Search for Psychological Clues," *Hartford Courant,* December 1, 2013.

2. "Race Not a Factor in Australian Baseball Player's Oklahoma Murder, DA Says," foxnews.com, August 24, 2014.

3. "Firesetting, Arson, Pyromania, and the Forensic Mental Health Expert," *Journal of the American Academy of Psychiatry and the Law* 40, 2010, 358.

4. "Jurors Find Man Simultaneously Sane and Insane," *National Psychologist,* July/August 2008, 1.

5. American Psychiatric Association, *Diagnostic and Statistical Manual of Mental Disorders, DSMIV-TR* (Arlington, VA: American Psychiatric Association, 2000), 519.

6. "Acquaintances Split on 'Brainwashing,'" *Washington Post,* November 17, 2003, A1, A12.

7. "The Sick World of the Snipers," *Newsweek,* November 4, 2002.

13. Locked Up

1. The Sentencing Project, "Trends in U.S. Corrections," sentencing project.org, 2012.

2. Bureau of Justice Statistics, "Prison Rape Elimination Act," 2003.

3. Michigan Family Impact Seminars, "Fathers in Prisons," family impactseminars.org/index.

4. Daniel P. Mears, "Evaluating the Effectiveness of Supermax Prisons," Research Report of the Urban Institute Justice Policy Center, March 2006, iii.

5. Stephen Gettinger, "Informer," *Corrections Magazine,* April 1980, 17–19.

6. "Suicides Kill More Inmates Than Homicide, Overdoses, Accidents Combined," usnews.nbcnews.com, September 2013.

7. Charles Colson, *Life Sentence* (Ada, MI: Chosen Books, 1979).

8. "Faith-Based Prisons: More Religion Equals Less Crime?" divinity .uchicago.edu/sightings/faith-based-prisons, December 19, 2013.

9. "Column: Nightmare of Prison Rape," usatoday.com/news/opinion/ forum/story, June 20, 2012.

10. "Drugs Inside Prison Walls," washingtontimes.com/news, January 27, 2010.

11. "Prison Drug Use Becoming Harder and Harder to Control," correctionsone.com/drug-issues, January 28, 2010.

12. "Prisoners with Gang Links to Be Isolated," journal-news.com/news, December 29, 2013.

13. "When Texas DA, Wife Were Slain . . . ," *USA Today,* April 12–14, 2013, 1A–2A.

14. "In Honduran Prison Talks, Wary Overtures of Peace," *Washington Post,* July 26, 2013, A10.

15. Shadd Maruna, *Making Good: How Ex-Convicts Reform and Rebuild their Lives* (Washington, D.C.: American Psychological Association, 2001), 152.

14. "Rehabilitation" Revisited

1. Robert Martinson, "What Works? Question and Answers About Prison Reform," *The Public Interest* 35, 22–54.

2. merriam-webster.com/dictionary/rehabilitation.

3. Department of Corrections and Rehabilitation, Division of Juvenile Justice, cdcr.ca.gov/Juvenile_Justice.

4. American Council on Education, "GED Testing in Correctional Centers," September 2011.

5. "GED Use Instead of School Decried," *Washington Post,* May 13, 2013, B1.

6. National Correctional Industries Association, "Correctional Industries," nationalcia.org/about/correctional-industries.

7. Pew Charitable Trusts, "Collateral Costs: Incarceration's Effect on Economic Mobility," 2010, 18.

8. Michigan Family Impact Seminars, "Fathers in Prisons," familyimpactseminars.org/index.

9. U.S. Department of Health and Human Services, ASPE research brief, aspe.hhs.gov/hsp, April 2010.

10. "Hiland Mountain Correctional Center Women's String Orchestra," artsontheedge.org/the-hiland-mountain-womens-string-orchestra-turns-ten, December 9, 2013.

11. Arts in Prison, artsinprison.org/about, Overland Park, Kansas.

12. American Psychological Association, "Punishment," *Monitor on Psychology,* October 2009, 54.

13. Stephen A. Ragusea, "Ethics, psychology and the prison mess," *National Psychologist,* November/December 2013, 13.

14. "S.F. Center Gives Ex-convicts Help at Starting Fresh," *San Francisco Chronicle,* June 19, 2013, A1.

15. Robert W. Reasoner, "Can the Use of Self-esteem Programs in Schools Actually Reduce Problem Behaviors and Create More Positive Climates?" self-esteem-international.org/Research/SEPrograms, undated.

16. U.S. Department of Justice, "Justice Department Discourages the Use of 'Scared Straight' Programs," ncjrs.gov/html/ojjdp/news_at_glance, March/April 2011.

17. U.S. Department of Justice, Bureau of Justice Statistics, "Recidivism," bjs.gov/index.cfrm?ty, undated.

18. Stephen Brake, "Recidivism and Reoffense Rates of Adult Sex Offenders" (Denver, CO: Stephen Brake Associates, 2011), 1–2.

19. "States Spend Almost Four Times More Per Cap Incarcerating Prisoners Than Educating Students, Studies Say," foxnews.com/politics/2011/03/14states-spend-times-incar, March 14, 2011.

15. To Change a Criminal

1. Ben Stein, "Taking the Lumps, Calling them Sugar," *Los Angeles Herald Examiner,* July 27, 1978.

2. Paul Hauck, *The Rational Management of Children* (New York: Libra, 1967), 100, 101.

16. "Habilitation" or More Crime?

1. "Commitment to Change" (video series in 3 volumes, 9 parts), FMS Productions, Georgetown, Texas.